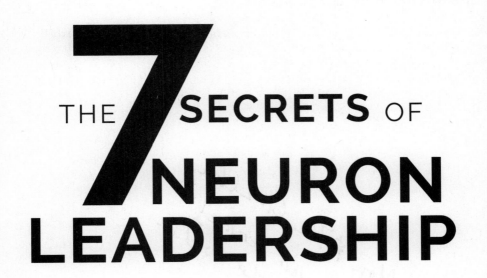

THE 7 SECRETS OF NEURON LEADERSHIP

Bob, Alon & The ClarkClon,
Thanks for your service!
Help me spread the word...
Commit to Lead,
Lead with Passion,
Build Dedicated Doers,
and Change the World!

Anthony Jose
Pg 121

THE 7 SECRETS OF NEURON LEADERSHIP

WHAT TOP MILITARY COMMANDERS,
NEUROSCIENTISTS, AND THE ANCIENT
GREEKS TEACH US ABOUT INSPIRING TEAMS

W. CRAIG REED

WILEY

Published by John Wiley & Sons, Inc., Hoboken, New Jersey.

Published simultaneously in Canada.

For general information about our other products and services, please contact our Customer Care Department within the United States at (800) 762-2974, outside the United States at (317) 572-3993 or fax (317) 572-4002.

Wiley publishes in a variety of print and electronic formats and by print-on-demand. Some material included with standard print versions of this book may not be included in e-books or in print-on-demand. If this book refers to media such as a CD or DVD that is not included in the version you purchased, you may download this material at http://booksupport.wiley.com. For more information about Wiley products, visit www.wiley.com.

Library of Congress Cataloging-in-Publication Data Is Available:

ISBN 978-1-119-42824-4 (hardback)
ISBN 978-1-119-42868-8 (ePDF)
ISBN 978-1-119-42871-8 (ePub)

Cover Design: Wiley

Cover Image: © duncan1890/Getty Images

Printed in the United States of America

10 9 8 7 6 5 4 3 2 1

Contents

Foreword

by Gordon R. England

Source: Photo courtesy of the U.S. government—archive.defense.gov.

I became the 72nd Secretary of the Navy on May 24, 2001. A little more than three months later, I was thrust into the middle of a terrifying situation where I needed to bring to bear every leadership principle I had ever learned.

Like many Americans, I watched in horror on the morning of 9/11 as terrorists crashed airplanes into the World Trade Center. Our entire military force went on high alert. We didn't yet know who was responsible for this heinous act or where they might be, or if they'd attack us again within hours or days. Tens of thousands of people working for the Navy all around the world wanted answers. Until we could learn more, we had none to give them.

Thousands of enlisted personnel, commissioned officers, and civilian employees stepped forward for their country and shouldered their burdens side by side to ensure that our bases, ships, and personnel were safe, secure, and vigilant. These dedicated men and women, many with different cultural backgrounds and belief systems, exhibited team leadership at every level and exemplified what retired four-star Air Force General John Michael Loh once told me when he said: "No one is more important than anyone else." I often tell people that I was not the Deputy Secretary of Defense or Secretary of the Navy. I served in those roles, but only on a temporary basis. The titles defined what I did; they did not define who I was.

One of the greatest leaders of our time, who I believe personified this philosophy, was President Dwight D. Eisenhower. When he was a young man, he loved history and spent a great deal of time reading stories about the ancient Greeks. Many historians have commented that Eisenhower gained much of his leadership wisdom from his study of the ancients.

Johann Wolfgang (von) Goethe, a famous German writer and statesman, once said: "He who cannot draw upon 3,000 years is living from hand to mouth." Like Eisenhower, great leaders often draw upon the wisdom of the ancients, including Aristotle, Socrates, and Plato. This book uniquely unearths interesting and inspirational enlightenment offered by these sages and others to illustrate what separates great and revered leaders from the rest of the pack.

Two additional leaders that I admire and respect are President George W. Bush and his father, President George H.W. Bush. When George W. Bush asked me to be the first Deputy Secretary of Homeland Security, I readily accepted even though I had to reluctantly leave my position as secretary of the Navy. Serving with Homeland Security afforded me the opportunity to leverage and hone my experience and leadership skills in an entirely new organization to protect our citizens from attacks at home.

When George H.W. Bush was only 19 years old, he earned his wings as a Navy pilot during World War II. He was shot down on a bombing run over a Pacific Island and, through excellent Navy teamwork, survived the ordeal. That experience served as a valuable lesson in military team leadership that Bush relied upon throughout his career.

This book contains interviews from dozens of respected military commanders, war heroes, and world leaders, many of whom have achieved great success in civilian roles as CEOs or executives of multibillion-dollar firms. They impart harrowing, fascinating, and informative stories and team leadership strategies that clarify and exemplify the seven secrets revealed in this book.

President John F. Kennedy once said that "man is still the most extraordinary computer of all" and "the human mind is our fundamental resource." He believed that "leadership and learning are indispensable," and understood the critical need for leaders to expand their thinking and inspire others to do the same. On May 21, 1962, he demonstrated his commitment to this goal by articulating his "commander's intent" to land a man on the moon by the end of the decade. While serving as an engineer at Honeywell, helping with the design of the Gemini spacecraft, I believed in Kennedy's vision and agreed with his statement that "science contributes to our culture in many ways, as a creative intellectual activity in its own right, as the light which has served to illuminate man's place in the universe, and as the source of understanding man's own nature."

This book reveals the latest scientific research into the human mind conducted by some of the world's most respected neuroscientists and psychologists. Within these pages we can discover why some leaders succeed while others fail, why some employees are fully engaged while others are not, and why it's important for leaders to transform hearts and minds.

Our world is in desperate need of leaders with the desire, courage, and vision to chart a new course toward a future where individual talents and initiatives are respected and teams are empowered, engaged, and effective. It is my sincere hope that as a current or aspiring leader, you will look in the mirror and deep inside your heart, for that is where leadership begins. Books, seminars, and coaches can help us improve our knowledge, our tactics, and our skills. They cannot fundamentally change who we are as human beings. We must first learn how to lead ourselves with courage, integrity, and a heart filled with love. For without these defining virtues, our leadership efforts will ring hollow and few will be inspired to follow us anywhere.

—Gordon R. England, former Deputy Secretary of Defense,
Deputy Secretary of Homeland Security,
72nd and 73rd Secretary of the Navy

Introduction

The Definition of a Leader

FIGURE I.1   Leadership

Source: Matthew Trommer, Dreamstime.com.

> If your actions inspire others to dream more, learn more,
> do more, and become more, you are a leader.
>
> —John Quincy Adams

Over the past decade, as an executive consultant and coach for dozens of the world's largest and most innovative companies, I've watched my clients spend millions with Big Five consulting firms to implement change management or leadership (Figure I.1) development initiatives. Many months later, these consulting firms delivered comprehensive and detailed Lean and Six Sigma roadmaps to a glorious future based on the latest management trends. That was the easy part. The hard part was inspiring individuals on each functional team to willingly grab the keys and drive toward the destination on the map.

A change management or leadership development roadmap outlines *what* we should do to get somewhere, but rarely does it address *how* we'll get there. Moreover, it does not usually articulate *why* we should go there in the first place. The real *why* is not about perceived problems we need to rectify, it's about defining purpose and passion, which far transcends a simple mission statement. The *how* is not really about the individual process steps we will take to get there, it's about *how* we'll convince our teams to go there enthusiastically. The *what* is not only about a comprehensive process to drive more efficiency, it's about the foundational leadership principles the organization and its leaders embrace.

With a sincere desire to make a difference in our organization, many of us have hired consultants or read great leadership books written by excellent authors. We started following the advice of these experts and perhaps we made some progress. Then we started taking one step forward and two steps back. Why?

It's because we have lives and brains. Our lives often get in the way of our brains and vice versa. We're juggling kids, soccer games, piano lessons, PTA meetings, volunteer organizations, social engagements, and the demands of our profession. We're hammering out emails to San Francisco or Beijing at 2 A.M. We want to start adopting that new leadership habit, but our busy lives make it nearly impossible to retrain our brain. Vanquishing our dusty old habits to adopt shiny new ones seems like an impossible task. How do we solve this problem?

The 7 Secrets of Neuron Leadership provides simple and clear answers to this pervasive question. This book offers startling new ways to train our brain by allowing us to better understand how our minds work considering recent neuroscientific discoveries. It also provides insights from dozens of top military commanders who have led small teams in some of the most demanding and dangerous environments imaginable. Many are now CEOs or senior executives with large firms. Finally, this book reveals ancient wisdom passed down from the Greeks that can help us understand how to lead teams with passion, compassion, and love.

Most other leadership books focus on the latest skills, practices, and habits. These are important, but they are primarily outward-reflective qualities. The best leaders understand that you can't judge a book by its cover. The true quality of a book is found on its pages, not on its jacket.

It's not enough to act like a leader. When we strip away the surface-level veneer that we display to the world, we must also embody the inner qualities of a leader down to the core of our being. While *The 7 Secrets of Neuron Leadership* does offer unique perspectives to improve our outward capabilities and skill sets, this book is primarily designed to help us better understand why leadership is an inside job.

In his book, *Intelligent Leadership: What You Need to Know to Unlock Your Full Potential*, John Mattone describes three key elements to successful leadership:

1. *Capability:* This refers to a leader's present skills and competencies that can be developed, nourished, and enhanced.
2. *Commitment:* This is about the motivational factors that drive leaders including passion, desire, motivation, and zeal.
3. *Connectedness:* Internally, great leaders are aligned with a set of values and character elements that drive success. Externally, they are aligned and connected to the mission values and goals of the organization.

Again, while this book does touch upon leadership *Capability*, it primarily focuses on the "inside" qualities of *Commitment* and *Connectedness*, but from an entirely new perspective.

WHAT'S THE PROBLEM?

Worldwide, bad leadership is costing organizations over one trillion dollars each year.

A Gallup poll conducted in 2015 revealed that about 50 percent of the adults surveyed left a job to get away from a manager. A similar Gallup study of more than 1 million U.S. workers found that the number one reason people quit their jobs is poor leadership.

In the 2013 Gallup State of the American Workplace study, researchers stunned U.S. firms by revealing that only one-third of workers are engaged in their jobs, leaving more than two-thirds who are completely or partially disengaged. The estimated cost to U.S. firms is over $500 billion each year in lost productivity and revenue. Given that only 48 percent of Americans have a full-time job, and only one-third are engaged, that means only 16 percent of the U.S. population is actively engaged in full-time work.

Gallup studies have concluded that work groups with bad leaders are 50 percent less productive and 44 percent less profitable than well-managed teams. A Barna Group study found that two in five Americans rank their boss as "bad," and just one in five assigns only positive attributes. They also discovered that 90 percent of Americans believe the nation is facing a crisis of leadership.

Researchers from Eastern Kentucky University's Bachelor of Science in Occupational Safety program uncovered that workplace stress is costing U.S. firms $300 billion each year for healthcare and lost work days. They created an infographic showing that 77 percent of workers exhibit physical symptoms caused by work stress and 60 percent said they wanted a new career.

The Society for Human Resource Management (SHRM) predicts that every time an organization has to replace a salaried employee, it costs between six and nine months of salary. The Center for American Progress (CAP) reports that for an educated executive, the cost is more like 213 percent of annual salary.

An infographic created by *Inc.* magazine is eye opening. The title reads: "The Real Productivity-Killer: Jerks." *Inc.* infers that bad bosses aren't just a pain, they're bad for business. Colorful graphics in this report disclose that 65 percent of employees would choose a better boss over a pay raise. Around one-third confessed to dialing back their productivity due to poor leadership. The *Inc.* study concludes that it's not what bosses do that makes them bad, it's what they *don't* do.

The number one thing they don't do is inspire their teams. The number two thing they don't do is improve productivity—because they accept mediocrity. The number three thing is not providing a clear vision, and number four is not being a good team leader.

Many experts believe that bad leadership is often related to a bad culture. A survey conducted on 200,000 employees across 500 firms indicated that 71 percent of those organizations have mediocre to poor cultures.[1]

Bad team leaders and mediocre cultures are not limited to the United States. The Chartered Institute of Management (CIM) found that almost half of all workers in Britain left at least one job solely because of a bad boss. In Australia, around two-thirds of workers who responded to a CareerOne survey rated their leaders as either "horrible" or "average."

Obviously, firms with bad leaders need to change, but so do many organizations with mostly good leaders. They need to change because everything around them is changing. They need to change because the difference between good leadership and great leadership could equate to tens or even hundreds of millions of dollars in profit.

Leaders who recognize the need to change, and are courageous enough to do so, can learn a great deal about leadership from three excellent sources of wisdom.

WHAT CAN LEADERS LEARN FROM NEUROSCIENTISTS?

The fastest supercomputer in the world is China's Tianhe-2. This beast has 18,000 times more moxie than your Sony PlayStation® and is 400,000 times faster than an iPhone 7®, but it will never know sadness, kindness, or joy. It will never understand the meaning of hope, failure, or inspiration. And it will never feel happiness, fear, or love. It will never be able to lead or inspire teams because human beings aren't computers. Trying to lead people without a thorough understanding of how their brains work is like trying to become a golf pro without learning how to properly swing a club. Some leaders are naturally gifted and may do well, but rarely does someone make it to the pros without studying the science of the swing.

The science behind the "leadership swing" is called neuroscience.

Some of the world's top neuroscientists, many of whom are associated with leading institutions like Harvard University, have made startling discoveries in the last decade about the human brain. Some of these insights can help leaders dramatically improve employee morale, productivity, and retention. For example, increasing oxytocin can substantially enhance organizational trust and customer brand loyalty. Dozens of blue-chip firms have also discovered that employing neuromarketing principles can offer marketers the equivalent of a flashlight and a roadmap into the decision-making centers of a customer's brain.

WHAT CAN LEADERS LEARN FROM THE ANCIENT GREEKS?

The Greeks knew more about love and each other than we do. They promulgated the Enneagram personality profiler, which some believe is far more precise than Myers-Briggs or similar systems. The modern world uses only one word for love; the ancient Greeks used seven. Each is directly related to and serves as a foundational element for the Seven Secrets of Neuron Leadership outlined in this book. For some readers, approaching leadership development from the perspective of "love" may seem a bit too touchy-feely. After all, isn't this a business book? Shouldn't we be discussing the net net and the bottom line and quarterly business reviews?

For those who see a disconnect between business and the science of love—including an understanding of why employees love their jobs and customers love your brand—I recommend a great business book titled *Conscious Capitalism*, co-written by John Mackey, the co-founder of Whole Foods Market. In this popular book, Mackey explains why firms that have a passion and purpose, and aspire to make an impact rather than only money, often financially outperform competitors by a factor of eleven to one on Wall Street.

The bottom line is that the Greeks have a lot to teach us about the net net.

WHAT CAN LEADERS LEARN FROM MILITARY COMMANDERS?

Before John F. Kennedy was president of the United States, he was a naval officer and the skipper of Motor Torpedo boat PT-109. He commanded a crew of two officers and 14 sailors. These brave men charged headlong toward enemy warships that carried orders of magnitude more firepower.

One fateful night, Kennedy's PT-109 was accidentally sliced in two by a Japanese destroyer. Kennedy led his team by example. He towed a badly burned enlisted man for four hours to reach a nearby island, and encouraged his men to help each other through their difficult ordeal. They were stranded on the island for almost a week, surviving on only coconuts and Kennedy's strong leadership. Many say this near-death experience helped to create one of the most iconic and inspirational leaders of our time. Those who have served in small military units understand that team leadership does not start with a catastrophe. It starts with comradery, respect, and teamwork.

In modern society, experts now agree that the bottom-up and top-down leadership models of the past are no longer effective. In today's fast-paced, internationally diverse, and Internet-driven society, we need an entirely new form of team leadership that empowers each person on the team to contribute as leaders in the most optimal way.

The best team leadership examples can be found in tight military units such as Special Forces, submarines, platoons, air squadrons, and PT boats. In this book, dozens of former generals, admirals, Navy SEAL officers, and other military commanders with expertise in team leadership, many of whom are now corporate executives, share fascinating stories and insights to help us solve expensive and pervasive leadership problems.

THE LONG GAME

The Greek philosopher Heraclitus once said, "No man ever steps in the same river twice, for it's not the same river, and he's not the same man." The speed of business today makes it impossible to stand still. The river of life will pass us by. To be successful leaders, we must continuously improve our knowledge and skills lest we become obsolete.

That said, if your only motivation to become a better team leader is to make more money, you bought the wrong book. Increased revenue and market share may well be the byproduct of improved leadership, but it should not be your only goal. This book is not a magical pair of slippers that can be clicked three times to find your way across a rainbow or to a pot of gold. It is not a get-rich-quick scheme or an instructional manual on how to bend the universe and everyone in it to your will. You will not consistently invoke positive change by manipulation, coercion, deceit, or force. People need to be inspired, not compelled.

Rather than focus outwardly on trying to change everyone else, great leaders seek to change themselves. They understand that we must first make the appropriate and wise changes to *our* life, to *our* reactions, to *our* expectations, to *our* attitudes, to *our* communication style, to *our* mind and heart, and to *our* leadership style. We can then see a *magical change in us—and perhaps in everyone we lead.*

It's obvious that our world is in desperate need of better leadership. My heartfelt desire is that the secrets revealed in this book will inspire, inform, and motivate you and others to lead us all toward a brighter and better future. If you agree to embark on this exciting journey, you must be open to new concepts, methodologies, sciences, viewpoints, teachings, and, of course, change. Your path will be lined with years of research, experience, and insights, as well as inspirational knowledge offered by dozens of military commanders, experts, philosophers, authors, executives, world leaders, and even poets.

One of these poets is the late Dr. James Kavanaugh. He was the best-selling author of more than a dozen books and the best friend of my late father, William J. Reed. Dr. Kavanaugh's widow, Cathy Kavanaugh, graciously granted permission for a few of her husband's writings and poems to be reprinted in this book.

Kavanaugh's books have touched the hearts of millions, starting with his first poetry book, *There Are Men Too Gentle to Live Among Wolves.* A dozen publishers turned down this inspirational book that eventually sold more than 1 million copies. Kavanaugh then wrote *Search: A Guide for Those Who Dare to Ask of Life Everything Good and Beautiful,* which launched a movement and a series of workshops based on his unique approach to introspection and self-healing.

Dr. Kavanaugh once told me that a "searcher" must be prepared for a journey, not an overnight stay in a motel. He called this "the long game," a philosophy that helps us view our profession, and our life's *purpose*, as a journey, not a temporary situation. We can't play a few holes, walk off the course, and expect miraculous changes to occur. Improving our team leadership skills requires playing all eighteen holes. In the next chapter, we'll tee off at the first hole and discover an ancient secret that many leaders have used to dramatically improve their game.

Grateful

Grateful for the sight
   of a single star,
Grateful for the memories
   salvaged from afar.
Grateful for this time of silent peace,
Grateful beyond all words
   when the mad echoes cease.
Grateful for deliverance
   from a private hell,

Grateful beyond
  what a human voice can tell.
Grateful for the wonder of human love.
Grateful for some strange guidance from above.
  Grateful for life.
Grateful for rebirth,
  Grateful forever to live joyously on the earth.

—Dr. James Kavanaugh, *Laughing Down Lonely Canyons*

CHAPTER 1

The Secret of Persuasion

FIGURE 1.1   Abraham Lincoln

Source: Historical photo from Wikimedia Commons, courtesy of Library of Congress, taken by Alexander Gardner.

> Do I not destroy my enemies when I make them my friends?
>
> —ABRAHAM LINCOLN (FIGURE 1.1)

On December 14, 1863, Ohio Congressman James Ashley opened more than a few eyes in the House of Representatives by introducing one of the most controversial constitutional amendments in history. Missouri Senator John Brooks Henderson brought the amendment to the Senate floor on January 11, 1864. Three months later, the Republican-majority Senate approved the Thirteenth Amendment to abolish slavery, but the Democrat-controlled House blocked the final passage. On June 15, 1864, the amendment failed to pass by a mere 13 votes.

During the heated summer of 1864, bloody battles pitted brother against brother on dusty fields across a dozen states. Convinced that final passage of the amendment might eventually heal a divided country, President Abraham Lincoln became impassioned to push it through. During his campaign, he called for the "utter and complete extirpation" of slavery as "a fitting, and necessary conclusion" to the war.

After winning the election, Lincoln kept his promise and petitioned for the passage of the Thirteenth Amendment. In December 1864, as part of his annual message to legislators, Lincoln made it clear that he would not wait until the March 1865 congressional inauguration, but intended to fight for immediate passage. He wrote, "The next Congress will pass the measure if this does not. May we not agree that the sooner the better?"

House Democrats stonewalled. Backed into a corner, Lincoln faced a difficult, uphill battle. What did he do? Did he stand on a podium and berate all the dissenters for being malicious, injudicious, or un-American? Did he blame them for all the perils of the world, or for potentially prolonging a costly and devastating war? Did he divide the country further by conceding defeat because winning was impossible?

He did none of these things. Instead, he gave the world a lasting and inspirational example of leadership. He climbed into his carriage and rode to the homes of every "fence-sitting" Democrat. He spent long hours negotiating, pleading, and most importantly, persuading his opponents. He reached across the acrimonious aisle and twisted intransigent arms and negotiated difficult deals.

He did whatever it took to win their minds and hearts.

Some historians argue that he gave away too much or used shady tactics. While it's true that patronage jobs were offered to some Democrats in exchange for breaking ranks, and purists may be correct in calling this move a bit shady, it is also true that Lincoln did not compromise his core principles or resort to illegal or immoral tactics. He did what all true and great leaders must do: He brought to bear an equal measure of compromise and courage to ensure a greater good.

On January 31, 1865, a nervous Lincoln paced the floor as the world awaited the outcome. The Confederates were on the brink of defeat, and the Republicans thought this might sway several "swing" Democrats from voting in favor of the amendment. A hushed silence swept across the floor of the chamber as House of Representatives Speaker Schuyler

Colfax stepped to the podium. He cleared his throat and said, "On the passage of the joint resolution to amend the Constitution of the United States, the ayes have 119, the noes 56."

Lincoln exhaled a sigh of relief. The Thirteenth Amendment had passed by a narrow margin. The president had succeeded in convincing 16 Democrats to join all the Republicans in voting in favor of the measure. The rules of parliament were temporarily overlooked to allow a throng of congressmen to cheer and "weep like children." One great leader, led by a heart filled with passion and purpose, had persuaded 16 minds and hearts to do the right thing. How had this one man changed the course of history?

By understanding and applying the art of persuasion.

Great leaders like Abraham Lincoln know that you can never force change. Using coercion or fear to get your way might work temporarily, but the inevitable consequences are usually dismal. To inspire long-term and effective change, leaders must win minds and hearts, which requires advanced skills in persuasion. Contrary to popular belief, this art is not new and has been around for thousands of years. The ancient Greek philosopher Aristotle invented the Persuasion Model, which theorizes that persuading someone requires three primary arguments that appeal to instincts (ethos), emotions (pathos), and logic (logos) (Figure 1.2).

Aristotle developed *The Art of Rhetoric* starting in 367 BC, which detailed his triangle of persuasive arguments. Today, top speakers and leaders incorporate these principles into their speeches or approaches to persuade and inspire audiences and followers.

One corner of Aristotle's triangle, which he called *Pathos*, is defined as a "pathetic appeal." From an emotional perspective, Pathos relates to feelings, suffering, pain, or calamity. Linguistic derivatives of Pathos include empathy, sympathy, and apathy. The goal of the speaker or leader is to appeal to heartstrings and create a shared emotional bond or connection.

Top leaders use a rhetorical approach called enumeration, which is strengthened by making an emotional appeal three times in succession while using three related but different examples. The speaker or leader seeks to trigger key audience emotions that can set up subsequent calls to action, which might be to take out your wallet or approve a purchase order.

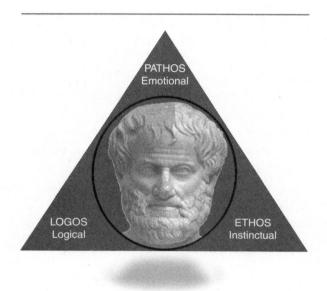

FIGURE 1.2   Aristotle Pyramid

Source: Graphic created by author. Aristotle (384–322 BC). Bust White photo is from Wikimedia Commons, attributed to jlorenz1.

Aristotle recommended seven positive emotions as compared to their contrasting negative emotions to accomplish this goal:

1. Calmness vs. Anger
2. Friendship vs. Enmity
3. Confidence vs. Fear
4. Shamelessness vs. Shame
5. Kindness vs. Unkindness
6. Pity vs. Indignation
7. Emulation vs. Envy

When employed properly and passionately, with the right motives and intent, Aristotle's Pathos moves an audience to feel what the speaker or leader feels, which in turn creates a bond similar to what one might feel for a close friend or loved one. People want to follow people they trust and like. The right emotional appeal allows us to connect with others and lay a solid foundation for the second mode of persuasion.

When you step onto the stage, whether in front of your team, a large audience, or a single person, it's critical to connect emotionally, which is Pathos. Once this has been accomplished as noted above, you then need to build credibility and trust, which Aristotle called *Ethos*. The best way to do this is to appeal to someone's instinctual drivers. As humans, we are wired to avoid fear, harm, or pain. By informing our audience about a potential risk or action that could cause them harm, we can gain their trust. We must do this honestly and factually by researching our topic.

Aristotle used three additional terms to define his views about Ethos. *Phronesis* means good sense. When we communicate, it should be relevant, tasteful, and appeal to our audience's good senses.

Arête stands for good moral character. By showing our honest vulnerability, authenticity, and true heart, we allow our audience to see our *arête*.

Finally, *eunoia* refers to goodwill. Our audience needs to sense that our intentions are selfless and that our honest goal is to be helpful by informing them about something important, such as a pending calamity or consequence.

The third leg of Aristotle's persuasion triangle is *Logos*. This is where we make a logical argument supported by facts, figures, numbers, validation, case studies, evidence, and reason. There are two types of arguments that ensure we are properly delivering Logos: deductive and inductive.

Deductive reasons, or arguments, are generally based on specific premises, delivered in small steps, that are true. If one small premise is true, then the next, which builds upon the first, must also be true, and therefore the logical conclusion must be valid. Socrates also used this approach by effectively gaining agreement for a small truth and then using that as a steppingstone for the next one. For example, we might say:

Do you agree that the sun will come up in the east tomorrow morning?

Yes, of course I do.

And that it will set in the west in the evening?

Yes, absolutely.

And do so again for the next 365 days?

Yes, without question.

And continue for all the years of your life?

Yes, for the rest of my life.

And that someday, for all of us, we will not witness this event once we're gone?

Yes, sadly that is true.

And you have no idea when that day may come, correct?

Yes, I have no idea when that will be.

Therefore, it's important to ensure that the family you leave behind is taken care of, yes?

Yes, very important.

Then wouldn't you agree that it's vitally important to have adequate life insurance?

After having said "yes" seven times to small unarguable truths, it's almost impossible for someone to then say "no" to question number eight.

Inductive reasoning, where the premises are not certain but offer strong evidence to support the truth, can also be used to invoke Logos. One application of this uses reverse psychology, and it can be a powerful technique to encourage someone to "sell themselves." As an example, a clever salesperson with a gleaming smile might say to a prospect:

"Are you working with anyone to help you solve your issues, John?"

"Yes, Linda, I contacted another vendor and they're researching answers now."

"Did they inform you of the consequences of deploying an inadequate solution that does not offer a whizzle stick umptifrats?"

"No, they didn't."

"That's very concerning, John. Without a whizzle stick umptifrats you could fry your whittle-me-rig. Even so, if you're happy with the other vendor, then you probably would not entertain a second opinion at this point. I hope I've at least been of some help and would be happy to answer any questions you might have in the future."

"Well, I haven't pulled the trigger with them yet, Linda. Tell me more about this whizzle stick umpti-whatever."

In this example, by offering a morsel of information that included strong evidence of truth, Linda used inductive reasoning to pique curiosity and then politely refused to satisfy the interest. She then used reverse psychology to "close" John by stating that he probably would not be interested.

Like many ancient Greeks, absent HBO® and Showtime®, Aristotle had a lot of time on his hands to conduct observational science to create his Persuasion Model. He studied how humans act and react and are persuaded through speech and action. He obviously had no idea that, more than 2,000 years later, modern neuroscientists would not only validate his theories but discover *why* they work from a scientific "human brain" standpoint.

CHAPTER **2**

What Leaders Need to Know About the Brain

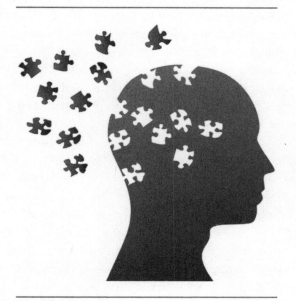

FIGURE 2.1   Brain Puzzle

Source: Gan Hui, Dreamstime.com.

> The brain is a wonderful organ; it starts working the
> moment you get up in the morning and does not stop until
> you get into the office.
>
> —ROBERT FROST

While many aspects involving the complexity of our brains are still
unsolved puzzles (Figure 2.1), Dr. Paul D. MacLean, a renowned

9

neuroscientist, postulated that humans don't have just one brain; we have three. He shared this theory with the world in his 1990 book *The Triune Brain in Evolution*. The late MacLean believed that each of our three brains evolved over time and formed three layers, like the layers of a cake, one atop the other. He served as the director of the Laboratory of Brain Evolution and Behavior in Poolesville, Maryland, and commented that our three brains work like three interconnected biological computers, and they each have their own intelligence, subjectivity, and sense of time, space, and memory.[1]

Some leading neuroscientists agree with MacLean while others do not. For example, Dr. German Garcia-Fresco is the director of the Adaptive Neuroscience Research Institute in West Hollywood, California. He has a PhD in molecular neurobiology from the University of North Carolina. He and his colleagues (also PhDs) published a paper titled "Neuroscience of Selling" wherein they refer to three brains—rational, emotional, and reptilian. Said Dr. Garcia-Fresco, "I agree that it's not exclusive, but for the most part, the human brain can be divided into three areas. The neocortex is more rational, or logical, and involved with reasoning and high-order thinking. The reptilian brain is the oldest part evolutionarily. It is more instinctual and consists of the brain stem and cerebellum. The limbic system or middle brain is where we find the hippocampus and amygdala, which produce most of our emotional chemicals and neurotransmitters."

In contrast to Garcia-Fresco and other neuroscientists, Dr. Paul Zak, a neuroeconomics expert with a PhD in economics, along with a few other neuroscientists, disagree with MacLean and argue that the human brain is a more unified system that is diverse in structure, connection, and function. While this is true, the MacLean camp PhDs point out that certain areas of our brain produce various chemicals and/or are more involved than other areas with respect to emotional, instinctual, or logical thought processes and responses.

Said Dr. Garcia-Fresco, "There will always be controversy as the science is still maturing, but I think it is best to align with the science that is best supported and the least disputed."

One could spend the next decade getting into the weeds and argue about which neurons fire at specific intervals in different regions of the brain, but I think we are safe to simplify things by assuming that Aristotle's observations were fairly accurate. Persuasion is a vital

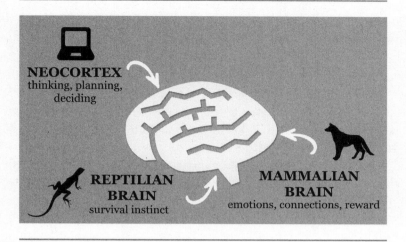

FIGURE 2.2   The Three Brains

Source: Alain Lacroix, Dreamstime.com.

leadership ingredient, and to persuade we need to appeal to someone emotionally (pathos), instinctually (ethos), and logically (logos). Dr. Zak and Dr. Garcia-Fresco concur that Aristotle was fairly accurate in his Persuasion Model conclusions.

For the purposes of simplification, we'll use the diagram shown in Figure 2.2 that refers to three parts of our brain, but I concede that many different areas may be involved rather than *only* three.

EMOTIONAL BRAIN

The limbic system, or the paleomammalian brain as neurobiologists call it, is comprised of the hippocampus, hypothalamus, and the amygdala. Again, some experts disagree that this part of our brain is "more emotional," however, leading neuroscientists state that the amygdala is a critical center for coordinating behavioral, autonomic, and endocrine responses to environmental stimuli, especially those with emotional content.

This part of our head is involved with our emotions, love, excitement, heart rate, blood pressure, sweat glands, appetite, sexual desires, and the desire to seek pleasure and avoid pain. Areas in our limbic system are stimulated by mild electrical currents that invoke a myriad of emotions including love, which is influenced by a neuropeptide hormone called oxytocin that is produced in the hypothalamus. For women, oxytocin is released during labor and breastfeeding, and during sex with a mate. For men, it's also released during sex, but far more so when there is a close bond, such as in a loving relationship. One study, published in 2012, noted that oxytocin levels are higher in lovers as compared to single individuals, and remains highest during the first six months of a relationship.

In a later chapter, we'll learn how to stimulate someone's oxytocin level to not only keep those love fires burning throughout a long-term relationship, but also how to inspire others to love your brand and trust you as a leader.

Our limbic system (again, not exclusively) is involved with our attention span, imprints emotionally charged memories, and determines our valence—whether we feel positive, negative, or neutral about something. It also affects our salience—whether something grabs and holds our attention or stimulates our creativity. Our middle brain influences our value judgments, action rationalizations, and decisions about whether an idea or leadership vision is good or bad. Should we become psychologically unhealthy, this part of our brain can plunge us into the depths of depression, paranoia, and addiction.

The non-MacLean camp disagrees that the limbic system is primarily responsible for more of our emotional responses, but they do concur that it's important for leaders to raise oxytocin to instill trust and love—including love for one's profession, company, vision, and leaders. They also agree with the biological fact that oxytocin is often referred to as the love hormone and has been dubbed the hug hormone or bliss hormone due to its effects on human behavior, most especially its role in love.

Oxytocin is obviously responsible for an emotional (loving) response, and it's produced in the limbic system. Therefore, I think it's safe to assume that when our goal is to stimulate an emotional "loving" or "trust" response, we are primarily lighting up the limbic.

Unless we're psychotic, we are all striving to be happy. Increasing our production of oxytocin makes this more readily possible. It also decreases our cortisol levels. This nasty hormone controls our instinctual fight or flight responses, which on a short-term basis can save our life. On the flip side, long-term cortisol production can be extremely detrimental to our health.

To illustrate, let's say that a subordinate found a unique way to royally tick you off. Maybe they accidentally deleted a critical file that took you weeks to create. What happens to your brain? Your cortisol level shoots through the roof. Your instinctual triggers scream at you to go all caveman and "fight" by ranting and raving and throwing things around your office. That's what you want to do, but your logical mind reminds you that doing so could get you fired, or at the very least, earn you the reputation of being a royal asshole.

So instead, you sit there at your desk and fume. Your face turns red, your fingers curl into your palms, your eyes bulge, and maybe a few flames shoot out your nose. That's what happens on the surface. Underneath your skin, your vagus nerve, which reaches from your brain stem down to your stomach and affects most of your major organs along the way, lights on fire. This nerve becomes inflamed by too much cortisol, the culprit responsible for almost every ailment known to humankind. Angering your vagus nerve with stress and inflammation is like poking a mean bulldog with a stick.

What's the antidote?

Oxytocin. This hormone is highly involved in creating love and life, but it's also a cortisol killer. That's why we feel so relaxed after sex. By the way, smoking a cigarette after an orgasm is a bad idea because it'll raise your cortisol levels.

Dopamine (Figure 2.3) is a neurotransmitter released by the hypothalamus, which is located in the limbic system. Both MacLean and non-MacLean groups agree that dopamine is involved with memory, pain/pleasure responses, behavior, cognition, learning, moods, and more. It's released during pleasurable situations, such as the anticipation of or indulgence in something exciting, interesting, and fun—like having sex, eating a juicy hamburger, going on vacation, winning a contest, or completing an important goal. One can argue that dopamine is also involved in instinctual "fight or flight" situations, but let's assume that, for the most part, dopamine is an emotional "feel-good" chemical. In simplistic terms, dopamine regulates how we *behave*.

Many other brain chemicals are involved with our emotions, but can we agree that two of the more important ones are directly related to love and pleasure? If so, dopamine and oxytocin are predominately produced in the limbic system, so can we nod our heads in agreement that the limbic system is more involved with emotional responses than other areas? If yes, then it's important to know that this part of our brain does

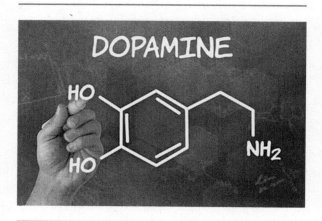

FIGURE 2.3   Dopamine

Source: Zerbor, Dreamstime.com.

not respond well to a communication style that is more logical and that employs lots of facts, figures, written copy, graphs, charts, and so on. Instead, pictures, video, audio, tactile, or olfactory (smell) stimuli will be more effective at eliciting an emotional response. To impact teams emotionally, leaders should therefore limit the use of spreadsheets and instead use more pictures, sounds, and vocal timbre.

INSTINCTUAL BRAIN

The MacLean followers say this part of our brain includes the stem and cerebellum and is responsible for safety responses, harm avoidance, motor balance, and survival instincts. It is also responsible for involuntary actions such as heart rate and food digestion. The anti-MacLeaners do not completely concur, but biologically both camps agree that the vagus nerve, discussed earlier, originates from the brainstem. MacLeaners note that the brainstem is located in the reptilian brain or R-Complex. Also as we learned earlier, the vagus nerve is where the cortisol "antagonist" resides. Since this hormone controls our instinctual fight or flight responses, can we not agree that our "instinctual brain" includes our cortisol brain?

In Dr. Zak's excellent book, *Trust Factor: The Science of Creating High Performance Companies*, he states that "trust begets oxytocin" and

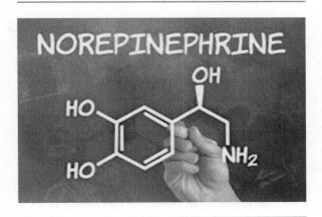

FIGURE 2.4   Norepinephrine

Source: Zerbor, Dreamstime.com.

"high levels of [chronic] stress inhibit the release of oxytocin." While this chemical obviously belongs in the emotional bucket, it is also the antidote to our cortisol-triggered instinctual fight or flight response. If we trust someone, we will not be instinctually inclined to run away or punch them in the nose. Who do we trust? Dr. Zak said, "Think of trust as the biological basis for the Golden Rule: if you treat me nice, my brain makes oxytocin, signaling that you are a person whom I want to be around, so I treat you nice in return."

The fear of pain is also an instinctual trigger. Norepinephrine (Figure 2.4) is produced by the adrenal medulla, which is located in an adrenal gland atop our kidneys. Does that mean our reptilian brain is located in our kidneys? Not quite. Norepinephrine (noradrenaline) is released by our kidneys, but it affects a part of our brain called the locus coerules, which is located in the R-Complex brainstem. So perhaps both the MacLean and non-MacLean scientists are correct. Our instinctual adrenaline hormones are not exclusively located in our brainstem, but that part of our brain does have some dominion over the norepinephrine neurotransmitter.

While still disputed by some neuroscientists, MacLean postulated that the reptilian brain (R-Complex) is the only part that most reptiles have. A snake, therefore, only acts out of instinctual self-preservation. This is probably why lawyers are often called snakes, but I digress.

Experts call it the archipallium, primitive, or "basal brain." Our instinctual brain (again, I'm referring to more than just the reptilian brainstem) is often obsessive/compulsive, rigid, paranoid, and ritualistic. It is crammed full of ancestral memories and, well, instincts. It drives us to keep repeating old behaviors over and over again because, if they kept us alive before, they will keep us alive again. Don't eat molded berries or that nasty yellow snow.

Our instinctual brain is always alert and never sleeps, which is why we can be instantly awakened by a potential threat, like someone trying to steal that candy bar we hid under our pillow. It's motivated by fear of loss, harm, or conflict, and is involved with aggression, dominance, and repetition. Here's another interesting fact: our instinctual brain does not respond well to the written word, numbers, statistics, or anything logical. It prefers sights, sounds, smells, and touch. If you're a leader, and you're trying to motivate your team to follow you, follow instructions, or follow their gut instincts, doing so with a presentation or speech filled with only a bunch of numbers may fail miserably.

In summary, our "instinctual brain" helps govern norepinephrine, an adrenaline neurotransmitter involved in fight or flight responses. In simplistic terms, it regulates how we *think*. This part of our brain also controls cortisol, which is the antithesis to oxytocin. We'll discover later when and how cortisol stimulation is desirable in certain situations, but for now it's important to note that encouraging oxytocin release will lead to happier and more trusting and productive workers. Robbing people of oxytocin and raising cortisol by using fear or other instinctual motivators will do just the opposite. Said Dr. Zak, "The science shows that fear-based management is a losing proposition because people acclimate to fear quickly. Fear-inducing leaders must ramp up threats to increase productivity, but there are only so many threats one can make."

Going forward, when I discuss the "instinctual brain," I am not referring exclusively to the reptilian brainstem, but to those parts of the brain that shoot us full of cortisol and norepinephrine and cause us to put on war paint or run for cover.

LOGICAL BRAIN

Our neocortex is the area of our brain that experts call the cerebrum, cortex, neopallium, neomammalian, superior, or rational brain. Why they need six names to define something defies logic, but this part of our brain is what separates us from the animals. Perhaps that's why we refer to animalistic individuals as "dogs."

Here's a strange fact: Our neocortex takes up two-thirds of our brain mass. In animals, it's just the opposite. Their neocortex is much smaller and has far fewer folds, which is indicative of less development and complexity. Remove the neocortex from a rat and it will act like a rat. Remove the neocortex from a man and he'll act like a vegetable. You can also accomplish that with a pint of tequila, so I've heard.

Our cortex is divided into two parts. This is where we get that famous left and right brain thing. The left cortex controls our right side and vice versa. As most of us know, our right brain is more artistic, musical, and abstract, while our left brain is more rational, verbal, and linear. The non-MacLean dissenters do not agree that our neocortex reigns supreme over our logical inclinations; however, *ScienceDaily* states that our neocortex is involved with the higher functions of our brain, including spatial reasoning, sensory perception, conscious thought, the generation of motor commands, and language processing. Leading psychologists agree that our neocortex receives and stores information for decision making and is involved with abstract reasoning and judgment.

If we agree with the above definitions, then it stands to reason that the neocortex is more involved than other parts of our brain in processing logical information. Non-MacLeaners point out that the neocortex is not the exclusive host of logical thought or action, but to keep things simple, when I refer to our "logical brain," I concede that it may include areas beyond the frontal lobe. Regardless, persuading someone from a logical perspective is better achieved by using facts, figures, written words, research, graphs, and so forth that will appeal more to the logical brain. Pictures, video, and audio can help reinforce concepts, but they will be more effective at stirring emotions than gaining rational agreement.

Also, because of the way our brains are wired, we humans will respond three times more often to a potential threat (instinctual) than to a potential gain (emotional or logical); so stop dwelling on all those "value propositions" to motivate employees and customers and instead focus on instinctual consequences. Then, develop trust and raise oxytocin levels by helping people avoid pain.

OUR SUBCONSCIOUS MIND

Can we agree that leaders can't lead effectively without persuading? If your team is not persuaded to follow you, accomplish the goals, or buy into the vision, then your ability to lead will be greatly diminished. Aristotle has shown us that to persuade, we need to appeal to someone's emotional, instinctual, and logical "brains." Many neuroscientists concur that the primary chemicals, hormones, functions, and so on, that trigger these three responses are conjured in or mostly affected by three parts of our brain.

Gerald Zaltman, a prominent neuroscientist from Harvard University, is the author or editor of over 20 books on various topics involving neuroscience. He stated that at least 95 percent of human cognition is subconscious, while our high-order consciousness is only involved with about 5 percent of decision making.

The higher-order consciousness he refers to is, predominately, the realm of our logical brain. In other words, we humans are allowing our emotions and instincts to dominate how we make decisions. We smell that new car leather and our logical brain, which is trying to warn us that we can't afford the car payment, is given only a 5 percent seat at the table.

Dr. Zak agrees with Zaltman that more than 95 percent of our decisions are ultimately made by our subconscious mind, which is usually not very logical. Therefore, we can't just win logical minds, we must also win emotional hearts and instinctual guts. To win someone's heart and gut, they must like and trust us, and to win their minds, they must believe our logic.

Zaltman patented some of his science under the term Zaltman Metaphor Elicitation Technique (ZMET). By employing ZMET, he explored unconscious behavior using emotional response testing and metaphors to stimulate purchase scenarios. The objective was to create foundational advertising elements, such as images, for commercials. This work, combined with other discoveries made by Harvard researchers, led to an exciting new field called neuromarketing, a term coined in 2002 by researcher Ale Smidts.

The use of neuromarketing is expanding rapidly at Yahoo!, eBay, CBS, Google, PepsiCo, Ford Motor Co., Hyundai, Hewlett-Packard, Frito-Lay, Coca Cola, Procter & Gamble, and many other companies worldwide.

While neuroscientists and neuromarketers would like to believe that these discoveries are groundbreaking, Aristotle obviously had a glimpse of this concept when he created his Persuasion Model eons ago. Also, George Ivanovitch Gurdjieff, a Russian philosopher and teacher (of Greek descent, by the way), often referred to humans as "three-brained beings." One brain for the body (gut), one for the spirit (head), and one for the soul (heart). Plato referred to similar concepts, as did Kabbalah spiritual leaders.

Throughout human history, our observational science has far preceded our learned science. For centuries, we observed the stars and recorded what they did, but until our astronomical science caught up, we didn't understand *why*. Likewise, for centuries we have observed how humans act and think and make decisions, but until the advent of neuroscience, we didn't understand *why*.

Now we do.

INNIES AND OUTTIES

Few of us blink an eye when asked whether we or someone we know is introverted or extroverted. Research on this topic dates to the Myers-Briggs Type Indicator of the 1940s. Today, around 2 million people each year take the test. Leading psychologists concur that introverts are not necessarily shy, but can become drained by social encounters and thus need to find time alone or with nature to recharge. Extroverts gain energy by interacting with others and can become drained by alone time or a simple walk in the woods. Extroverts often have a lot of friends, while introverts are more selective and prefer a few close relationships.

The ratio of introverts to extroverts is changing with generations. CPP (formerly Consulting Psychologists Press), publishers of the Myers-Briggs assessments, reports that Baby Boomers, born before 1964, are roughly 50 percent extroverted; Generation Xers, born between 1965 and 1981, are 59 percent extroverted, while Millennials, born after 1981, are 62 percent extroverted.

There are varying degrees of introversion and extroversion, and some of us can cross the line upon occasion. However, if we take a hard look at our personality traits, we will discover that we tend to favor one side or the other most of the time. Why is this important?

During the 1940s, leadership researchers started analyzing the effects of introverted and extroverted managers, which led to research on specific leadership behaviors. They created two buckets in which these managers were dumped: You were either a *task-oriented* or *relationship-oriented* leader.

Task-oriented leaders may be a bit more introverted and are focused on getting the job done, completing tasks, or achieving goals. These leaders exhibit modest concern for employee relationships and place more emphasis on achievements, organization, and structure. The upside is higher productivity, but at the cost of morale, which can eventually affect productivity. These leaders may seem a bit harsh or uncaring, but that's usually just their exterior demeanor and they often act this way to get results. Inside, most of them are just as much marshmallow as anyone.

Relationship-oriented leaders may tend to be more extroverted and focus on people, relationships, teams, motivation, and support. They encourage collaboration and frequent communication, and emphasize employee well-being and happiness. They understand that reducing workplace conflicts and stress can lead to higher productivity. The upside is higher morale and job satisfaction, but sometimes at the expense of productivity and profitability. Those who prefer task orientation might call these leaders "wimps," but that's usually due to a differing perspective. Many relationship-oriented leaders can make tough decisions and tackle rough seas with the best.

Which style is better? Management theorists from Ohio State University and the University of Michigan published a series of studies in the 1950s that sought to answer this question. They discovered that it really doesn't matter, and that either style can be successful depending upon the situation. This led to a new management approach called *Situational Leadership*, which I studied at length a few decades ago.

This approach recommends that leaders should use either style depending upon who you are leading and when. In other words, some people respond better to a Task-oriented rather than a Relationship-oriented style, and vice versa. This can also change depending upon the circumstances. For example, if the firm has a critical deadline, a Task style may be better. The problem with this approach is determining which style to use when and with whom, which can become confusing and almost impossible to memorize.

Perhaps it's time to introduce a new term called *Neuron Leadership* that encourages us to adjust our team leadership style to a person's situation based on their neuroscientific personality, demeanor, and psychological health. Also, to their role and responsibilities within a team unit. In the pages to follow, we'll explore this new concept in greater detail and uncover seven secrets to optimizing this approach.

In the next chapter, we'll see just how deep this rabbit hole goes, and find out how mysterious our minds really are.

CHAPTER **3**

What Leaders Need to Know About Personalities

FIGURE 3.1   Shrinking Leadership

Source: Bachol12345, Dreamstime.com.

> If you think you can do a thing or think you can't do a thing, you're right.
>
> —HENRY FORD

The term *psychology* is derived from the Greek words *psyche*, meaning "spirit, soul, and breath," and *logia*, which means "the study of something." Psychology is the study of us: our mental and behavioral processes; how we interact with and react to the world around us. Ancient Greek philosophers were the founders of psychology, but the German psychologist Wilhelm Wundt set up the first "psych lab" back in

1879. Since then, the science has spurred dozens of studies and theories about what makes us tick.

Full disclosure: Although I have studied various aspects of this science for decades, have consulted with dozens of experts, and also have three decades of management, leadership, and consulting expertise, I do not have a degree in psychology. I'm not a "leadership shrink" (Figure 3.1). Thus, a PhD somewhere might disagree with some of my conclusions, regardless of whether most of his peers concur. The science of our minds is anything but exact, and psychologists have frequently disagreed with each other throughout history. While researching this topic, I discovered that the "raw data" collected by field observations, ever since the time of the Greeks, is quite harmonious. *Moreover, when the observational science is examined against the light of neuroscience, the revelations are astounding.*

One of the most well-known psychologists in history is Sigmund Freud. Born in 1865, Freud spent most of his life in Vienna where he wrote three books about dream interpretation, psychopathology, and sexuality. He is remembered most for the latter, but Freud gave us many of our modern concepts about the human *Id, Ego,* and *Superego.* Freud observed that we have three brains, but, lacking neuroscientific knowledge, he did not understand *why.*

The Id refers to that unorganized portion of our personality structure related to our basic animal instincts and bodily needs. Our Id is motivated by pain and pleasure. Naturally, we want to avoid one and seek the other. As babies, we were controlled almost entirely by our Id, which is why we cried every time we got hungry. Some of us still do that: you know who you are.

As we became adults, we learned to control these impulses lest we pee in our pants or attack the waiter at a fancy restaurant with a fork rather than wait patiently to be served. Addictions and severe temper tantrums stem from an inability to properly control our Id impulses. Our Id is the raw animal within each of us, the untamed beast, unconcerned with right, wrong, good, evil, or morality. *Within the Id resides our instinctual drive to survive.*

Superego is the learned stuff. Rules, guidelines, boundaries, etiquette, proper communication skills, flushing the toilet, saying thank you, and so on, all reside in the Superego domain. Most of us learned these appropriate behaviors from parents, teachers, siblings, friends, and so forth. When we did something bad, probably because that devil Id sat on our shoulder and told us to, we were given pain, such as a belt whipping from Dad. When we did something good, we got a dose of pleasure, like ice cream from Mom. Our Superego learned how to behave appropriately through this process of *emotional pain and pleasure learning*.

Our Ego deals with the part of our personality structure that controls our perceptive, defensive, cognitive, and executive functions. Reason and common sense stem from the Ego. A primary Ego function is to mediate between our Id and Superego while striking the right balance between our primitive drive and reality. *Our Ego lets us logically organize our thoughts and make sense of them.* Unlike the Id, in which our raw passions reside, the Ego deals with reason and common sense. When our Ego is healthy, we have better control over our base instincts, such as the need to lash out in anger or run from potential conflict. Our Ego may know that we should respond to bad behavior with patience, reason, and intelligence, but if we're operating on two hours of sleep, our Id may take over and have us smash a fist into our computer monitor.

Freud's conclusions intimate that the Id is predominately involved with our instinctual brain functions. The Superego appears to be more involved with our emotional functions, and the Ego is rational and pragmatic and more logical. Could it be that Freud had the same observations as the ancient Greeks? It seems that Freud and the Greeks, as well, proffered the concept that humans have three distinct brains that tend to be emotional, instinctual, or logical.

DOG BRAIN

Ivan Pavlov, a psychologist born in Russia in 1849, gave us another interesting viewpoint about our behaviors. Although his theories predate Freud's, they help us see why we might be reacting in certain ways with certain people in certain situations. Pavlov's conditioned reflex experiments led to the famous *Pavlov's dog* term. A conditioned reflex is a response associated with a previously unrelated stimulus. In Pavlov's experiments, he placed food in front of a dog and the dog salivated. He then rang a bell. The dog did nothing. Then he rang a bell *and* put food in front of the dog. The dog salivated. Thereafter, whenever Pavlov rang the bell, even without the food present, the dog salivated.

What does Pavlov's dog have to do with leading? How we interact with others, including those we lead, is often directly related to learned responses. For example, what if as a child one of your subordinates had a parental or other authoritative figure bully, mistreat, ridicule, or upset them in some way? Perhaps this figure used a certain vocal tone or facial expression during these episodes. If so, these figures "rang a bell" before they metaphorically slapped your subordinate around. Today, whenever you use a similar tone or look, is it possible that you're ringing your subordinate's bell?

PERSONALITIES AND OBSERVATIONAL SCIENCE

During the early 1900s, humanist psychologist Carl Rogers proffered his *self-theory*. He believed that all humans are infused with a single driving motivation: to self-actualize. He defined this state as achieving the highest level of "human-beingness." He obviously never watched a hockey game. Others have simplified this theory to being happy or filled with joy in every aspect of one's life—including our professions.

Modern psychology views personality through the lens of an individual's emotions, behaviors, thoughts, actions, and reactions. These make us unique in relation to others, and are referred to as our *mental system*. Although we exhibit our personality characteristics in individualized ways, there are definite commonalities. Our traits remain relatively constant throughout our entire lives. The caveat here is whether we are acting in healthy or unhealthy ways. Most people slip in and out of these categories upon occasion.

In addition, individual or not, people tend to behave in similar and sometimes predictable ways when faced with certain situations or decisions. Although the study of personality is decidedly a psychological science, many experts now agree that our personalities are impacted by neurological wiring and processes. Some psychologists, like Sigmund Freud, subscribe to the *nature theory*, in which they believe that biology (today more commonly referred to as neurobiology) entirely governs our personalities. Others, like Alfred Adler, lean toward the *"nurture" theory* in which personalities are governed entirely by experiences, environment, and societal factors.

Many other experts have a leg in both camps. They point to identical twins or triplets exposed to similar environments and home situations who exhibit completely different personalities. They claim that nature is to blame for our core personality types, but different nurturing aspects can alter levels of psychological health and account for diverse individuality. Based on direct observation and years of research, many leading psychologists I've interviewed believe this theory is the most accurate. I'll reveal some of the science behind their conclusions in a moment. These insights may, as they did for me, *alter your concepts about personalities forever*.

In the mid-1930s, Gordon Allport, a Harvard graduate, became the first psychologist in the United States to teach a class about personalities. He also created a trait theory that used more than 4,500 dictionary words to describe different traits. He divided these traits into three categories he named *Cardinal (individual), Central (common),* and *Secondary (conditional) traits*. Years later, Raymond Cattell reduced Allport's long list to 171 traits by combining and reclassifying similarities and removing uncommon ones. Using questionnaires completed by individual subjects, he narrowed the list even further to only 16 types that include perfectionism, dominance, apprehension, warmth, and so on. Allport's observations provided some of the foundational elements used in the 16 Myers-Briggs personality profiles.

NINE TYPES

When speaking Greek, *Ennea* means nine and *gram* means point, so the term *Enneagram* (pronounced any-a-gram) means nine points. I first learned about the Enneagram in writing circles. I've used it frequently to create distinct fictional characters for my novels. At first I thought this stuff was all mumbo jumbo, but upon further research, aided by my son, Brandon Reed, *I discovered some rather amazing and enlightening information about the Enneagram*.

Brandon's friend in middle school was the son of Helen Palmer, a well-known author on the Enneagram. By asking questions and scouring books, I learned that this personality theory had gained ground in scientific circles and was used for jury selection, employee hiring, and Internet matchmaking. This theory also aligns well with Myers-Briggs and the 32-trait Occupational Personality Questionnaire (OPQ32) initiated by Saville and Holdsworth Ltd. in 1984.

OPQ32 is a personality "test" widely used in professional and employment circles for selection, development, team building, succession planning, and organizational change. The SHL Group, purveyors of the OPQ, completed a study in 2005 in concert with The Enneagram Institute and discovered that the nine personality types promulgated by the ancient Greeks are real and objective and stand on a par with Myers-Briggs, the Big Five, and other prominent psychological systems.

The OPQ32, backed by hundreds of validation studies across tens of thousands of individuals, is one of the most widely used and highly regarded measures of personality in the workplace. Professors Dave Bartram and Anna Brown conducted an independent study of the Enneagram Institute interpretation made by authors Don Riso and Russ Hudson to see if it related to the OPQ32, and discovered a clear match.

Bartram and Brown reviewed information from hundreds of volunteer participants from different countries. The results indicated a strong relationship between the nine Enneagram personality types and OPQ32 traits. In fact, based on a person's OPQ32 profile, someone could predict the Enneagram type 75 percent of the time. One could do this only 11 percent of the time by guessing. The conclusion is that modern researchers have all but validated the observational science recorded by ancient researchers from as long ago as 2000 BC.

The Enneagram symbol is an interconnected circle made of nine points used to depict nine distinct personality types. Many believe the ancient Greeks invented the diagram and science, but evidence of its origination can be found in 4,000-year-old Pythagorean geometry (Figure 3.2). The Pythagoreans were an inquisitive bunch and were captivated by the deeper meaning and significance of numbers. Plato apparently studied the Enneagram theories and passed them on to his disciple Plotinus and other followers.

George Gurdjieff, a Russian teacher and follower of Freud, learned about the Enneagram in the 1920s while visiting a Sufi monastery in Afghanistan. Oscar Ichazo learned about it from Gurdjieff, and Claudio Naranjo heard about it from Ichazo. Robert Ochs and Helen Palmer researched the Enneagram by studying Naranjo's concepts, but the most famous authors on the Enneagram are Riso and Hudson of The Enneagram Institute.

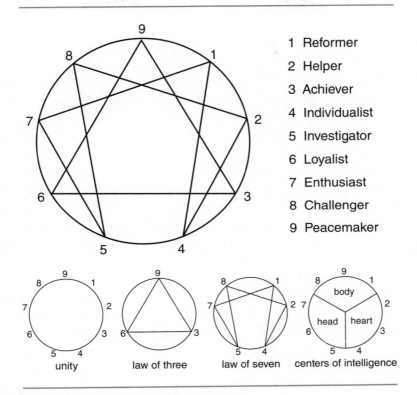

FIGURE 3.2   The Enneagram Symbol

Source: Peter Hermes Furian, Dreamstime.com.

Is the Enneagram accurate? The ancient Greeks invented the water mill, odometer, alarm clock, cartography, geometry, medicine, philosophy, and democracy. They excelled in the fields of astronomy, biology, and physics. Aristotle postulated that our world was round, and the Pythagoreans proposed that the earth revolved around the sun. Archimedes discovered that submerging a solid object displaces a like measure of weight. The Greeks weren't infallible, but they were obviously highly observant and accurate. It is possible that the research conducted by the ancients on human personalities is bunk, but it's highly unlikely.

If we assume that the Enneagram is reasonably precise, and there are indeed nine distinct personality types, how then might modern neuroscience validate this theory?

PERSONALITIES AND NEUROSCIENCE

Most experts seem to agree that neurotransmitters and chemicals modulate brain activity in predictable patterns and influence how we humans act and react to the world around us. Three primary neurotransmitters that appear to be more involved with our personalities than others are dopamine, serotonin, and norepinephrine.

Dopamine is a basic modulator of attention, motivation, pain, and pleasure and regulates how we *behave*. Serotonin modulates obsession, compulsions, and psychological well-being and regulates how we *feel*. Norepinephrine is involved with focused thinking, mental activity, alertness, and energy and regulates how we *think*. For all of us, each neurotransmitter's production, or level, is either high, medium, or low. Apparent levels can also be determined by the length of a neurotransmitter's pathway in our brain. Neuron Profiles are divided into three groups: logical, emotional, and instinctual (Figure 3.3).

How does this relate to Aristotle's Persuasion Model or the emotional, logical, or instinctual brain functions we previously discussed? Here's where it gets tricky and controversial. Some experts flatly disagree with the above premise. They do not believe that the three neurotransmitters noted are the ones primarily involved with personalities, or

FIGURE 3.3   Neuron Profiles Venn Diagram

Source: Illustration by author.

that humans are genetically predisposed to have high, medium, or low levels. In fact, they disagree that we can have "levels" at all. Conversely, many other experts state that genetic predispositions *are* factors that can cause low, medium, or high levels, and they specifically use the word "levels."

For example, a May 9, 2015, article in *Psychology Today* states that around 20 percent of the population is likely more sensitive in nature. The article cites findings from the University of British Columbia and Cornell University neuroscientists, who discovered that human genes may influence how sensitive certain people are to emotional information.

In other words, some of us may be genetically wired to be more emotional.

Furthermore, the researchers determined that some people have a genetic variation called ADRA2b, which influences the norepinephrine neurotransmitter. ADRA2b is linked to heightened activity in certain brain areas that can trigger intense emotional sensitivity and responses.

To summarize, neuroscientists from two respected universities validated that a percentage of the human population is genetically wired to be more emotional, which may be directly related to their levels of norepinephrine. Furthermore, their research shows how the norepinephrine pathways connect directly to the hippocampus and amygdala, which are located in the limbic system.

How is this emotional disposition linked to our personality type? Adam Anderson, professor of human development at Cornell University and senior author of the study, intimated that it is. He stated that emotions aren't just about how someone feels about the world, but also how a person's brain influences perception. Human genes can influence how we visualize negative and positive aspects in our environment.

The American Psychological Association defines personality as the differences in characteristic patterns of thinking, feeling, and behaving. So it appears safe to assume that, to some degree, norepinephrine influences our personality, and our levels of this neurotransmitter are genetically predisposed.

What about serotonin and dopamine? Can they also influence our personalities?

The research study referenced above states that there is reciprocal activity between norepinephrine and serotonergic and dopaminergic systems, which refer to serotonin and dopamine production, respectively.

Several additional resources validate that neurotransmitter levels are directly related to personality types. In his book, *The Edge Effect*, Dr. Eric Braverman shows how four main neurotransmitter or chemical levels in the brain can determine our personality profile. To validate this, he used a quantitative electroencephalogram (EEG) called BEAM (Brain Electrical Activity Mapping). Some skeptics question Braverman's research and even his credibility, but his studies do appear to be thorough and match research conducted by two PhDs that I personally know are quite reputable.

What are the four neurotransmitters or chemicals Braverman researched?

Dopamine is an assertive "power" neurotransmitter that dominates our frontal lobe. Braverman found that those with high dopamine levels enjoy power, theories, language precision, and strategy.

GABA (Figure 3.4) is found in our temporal lobe. Those with high "calming" GABA levels are more traditional and conventional, dependable and punctual, organized and confident. GABA is an "inhibitory" neurotransmitter that can lower "excitatory" ones, most especially norepinephrine.

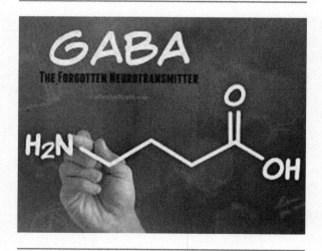

FIGURE 3.4   GABA

Source: Zerbor, Dreamstime.com.

Norepinephrine makes us more alert and ready for active body movement, which increases our energy use. Its effect can be offset by GABA and acetylcholine, which act on most of the same organs to make us more conducive to calmness, rest, recovery, and food digestion.

Acetylcholine is related to motor and memory functions and is produced in the parietal lobes. Braverman says that individuals with high levels are more creative, empathetic, authentic, and benevolent. As noted above, it can affect our norepinephrine level. Other studies show a direct connection with this chemical and introversion and extroversion. Introverts apparently have long acetylcholine pathways. For extroverts, it's shorter. Visualize a hose pumping water into your brain. You won't necessarily have a higher "level" of water with a longer hose, but it will take longer to fill up your brain. That's why introverts can handle large crowds temporarily but eventually grow weary of them. Their brains are slowly filling up with acetylcholine.

Serotonin (Figure 3.5) is in the occipital lobe and is associated with delta waves. Those with high serotonin are playful, adventurous, optimistic, achievement-oriented, and have a positive mental attitude.

If Braverman's research is accurate, it could prove to be ground-breaking, but does it align with the ancient Enneagram?

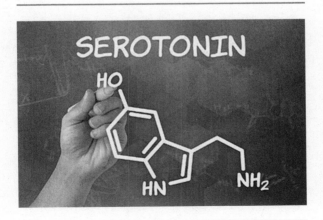

FIGURE 3.5   Serotonin

Source: Zerbor, Dreamstime.com.

NEUROSCIENCE AND THE ENNEAGRAM

Renowned experts Dr. Eric S. Schulze and Dr. Tina Thomas conducted research studies similar to Braverman's. Dr. Thomas documented these findings in her book *Who Do You Think You Are?: Understanding Your Personality from the Inside Out*. These two PhDs discovered that the Enneagram's observational science can be explained by genetically determined high, medium, or low levels of dopamine, serotonin, and norepinephrine.

We know that the Enneagram's nine types are divided into three distinct groups of three personality types each (Figure 3.6). The three groups, or triads, can be defined as "head types" (more logical), "heart types" (more emotional), and "gut types" (more instinctual). Schulze and Thomas discovered that thinking group types appear to have high levels

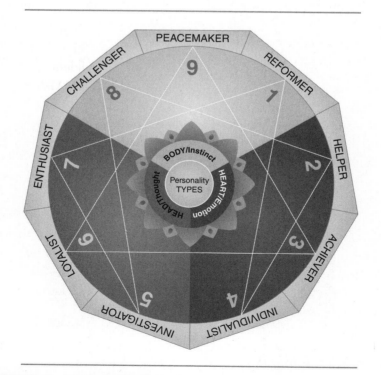

FIGURE 3.6   Personality Types

Source: Artellia, Dreamstime.com.

of norepinephrine activity and are generally mentally active. The instinctual types have relatively low norepinephrine activity, and the heart types have medium levels. There is also an assertive group, which has high levels of dopamine activity and a lot of energy and drive. The passive group has low levels, while the compliant group has medium levels.

How does their research compare to Braverman's work? A close examination reveals that they are quite compatible (Figure 3.7). Here's how:

Norepinephrine: Schulze and Thomas found that this neurotransmitter regulates how quickly and how often a person thinks and solves problems. Thomas reports that "people who have a high set point of norep [norepinephrine] are people whose brain 'engines' are set at a high idle. They are almost always revved up and ready to think." They also tend to speak quickly and may be perceived as "high-strung" individuals. They may have difficulty "turning their brain off," so sleeping soundly could be a challenge. People in this category are logical "head types."

Those with low levels are referred to as the three instinctual "gut" personality types. They are more solid and steady, traditional and conventional, dependable and punctual, organized and confident, and "calm." They rarely have a problem falling asleep. Recall that GABA is calming and throttles norepinephrine, and Braverman said that those with high levels have similar attributes. High GABA and low norepinephrine are essentially peas in the same pod, so it appears that the two viewpoints are similar.

Schulze and Thomas determined that people with medium levels of norepinephrine fall into the emotional and feeling "heart" triad. They are "intermittent thinkers" and may cycle in and out of daydreaming. These types are also more creative, caring, and empathetic. Braverman said that those with high levels of acetylcholine are creative, empathetic, authentic, and benevolent. The effects of norepinephrine are offset by acetylcholine, so it's quite possible that high levels of the latter will create medium levels of the former. Again, a potential fit.

Dopamine: Braverman said that those with high levels are assertive and enjoy power, precision, and strategy. Schulze and Thomas concur. They show high dopamine types as falling into the assertive triad and they like power, control, precise diction, and strategic goal setting. Again, a close alignment.

Schulze and Thomas also note that dopamine levels can dictate whether or not someone is more extroverted or introverted. This aligns with research completed by Dr. Marti Olsen in her book, *The Introvert Advantage: How to Thrive in an Extrovert World*, wherein Olsen concludes that extroverts have a low sensitivity to dopamine and need more of it, while introverts are highly sensitive and prefer lower amounts.

Serotonin: Schulze and Thomas show high serotonin types as being in the "positive outlook" triad. Braverman said these individuals are playful, adventurous, and have positive orientations. Close enough.

Based on the above research (backed by studies and neurobiological facts) it appears that we might be able to conclude the following:

1. Our personality types are, for the most part (not exclusively), influenced by a handful of primary neurotransmitters and brain chemicals.
2. The levels (production) of norepinephrine and serotonin neurotransmitters are either high, medium, or low, which equals nine types. Our levels of dopamine and acetylcholine create what is referred to as "wings," meaning we may tend to have a few of the attributes of an adjacent personality type that has a higher or lower level.
3. The nine types described by the ancient Greek Enneagram align closely with the neurotransmitter studies done by leading researchers.
4. The Enneagram aligns with top personality profiling systems like Myers-Briggs and the OPQ32.
5. It appears that the ancients observed what recent neuroscientific research has possibly validated.
6. If true, it only took us a few thousand years to relearn what we already knew.

Why should you care? Because leading requires persuasion, which necessitates effective communication. Remember the book *Men Are from Mars, Women Are from Venus*? Therein, John Gray, PhD, discussed how men and women use different "languages" to convey thoughts and feelings. Perhaps the truth goes much deeper than this.

To lead effectively, we must understand someone else's viewpoints, motivations, and communication styles so we can *listen* to what they are saying, respond in kind, and better persuade them to embrace our vision or complete a task. For example, if someone is more logical, they may respond better to numbers, facts, figures, logic, etc. If emotional, to the "touchy-feely," warm and fuzzy, heart strings, emotions, etc. If instinctual, to messages about survival, security, fight or flight, avoidance of harm or loss, and so on.

Below is a chart outlining how several research studies align with the ancient Greek Enneagram. You can visit www.neuronleaders.com to use a free app to determine your Neuron Personality Profile and download a comprehensive description that includes diet and lifestyle recommendations to improve your leadership ability. You can also determine the Profile of anyone you interact with and receive a detailed guide on how to better persuade, communicate with, and motivate them to perform at their best.

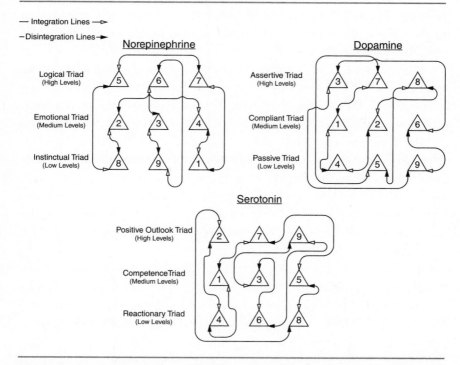

FIGURE 3.7 Enneagram Traits as Related to Neurotransmitter Levels. Includes Lines of Psychological Health Integration and Disintegration.

Source: Chart created by Brandon Reed.

MIRROR NEURONS

The key difference between this book and most others on the topic of leadership may well come down to this one neuroscientific term: *mirror neurons*. I've talked with dozens of well-meaning executives who have read excellent leadership books. They resonated with many of the concepts, scheduled meetings with their department heads, and asked them to implement the author's recommendations.

Now. ASAP. Then report back.

The department heads ran off, ran in circles, and ran out of steam while trying to deploy the concept or best practice in the midst of juggling 2 million emails and 5,000 meetings. They did their best to make changes, encouraged participation from the troops, and got some results, but the new behaviors never stuck. Eventually, enthusiasm waned and the project failed. The initiating executive blamed either the department heads or the author of the book—which he quickly tossed into the trash.

What went wrong?

Modern neuroscience tells us that forcing everyone else to do something the leader doesn't do habitually is a recipe for failure. Leadership is an inside job. We must first make the needed changes between our own ears before we can inspire others to follow our lead.

Studies show that the qualities exhibited by a leader account for up to 70 percent of the engagement of their followers.[1] McKinsey & Company,[2] one of the world's most respected management consulting firms, determined that around 50 percent of cultural change management efforts fail when leaders do not set good examples by adopting the recommended changes or new behaviors.

Workers do what their leaders do, not what they say.

As children, we emulated our parents. Doing so helped us learn how to walk and talk. As adults, we often look to others we want to emulate and mimic what they do. Modern neuroscience now explains how and why this works. Mirror neurons were discovered in the 1980s by neuroscientist Dr. Giacomo Rizzolati and his team from the University of Parma in Italy. They were conducting experiments on monkeys related to motor neurons, which carry signals from the spinal cord to the muscles to allow for movement. One of Rizzolati's lab assistants came waltzing in one day while chomping on an ice cream cone. One of the monkeys, who was still wired up to the monitors, observed the assistant. On the monitor, the monkey's readings lit up with electrical brain activity as if the animal was also eating the ice cream. The primate mimicked the assistant and even moved its arms and mouth as if also enjoying the cone.

Rizzolati's team conducted further research using peanuts and found that the same motor neurons fired in the same way whether the monkeys were handling the peanuts or observing others doing so. Subsequent research on humans led to the theory that mirror neurons trigger our brain to simulate the action of those we observe. We can also mimic the emotions we witness when expressed by others. This is why we cry during a sad scene in a movie. We actually feel the same emotions we observe on the big screen.

Experts believe that mirror neurons play an important role in our learning process, which is why storytelling is so powerful. We'll dive deeper into that topic in a later chapter. For leaders, an understanding of mirror neurons now places on our shoulders the grave responsibility of setting the right examples. It's easy to say "do what I say and not what I do," but the human brain will do just the opposite. It is therefore vitally important to maintain proper and good daily habits. Your team will observe your discipline, dedication, and actions. They will then do what you do and not what you tell them to do.

Vanguard Group is a Fortune 500 company and was once ranked number 18 on *Fortune*'s list of the 100 Best Companies to Work For.[3] Jack Brennan, the company's CEO during that time, once said that workers will emulate what a leader does, good or bad.

Plutarch was an ancient Greek educator and historian. He felt that most people, whether introverted or extroverted, preferred not to live in a vacuum. Instead, he believed we are naturally curious and social creatures that imitate others through close observation. If someone is cursed with a bad role model, they may unfortunately adopt bad behaviors. Therefore, all leaders have a responsibility to lead by example. Plutarch taught us how to do this through his famous Parallel Lives biographical sketches, which pictorially told positive stories about Greek and Roman heroes including Alexander the Great, Caesar, Cicero, Pericles, and others. His goal was to offer children examples of heroism that they could emulate.

When leading, are you a positive role model that your team will emulate? Are you constantly striving to become a better person, a better listener, and a better leader? Do you take full responsibility for your actions when things go wrong, or do you focus outwardly and blame others for setbacks and failures?

As mentioned in the Introduction, rather than focus outwardly on trying to change everyone else, great leaders seek to change themselves first. Once they do this, miracles can happen … within themselves and everyone they lead.

THE LAND OF OZ

An easy way to remember the concepts we've discussed in this chapter is by recalling *The Wonderful Wizard of Oz* book, written by L. Frank Baum and published in 1900 (Figure 3.8). As Baum tells us, the only thing the Tin Woodsman wanted was a heart. He appeared to lack the

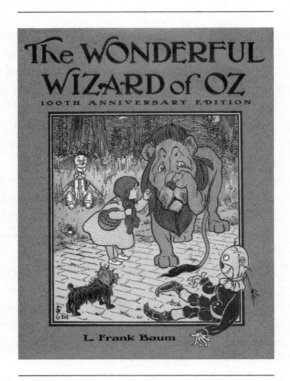

FIGURE 3.8 *The Wonderful Wizard of Oz*

Source: Cover art from *The Wonderful Wizard of Oz* by L. Frank Baum, public domain.

ability to tap into and use his emotional brain, and so could not feel or impart emotions to the extent he desired. By the end of the book, his tears were rusting his metal. If those we lead appear to be heartless, perhaps we need to do a better of job of getting past their hardened metal exteriors to see the beating hearts inside.

The Lion thought he lacked courage. In the end, he discovered that fear and courage are the opposite sides of the same coin. He had been ruled by his instinctual brain, which governs fight or flight responses. When controlled by fear, as was the case with the Lion, our gut tells us to run. When courage takes over, we can fearlessly stand our ground. If someone on your team appears to be ruled by fear and caution, and tends to delay action until the path is clearly safe, perhaps becoming frustrated and angry with them is not the answer. Maybe they just need you to lead them by example and take that first courageous step.

The Scarecrow imagined himself as an uneducated simpleton. With a head full of straw, he had convinced himself that knowledge was unattainable. He was certain that he lacked a well-developed rational brain. The Wizard eventually handed him a diploma and helped him realize that we are all wise in our own way. If those we lead tend to act more like the Scarecrow, instead of assuming they are "dumber than bricks," perhaps we need to come out from behind our curtain and find out what they do know. The wisdom they display in areas we hadn't considered may surprise us. Also, rather than assume they should instantly know everything we know, perhaps we should invoke some patience and become mentors and teachers rather than "straw bosses" on the pyramid.

In summary, *from a simplistic perspective, three primary areas of our brains influence our emotional, instinctual, and logical responses. We also have three dominant personality neurotransmitters that affect how we act, react, and deal with everything and everyone in our world.* The levels of these three neurotransmitters are either high, medium, or low.

Our three neurotransmitters influence our emotional "Tin Woodsman" brain functions, instinctual "Lion" brain, and logical "Scarecrow" brain. Based on the levels of our neurotransmitters, we tend to act more emotional, instinctual, or logical.

If we believe the ancient Greeks and several modern neuroscientists, human beings exhibit one of nine distinct personality behavioral patterns. If we can better align our communication and leadership styles with the profiles and perceptions of individuals on our team, *we can dramatically improve our ability to persuade and to lead*.

PREFACE TO THE 7 NEURON SECRETS

We think of ourselves as modern and contemporary. We can Tweet, Skype, text, Google, post, download, and SnapChat. At our local Starbucks, we can choose between Grande or Venti, whip or no whip, macchiato or mocha, blended or Americano. We can use emojis to express ourselves and make light of feelings that are often misunderstood or rarely felt.

When we do speak of love, we use a single, vague term to describe a universe of concepts that encompass playfulness, friendship, romance, marriage, relatives, professions, tastes, sounds, smells, and all sorts of feelings. As teenagers, we "love" that song or that chocolate bar, fall madly in "love" with that cheerleader or football star, or casually tell our parents that we "love" them on our way out the door.

In our thirties, we "love" our spouse and our children, we "love" our professions, we "love" our leisure time with friends, or we "love" that favorite restaurant or football team. In our sunset years, we have grown to "love" our mate, our close friends, and the fact that we can still chew our food.

We use the same word to describe all these variations that have vastly different meanings. In contrast, the ancient Greeks might have admired our technological advances, but would have been quick to criticize the unsophisticated ways in which we express the most important emotion we share with each other. The typical Athenian might have shaken a sad head toward the typical New Yorker, perhaps while trying to enlighten our generation about the meaning of seven different types of love.

In the chapters to follow, we'll explore all seven of these. *We'll also discover an astonishing truth: all seven align surprisingly well with modern neuropsychology*. By blending this ancient wisdom with the latest scientific revelations, combined with advanced team leadership concepts imparted by top military leaders, we form the Seven Secrets of Neuron Leadership. Leaders who understand and practice these principles can transform hearts and minds, starting with their own, and become revered as the most successful and "loved" team leaders in the world.

The previous chapters you've read were designed to lay the proper foundation to help you learn about the seven secrets we'll now discuss so you can ingrain them into your everyday life. Whether you have been in various leadership roles for decades, have only recently become a leader, or are aspiring to be one, you can always benefit from improving your foundational leadership knowledge and skills. Hopefully, the information provided in this book so far has helped you take some useful steps toward your leadership goals, and now it's time to explore the seven secrets.

These principles are offered in a specific order, based on the neuroscience we've explored. We begin with Dorothy from the book *The Wonderful Wizard of Oz*. She was in her ordinary world before she embarked on her journey. The first secret is discussed in this chapter, followed by the remaining six in subsequent chapters. Secret One speaks to all three of our brains, while Secrets Two and Three are more emotional.

Secrets Four and Five are more instinctually oriented, and Secrets Six and Seven are more logical. We conclude with a summary of the secrets and suggestions of how to use them in our daily lives.

Interviews, stories, and examples in every chapter will show why an understanding of all seven forms of Greek love, combined with knowledge about modern neuroscience and military team leadership, can transform the way we lead.

CHAPTER 4

Dorothy's Journey—Neuron Secret One

FIGURE 4.1   Dorothy

Source: Anna Velichkovsky, Dreamstime.com.

> If we walk far enough, we shall sometime come to someplace.
>
> —DOROTHY (FIGURE 4.1) IN *THE WONDERFUL WIZARD OF OZ*

NEURON SECRET ONE

The Principle of Prosperity: To prosper, you must love yourself by being humble and teachable.

Captain E. Royce Williams grew up in the small rural town of Clinton, Minnesota. He got a taste of the military life in high school by becoming a corporal in the Minnesota Guard. He recalls living through the depressing years of the Great Depression and hearing his mother and father whisper with worry about keeping food on the table. Scarcity became a way of life, and Royce's parents often admonished him to be frugal and stay alert—the latter to ensure he did not make mistakes that could cost them money they did not have. Royce learned early on to listen to and respect his elders, and to remain humble and teachable.

When Royce was 11, one of his idols was a man named Ted Swank. The man owned a local gas station and used his profits to buy fast toys. Swank bought a motorcycle and charged people for rides around the town. One day Royce climbed onto the back of Swank's bike and strapped on a helmet. When Swank punched it, Royce almost fell off the back. Then he grinned.

"I think I always had the need for speed," said Royce, "but once I got a taste of it on Ted's bike, I knew I could never lead a slow life."

Swank tired of his motorbike and decided to buy a plane. He invested in a World War I Navy Aircraft Factory N2N biplane. It came with two open cockpit seats and no canopy. When Royce saw it, he fell in love and his desire to someday be a pilot climbed toward the sky. He quickly cut a deal with Swank: He'd sell plane ride tickets to locals in exchange for free rides for himself. Swank and Royce shook hands, and Royce went to work.

"I was motivated to sell tickets because I really wanted to ride in that plane whenever I got the chance," said Royce.

Swank had a wild streak and thrived on "pushing the envelope." He cut corners and took risks that others thought were far too daring. To satisfy his thrill-seeking nature, Swank became a "barnstormer" and performed aerial acrobatics at shows in the area. He soon earned a reputation for his wild antics, and whenever Royce rode in the second seat of the N2N, he asked Swank to show him a trick or two.

"Swank liked to bring a big roll of toilet paper with him in the plane," said Royce. "He'd throw it out the cockpit and then spin around in circles to slice the paper into dozens of white ribbons that fluttered and floated to the ground. It was a hell of a thing to see."

Royce recalls that while Swank was a talented pilot, he was also a little cocky. He thought he knew it all and didn't need any advice. When other experienced pilots tried to give him pointers or admonish him to be more cautious, Swank just laughed and told them to get lost. He was not at all humble or teachable, and that attitude almost got him killed.

"He used to fly with a buddy in the back seat," said Royce. "His friend carried a rifle, and Swank would swoop down low enough so his buddy could shoot wild coyotes. They'd later collect the pelts and sell them to traders."

One day, when Swank wasn't being cautious enough, he crashed his plane into a remote field. When the N2N hit the ground, one of Swank's legs broke and a splintered bone drove into the hard ground. His buddy in the back seat almost died on impact. Swank was trapped in the cockpit for hours with his leg bleeding and the engine sitting in his lap. He lived, but he never flew again.

That incident taught Royce three things: (1) be humble and don't assume you know it all, (2) be teachable and listen to other experts who may know more than you, and (3) you need to love yourself enough not to take unwarranted risks.

Those lessons helped save his life many years later when the bullets started flying.

Royce enlisted in the Navy in August 1943 and attended flight school in Pensacola, Florida. One of his flight instructors was an old crop-dusting pilot who'd flown during World War I. At first Royce thought the guy's flight training knowledge might be a bit dated. When his instructor showed him a few maneuvers that he'd learned as a crop duster, Royce rolled his eyes and started to question whether he should listen. Then he recalled his father's words about being humble and teachable. He also remembered how Swank had done just the opposite and almost died. Royce decided to open his ears and learn. Years later, he was glad he did.

Royce Williams earned his wings in November 1945. He flew various propeller-driven aircraft, and then his need for speed was assuaged when they handed him the keys to a modern jet fighter. During the Korean War, Royce was assigned to Navy Fighter Squadron 781 and flew F9F-5 Panther jets off the aircraft carrier USS *Oriskany*. His missions included combat operations over North Korea to thwart attacks against the South Koreans.

"We strafed a lot of ground targets and conducted close air support missions," said Royce. "We blasted ground troops and weapons platforms but never had any dogfights because the North Koreans didn't have much of an air force. We knew the Soviets were helping them and were flying some MiG-15s in the area, but we'd never seen any."

On November 18, 1952, the *Oriskany* received orders to operate near Chongjin off the northern coast of Korea. Their operating area placed them near a Soviet airbase in Vladivostok, Russia. That morning, the weather near the carrier turned sour. Dark clouds created a thick overcast at 500 feet, and blowing snow dropped visibility down to around two miles. Bad conditions dictated radar approaches and departures for all flight operations.

Royce strapped in to his Panther and felt the jolt as the catapult rocketed him off the deck of the carrier. He pulled back on his stick, shot upward, and joined his squadron of three other Panthers. Their orders were to rain down hell on North Korean industrial targets near the Soviet border.

"We lined up with our targets and descended for our runs," said Royce. "We were expecting some heavy anti-aircraft fire, but we didn't get much. We made several bomb and strafing runs and headed back to the *Oriskany*."

Royce landed on the deck, grabbed some chow, and prepared for his second mission of the day. He'd been assigned to a CAP mission around the *Oriskany* along with three other Panthers. If any bad guys approached the carrier, Royce and his team had orders to repel them by flying close enough to warn them away. If they didn't get the message, the Panther pilots had permission to shoot them down.

"We'd flown a bunch of these CAPs and had never seen a hostile bird, let alone an enemy aircraft," said Royce. "I was planning on a routine and boring flight when I launched off the deck for the second time that day."

Fate had other plans.

Royce and the three other Panthers in his section climbed toward the clouds at around one in the afternoon. They broke through the grey cover and found clear skies above 12,000 feet. The sun glinted off Royce's canopy and splashed beams of yellow that flickered across a clear blue backdrop. He recalled the excitement he'd felt when he'd climbed into the backseat of Swank's N2N. He remembered the rattle of the biplane's engine as it rolled down a makeshift runway and the feel of freedom when Swank propelled them toward the heavens. Ever since those days, Royce had known that the sky was his home, his domain, his sanctuary.

While in his element above the clouds, Royce had been hammered by guns and rockets from the ground, but no one had yet challenged him in a dogfight, and he was beginning to wonder if they ever would.

"My radio lit up with an excited voice," said Royce, "The radar controller on the *Oriskany* blurted out a frantic report. They had spotted several bogies only eighty-three miles north of us and the bad guys were on a direct course for the carrier."

Royce and his team were ordered to intercept and repel. They ascended to 16,000 feet and scanned the horizon. Nothing. Royce looked up and down and craned his neck in a circle. Still nothing. He started to wonder if the radar contact had been a false-positive signal. He glanced upward again and spotted the smoky contrails of jet fighters. Seven of them. His adrenaline surged. Then his heart raced when he saw rays of sunlight glitter off the sides of seven silver-shiny Soviet MiG-15s. They were high above him at about 35,000 feet.

Royce forced himself to remain calm. He knew that the North Koreans only had World War II–vintage Soviet propeller-driven airplanes. They did not have jets. The Soviets had tried to fool NATO forces by painting Chinese or North Korean insignia on MiG fuselages, and disguising their pilots by having them wear false uniforms. The trick had not worked. NATO had little doubt as to who was flying those planes, and Royce was also certain that these seven MiG-15s were being flown by experienced Soviet pilots.

"I knew that MiG-15s were faster and more maneuverable than our Panthers," said Royce. "I was really hoping we could scare them off because I didn't think we'd survive a head-to-head dogfight."

Royce's radio crackled again. He heard his flight leader, LT Elwood, call down to the *Oriskany* and report that his fuel pump warning light was on. A radio operator in the Combat Information Center (CIC) on the carrier gave Elwood a green light to return to the *Oriskany*. Elwood handed off command to Royce and descended back through the cloud cover. Royce acknowledged and turned his head to the left. He saw the outline of another Panther as it banked and followed Elwood downward. He knew that LTJG Middleton, Elwood's wingman, was obligated to stay with his boss and also return to the carrier.

"I felt my heart flutter," said Royce. "I suddenly realized that if things turned hot, the odds had just dropped from four against seven to only two against seven."

Royce glanced to his right. From the cockpit of another Panther, wingman LTJG Rowland flashed him an okay sign. Royce looked upward as the seven MiGs screamed overhead and made an about-face to head back toward Vladivostok. He breathed a sigh of relief. Maybe the Soviets were heading home.

The MiGs had closed to within 45 miles of the *Oriskany*, well inside the threat zone, before heading away. Not wanting to take any chances, Royce and Rowland climbed up to 26,000 feet to shadow the Soviets and warn them off. They'd only gone a short distance before the MiGs made a sudden about-face.

"I saw their burners ignite as the seven MiGs made a sharp turn back toward the *Oriskany*," said Royce. "They broke into two formations of three and four aircraft each and dove toward the carrier. As they passed through the cloud cover, their vapor trails vanished and we lost contact. I radioed the *Oriskany* and called out 'lost contact' to warn them. They radioed back and said that the bogey blips were no longer visible on radar."

Worried that they might attack the carrier, Royce dove toward the last known position of the MiGs. Seconds later, four of the Soviet MiGs burst upward through the clouds and started firing at Royce and Rowland. Their cannons flashed orange as 23- and 37-mm rounds raced toward the Panthers. Instinct kicked in and Royce banked to avoid the gunfire. Then anger flushed his cheeks. He focused his eyes on the lead MiG and dove. He clicked his guns and fired a burst. A stream of 20-mm rounds shot from his cannon and pounded into the MiG's fuselage.

"The MiG's pilot jerked left and right to avoid my cannon fire, but not in time," Royce said. "The guy fell out of formation trailing black smoke and a spray of airplane parts."

Royce's wingman saw the lead MiG break away and followed him downward to 8,000 feet to ensure he didn't crash into the carrier. Rowland tried to fire his guns at the MiG to finish him off, but his gun jammed. He finally broke off and turned upward to rejoin Royce.

The three remaining MiGs in the formation of four wanted retribution. They pointed toward Royce and blasted him with more cannon fire. Royce heard a dozen rounds pound into the metal of his Panther. For a fleeting moment, he felt a wave of panic well up inside his chest. Rowland had not yet returned. Royce was all alone and now faced three superior aircraft. They were racing toward him with guns blazing and Royce wondered if his first dogfight would be his last.

He took a deep breath and recalled his training. The old crop-dusting instructor he'd once doubted had taught him a few tricks. Royce let his muscle memory take control as he rolled and jinked and banked. Just when he thought he might survive the day, the three MiGs from the other sortie broke through the clouds to join their cohorts.

"One MiG managed to get behind me on my six," said Royce. "I used a trick I'd been taught to make him overshoot my position. Then I did a loop and got on his six. I locked on and fired."

The Panther's high-explosive armor-piercing rounds detonated against the MiG's shiny fuselage. The plane disintegrated. Parts flew into the air and forced Royce to dodge the debris. Using a few more ruses he'd learned, he lined up on another MiG and fired. The Soviet plane broke away as the rounds appeared to hit, but Royce didn't follow to verify. He was too busy trying to shake two more Soviets off his six. Yellow tracers from cannon fire raced passed Royce's cockpit as he executed rollercoaster maneuvers to avoid the rounds. He heard several hit with dull thuds. He held his breath and waited for his plane to explode into a ball of fire.

When it didn't, Royce went after another MiG and pounded it with 20-mm cannon fire. The MiG broke off in a trail of smoke. Then he heard several more rounds slam into the side of his plane. He felt the Panther shudder and knew instantly that he'd lost most of his rudder and aileron control. Only his elevators were still functioning normally. Then his low fuel light lit up.

"I didn't have any choice at that point," said Royce. "Due to the patchy cloud cover, Rowland had not been able to find me again, and I was badly damaged. I had to break off and return to the *Oriskany*."

With 37-mm rounds whizzing past his canopy, Royce dove his wounded plane toward the dark cumulus cover. He raced past 12,000 feet and struggled to keep his plane pointed toward home. He broke through the clouds and searched for the carrier. Nothing. Only empty ocean filled his view. He began to wonder if he'd crash into the cold ocean and drown in the Sea of Japan before they could rescue him. He shook off the thought and glanced downward.

He saw a formation of U.S. warships and dropped down to 5,000 feet. A few of the ships did not at first recognize his aircraft, which had been badly damaged. They opened fire. Royce almost laughed at the irony. They finally stopped firing when they realized he wasn't a MiG.

Royce clicked his radio and reported his situation to the *Oriskany's* CIC. He informed them that his plane was barely controllable above 170 knots and that, with his damaged controls, he did not believe he could properly line up with the carrier for a landing. By then he was flying too low to eject.

Any carrier landing is a bitch. If you don't line up right, you could die. If you come in too fast or too slow, you could die. Or, you could just die. Landing with a damaged plane is a bitch on steroids. You lack the ability to make small adjustments as the deck pitches and rolls and surges up and down in the roiling sea. Fortunately, the captain aboard the *Oriskany* made the course corrections needed by moving his ship into position and by adjusting as required to allow Royce to land.

"My Panther nearly slammed onto the deck and skidded from side to side when I hit the tailhook, but she held together," said Royce. "I climbed out of the cockpit and thanked God that those Soviet pilots hadn't been better shots. I still don't know how I made it back in one piece."

Royce hadn't made it back in one piece. The next day, the deck crew circled all the holes on Royce's plane. Some were made by 23-mm rounds, others by 30-mm cannon fire, and others by parts that had broken loose and ripped through the metal. Royce climbed up on one wing while someone snapped a photo (Figure 4.2).

"They counted 263 holes in my plane," said Royce. "It's a miracle she held together long enough for me to get back to the *Oriskany*."

Sometime later, Vice Admiral Robert Briscoe informed Royce that he'd shot down at least three of the MiGs, but he was cautioned that he could tell no one about the encounter. Details of Royce's 35-minute dogfight with seven Soviet MiGs remained top secret for another 50 years. When Russia finally declassified the incident, they reported the names of the four lost MiG pilots.

"I feel bad for those guys I shot down," said Royce. "They were just pilots doing their job, just like me. But I'm damn glad I survived that day. If I hadn't remembered what I'd been taught, I wouldn't have. My advice to leaders, and to anyone, is to be humble and teachable. You never know if it might one day save your life."

When I visited Royce at his canyon home in Escondido, California, he met me at the door with a grin and a glass. He asked if I wanted to join him for a drink. I said I'd have whatever he was having.

FIGURE 4.2   Captain Royce Williams

Source: Photo courtesy of CAPT Royce Williams.

He said, "Well, I used to drink Bourbon until President Eisenhower told me he had some damn fine Scotch and that I should consider switching. I've always tried to be humble and teachable, so I did."

Today, spry at the age of 92, E. Royce Williams is one of only 200 members who belong to an elite club of the finest aviators in history called the Golden Eagles. Photojournalist and screenwriter C.J. Machado is spearheading a project to document Royce's story in a short film titled *The Forgotten Hero of the Forgotten War*. Visit www.love amazinglyproductions.com/sd-ride-for-vets.html for more information and updates, or to provide support.

PHILAUTIA LOVE

Captain Williams's story illustrates the First Neuron Secret: The Principle of Prosperity: To prosper, you must love yourself by being humble and teachable.

The Greek word for prosperity is *euodoó*, pronounced as "you do," which seems apropos. In its purest sense, *euodoó* means "to have a prosperous journey." A sibling to *euodoó* is the Greek word *sozo*, which translates to "save, deliver, protect, heal, preserve, do well, and be made whole."

In an earlier chapter, we mentioned another Greek word, *arête*, which is a close cousin to *euodoó*. Translating *arête* into English requires some creativity. Some translators call it "excellence," while others say it means "goodness." A few believe it stands for "virtue." The most common reference, and the one most relevant to our discussion, is "becoming the best that you can be."

In the epic tale *The Iliad*, the Greeks used *arête* to depict the brave warriors who exemplified the best physical skill and fortitude on the battlefield. The ancients cherished heroes like Hector and Achilles and told and retold their stories time and again. The Greeks honored the examples of humanity and courage these champions brought to bear against all odds, and against the backdrop of a brutal, tribal society.

The Greeks also gave us Odysseus in *The Odyssey*, in which *arête* is used to show the embodiment of resourcefulness, cunning, and courage. Odysseus's wife, Penelope, depicts the female side of *arête* when she shows us that even while enveloped in disaster, turmoil, and grief, we can still raise our chins and exhibit excellence and mettle.

The Athenian Socrates lived during the fifth century BC and stood as a shining example of someone who strived to attain the highest degree of intellectual and moral excellence.

What can we learn from the examples set by Socrates, Odysseus, Penelope, Hector, and Achilles? As leaders, we should seek to attain *arête* in all our endeavors and encourage our teams to do the same. By doing so, we can become the best leaders we can be, and we can also become shining examples for others to follow.

Before others will believe in us, and therefore follow us, we must learn to love ourselves by embedding *arête* into our psyche. The Greeks described self-love as *philautia*. They divided this into two categories: selfish and selfless. The former describes an unhealthy narcissistic type of self-love. The latter embodies selfless *philautia*, which reflects *arête*.

The Greeks believed that our capacity to love ourselves constrained our capacity to love others. They believed it was impossible to reflect love and kindness to others if you did not first love yourself. The only way we can truly love ourselves is to be humble and teachable enough to learn and practice *arête*. If we are not humble, we are instead arrogant, pretentious, and conceited. If we are any of these, how can we love ourselves? And if we are not teachable, we will never learn how to be humble.

Philautia is emotional, instinctual, and logical all rolled into one. Loving ourselves requires knowing ourselves. We must open our hearts and minds and let go of our fears to adopt *philautia* into our lives. In the beginning of this book, I referred to leadership as an "inside job." This is *philautia*. We can lead no one if we can't lead ourselves. We can't lead ourselves unless we learn to love ourselves.

Philautia love means setting aside our egos, being honest with ourselves, and taking better care of ourselves so we can be better leaders whom others will emulate. Every day, every hour, and every minute your team will observe what you do and how you lead. If you set a great example, you will have a great team. If not, chances are, you will eventually have no team at all.

Aristotle once said, "We are what we repeatedly do. Excellence then, is not an act, but a habit." What are your daily habits? Are they healthy or unhealthy? Do they propel you toward your life's passion and purpose or toward the rocks of doom? If the latter, your team will do what you do and follow you there.

Some historians called Musonius Rufus the "Socrates of Rome." He was a famous Stoic philosopher, who taught his followers to form good habits. He believed that one could not just study a discipline, such as ethics, but instead must live it every day. In fact, the ancient word for ethics is synonymous with habits. Rufus believed that you could not rely solely upon intuitions, as they could be wrong. He advised tracking progress toward better daily habits by writing them down in journals. You may wish to attain leadership *arête*, but unless you track your journey daily, how will you know if you're making progress?

CHIEF *EUDAIMONIA* OFFICER

In my opinion, the word that all leaders should memorize is *eudaimonia*, which the ancient Greeks used to indicate a state of being happy, healthy, and prosperous. Also, having good "indwelling spirit," which we can attain by practicing *arête*. I believe that the true function of every leader isn't just to ensure a properly functioning firm, as in a "well-oiled machine," or to solely ensure a profitable organization with a high EBITDA and stock value. It is to embody *philautia* by striving to attain *arête* and create an atmosphere of *eudaimonia*.

The chief executive officer of any company should also be the chief *eudaimonia* officer. We live in a capricious world. Most people judge leaders based on logical values. Quarterly growth, P to E valuations, profits, market share, cost cutting, and so on. They take out calculators and form opinions based on a set of numbers, statistics, and percentages. They judge the book by its cover.

Do you buy a company's stock based solely on a set of numbers, or do you "crack the book" to see what's inside? Do the company's leaders care more about people than profits? Do they strive to create an atmosphere of *eudaimonia*? Do they attract the best talent by building a reputation for fairness, trust, mindfulness, autonomy, altruistic endeavors, "families first," and prosperity in all aspects of life?

If not, how might that affect their long-term performance?

Wall Street hates the word *eudaimonia*. At best, they are indifferent to its meaning. Workers are slaves, right? They are only means to an end, which is to drive up stock values. If employees don't like where they work, they can quit. If a CEO wants to write a personal check to save a whale, go for it, but forget about doing so from the company's checkbook.

Obviously, investors with such attitudes have not done their homework. They have not yet discovered that Conscious Capitalists lead companies that are an order of magnitude more profitable on Wall Street. Stockbrokers should be encouraging that CEOs live by the definition of *eudaimonia*.

In the introduction to this book, we learned that most workers are checked out and are just trying to muddle through each day at the office. Recall that Gallup's State of the American Workplace report determined that 20 percent of respondents were actively disengaged. These employees hate their jobs, complain continuously, do just enough to keep from getting fired, and frequently surf the Internet in search of another job they can hate. Another 47 percent of workers are mostly disengaged. They report to work but are lackluster in their daily efforts. They are not inspired by their managers. Leaders offering free lunches, nap rooms, massages, and other benefits fail to engage these workers.

The implications and consequences are far reaching. As noted earlier, the hit to the world's economy is around $1 trillion each year. If this does not herald the need for better leadership, what does?

Perhaps we measure our everyday leadership accomplishments in terms of graphs, charts, numbers, statistics, accolades, and wins. Maybe the arrows point upward most of the time, but sometimes our success feels empty. Maybe, if we're honest with ourselves, we're one of the 67 percent who's not fully engaged, motivated, or inspired. Perhaps we're showing up just to earn a living so we can enjoy life outside of the office. We want to be one of the 33 percent that's fully engaged, or even part of the top 5 percent that's inspired, motivated, and fulfilled by our profession.

We're just not sure how to get there.

THE BUCK STARTS HERE

When Dorothy was in her dull and gray ordinary world at home, she didn't really appreciate what she had. She wasn't as grateful as she could have been because she didn't love herself unconditionally. Then she got swept up by a tornado and landed in the Land of Oz. Initially she saw it as an adventurous departure from her ordinary world. She met new friends, explored interesting new surroundings, and got caught up in a worthwhile quest. Then scary and strange things happened. The witch got bitchy, monkeys attacked, the wizard helped Dorothy's friends get a bunch of cool stuff they already had, and Dorothy finally had to eat some humble pie. She had to admit that her previous dreary thoughts about home were unfounded. She hadn't been humble and teachable by those in her ordinary world. She also didn't love herself enough to love her life. Finally, she clicked her heels three times and discovered that "there's no place like home."

Many of us, fresh out of college or the military or whatever, embarked on our career paths full of "piss and vinegar" as they say. We were determined to change the world. Decades later, many of us have discovered that there's no place like home. Along the path of our own journey, we found the elixir and decided to come back home to offer what we've learned to others. What was the secret we discovered along our path?

We learned that *Leadership is Love*.

In fact, it's seven forms of love. To incorporate all seven forms into our lives and professions, and to embrace the Seven Secrets of Neuron Leadership, we must start with the first form. We must learn how to love ourselves unconditionally. To do this, we must undertake a *Hero's Journey*.

Author Joseph Campbell adapted this ancient format of storytelling, which has underpinned human interaction since the dawn of our species, and delivered it to the world as a monomyth—a pattern that we all recognize and try to emulate in our own life journeys. With the Hero's Journey pattern, one that we've experienced in nearly every book or movie, we start with a hero found in a mundane and normal "everyday" life.

For the purposes of our journey from where we are to where we want to be, we must place ourselves in the role of the hero. We are now standing on the edge of a large ocean. We can't see the other side, but we know the shore we stand upon today is not where we belong. Something tugs at our heart, whispers in our ears, and shoves us closer to the edge. Perhaps we are afraid. Maybe we're tired from the deluge of our daily struggles. We may have found comfort in the familiar, much like our favorite childhood blanket or those cozy faded jeans we cherish. We must be willing to step out of our comfort zones and find the courage to board the ship of dreams and sail to a new land.

Campbell describes the impetus to embark on the Hero's Journey as an act of volition akin to Theseus when he heard about the Minotaur, or Odysseus who was swept away by a malignant agent, or as a "mere blunder" when our hero stumbles across an event or person that pushes him or her toward the edge. In our case, as the hero of our story, we must mimic Theseus and be willing to undertake our adventure of our own free will. We must set aside fear, pride, sloth, repose, and the advice of well-meaning friends or loved ones and risk stepping out of our comfortable world. We must learn that a hero is anyone who has survived pain and overcome obstacles and has been transformed by his or her struggles.

A true hero is willing to learn how to love themselves unconditionally, warts and all.

In the book *The Wonderful Wizard of Oz*, L. Frank Baum describes Dorothy in her ordinary world before the tornado whisked her and Toto away to the Land of Oz:

When Dorothy stood in the doorway and looked around, she could see nothing but the great gray prairie on every side. Not a tree nor a house broke the broad sweep of flat country that reached to the edge of the sky in all directions. The sun had baked the plowed land into a gray mass, with little cracks running through it. Even the grass was not green, for the sun had burned the tops of the long blades until they were the same gray color to be seen everywhere. Once the house had been painted, but the sun blistered the paint and the rains washed it away, and now the house was as dull and gray as everything else.

Dorothy was obviously not happy in her gray home, but she was also reluctant to leave because, after all, it was her home. In truth, it was not the dull house or gray land that Dorothy dreaded, it was the perception of the ordinary world that she had created between her own two ears. In truth, she was unhappy with herself.

Finally, a dark and ominous tornado launched her house into the air and hurled her toward the Land of Oz so she could begin her Hero's Journey.

There are three phases in the Hero's Journey: Departure, Struggle, and Return. In the Departure phase, our hero usually refuses the call. It's natural for us to be reluctant, to question whether a new path is right for us, or to wonder if we should take any risks at all. If our pain or desire is not high enough yet to overcome our trepidation or to motivate us to do something to attain the life we've always wanted, to become the leader we were meant to be, to find the true purpose for our life, then this book may not be right for us—at least not yet. However, if our desire *is* high enough, then it's time to start our journey.

When we muster the courage to step outside our comfort zone and change from the inside, we can finally depart on our journey.

As we do our exercises and work on changing our attitudes and our ability to improve our situations and relationships, we will be in the Struggle portion of our journey. This will not be easy, but it will be enlightening, uplifting, renovating, exciting, and fulfilling. We will learn things about ourselves we never knew, and accomplish things we never thought possible. We will see miraculous changes, some subtle, some eye-opening, all necessary. We will become more emotionally and professionally healthy, and become ready for the Return.

In the final phase of our journey, we can return with the "magic elixir" of wisdom we've discovered and impart that gift to others—perhaps to our subordinates, colleagues, or even our boss. We will be grateful for our situation, our profession, our income, our responsibilities, our challenges, our subordinates, our colleagues, our opportunities, our abundance, our friends, our team, our loved ones, and, most importantly, ourselves. We will be thankful each day we are granted another sunrise on this planet, for our journey is never at an end.

As Campbell says, the hero is the champion of things becoming, not of things become.

ILLUSIONS

To depart and cross the Hero's Journey threshold from our ordinary world, sail upon the turbulent ocean of challenges and tests we must face to reach the other shore, and finally return with the elixir that will take us to new levels of success, we must be willing to let go of the things we learned to hang on to—mainly our illusions. The first illusion is control. Even the strongest of us needs to be "big" enough to admit that we fear losing control. We do not need to be ashamed of our control illusions. In fact, they are merely a part of our survival instincts, deeply engrained in our instinctual brain. We all feel the need to be in control, to varying degrees, to survive.

Although some of us may thrive on chaos, even the most chaotic must admit they prefer to fashion some form of control out of the chaos. We all fear the loss of approval, a lack of recognition, or being forced into battles we did not create. Mostly, we fear letting go and letting the coin fall to one side or the other. When we want "heads," we *really* want heads, not tails. We want to manipulate outcomes to our benefit, or better phrased, to our *perceived* benefit. What we may not realize is that what we want is often not what we *need*, and may be to our detriment.

As difficult as this may sound, we must learn to let the flipped coin fall where it may without interfering. The more we try to force our will on circumstances and other people, the more the universe and others will rebel against us. For every action, there is an equal and opposite reaction. Do we really want to continue fighting the currents of life and exhaust ourselves by paddling upstream? Could it be that our desire to manipulate and control ourselves and others will lead to the wreckage of our craft along the shores of life? Often, trying to control people, places, and things is a path to disaster more than bliss.

Rather than trying to bend every outcome to our will, can we be willing to let go of our illusions and set aside our fears over outcomes we are usually powerless to control? Chances are, we will be surprised and delighted when, after we let go and let things be as they should be, we are even more pleased with the results. We may see that what "was meant to be" is far more to our liking than any envisioned conclusion that our limited imagination could possibly have perceived.

When Epictetus was a young boy, he was a slave to Roman aristocrats. While in bondage, he could have been beaten or killed by his owners. He later shed the shackles and became a Stoic philosopher. Although a free man, he still lived on the edge of a knife. As a philosopher, if he rubbed an imperial Roman authority the wrong way, he might have wound up in chains. In fact, he was later exiled because of his views.

Epictetus dealt with both of these precarious situations by focusing on what he could and could not control. He advised that we can only have control over our own beliefs, thoughts, attitudes, and actions. Everything else, despite our well-meaning desires or constant forcing and meddling, is not controllable.

The U.S. Army apparently understands this concept given that they incorporate it into their Master Resilience Training Course, which is designed to produce platoon and squad leaders. Soldiers learn why resilience is critical for success and well-being and about factors that predict resilience, with a specific focus on change. They are taught that even in adverse conditions, they may not have control over the circumstance, but they do have control over their tongues and actions.

If we are humble and teachable, we can learn how to better discern what we can and should control and let go of any expectations over what we can't. Once we know just how far our arms and legs can reach, we can learn to love ourselves unconditionally.

HUMBLE AND TEACHABLE

Despite being the class valedictorian, Greg Keithley decided to enlist in the Navy after he graduated from high school. Over the next 31 years, inspirational and impactful leaders motivated and helped Greg earn a master's degree, earn his wings, fly F-14 and F/A-18 fighter aircraft, graduate from the Navy's famous TOPGUN training program, become a tactics instructor, complete five combat deployments, command a Strike Fighter squadron, and command the Navy's West Coast Strike Fighter Wing. Along the way, he gained the nickname call sign "Chaser" and retired as a captain.

When asked to define the meaning of leadership, Chaser said, "It's simple but not easy. Leaders must have the ability to inspire and impact others."

During his first few years in the Navy, while working as a hull maintenance "welding" technician, Chaser was inspired and impacted by Chief Roque, a Filipino who had enlisted to earn his U.S. citizenship.

"Chief Roque invested in me and took the time to know me. He encouraged me to stay in the Navy. When I asked him why he cared so much about others he said, 'show somebody you care and watch what happens.' Roque cared for others, but he did not coddle them. Instead, he used tough love to push them beyond self-imposed boundaries."

After Chaser graduated from the University of San Diego, he earned his commission and was accepted into Navy flight school. During the six-month wait for flight training, he reported to the Naval Air Station at Miramar in San Diego, California, and worked for Commander John "Bug" Roach—a legend in the fighter community.

"What became obvious to me from the first day I met Bug was how many people gravitated toward him. He cared for everyone, including me, even though I was a green ensign who hadn't yet been to flight school. He was the epitome of a leader who inspired and impacted others."

Not long after Chaser started F-14 flight training, Bug was lost in an A-4 accident off the coast of San Diego.

"I saw him that morning," said Chaser. "He was riding his motorized scooter. He pulled up next to me and asked about my schedule for the day. I told him I had two simulators to complete. He just grinned and said he was going flying in an hour and that one day I'd get to fly the real thing, too. His said, 'come get me after I land and we'll go to the club.' I completed my second simulator and walked down the hallway at the Wing. I wondered why everyone was so quiet and somber, and then I learned that Bug was gone. I had a hollow feeling in my gut that I carry with me to this day.

"I could write a book about Bug, but what I remember most is how he treated people with respect and kindness. For the rest of my career, that's what I looked for in a leader, and what I tried to emulate when leading others."

Years later, after earning his wings and a few more stripes on his sleeve, Chaser was thrust into a change management leadership situation where the ugly cancer of apathy and discontent had taken root.

"I was given command of an airwing aboard an aircraft carrier," said Chaser. "We were headed toward a war zone, and my orders were to get my team ready for action. That was a tall order because they were disheartened, unmotivated, and lacked confidence. On one bulkhead, they'd hung a big sign that said 'We Suck.' At first I thought it was a joke. Then I learned that they actually believed it."

Chaser encouraged his guys to open up and talk freely. He allowed them ample time to vent, complain, and bitch without interruption. When chests were finally clear, he asked them one simple question: "where do you want to be?" He asked if they wanted to remain where they were, in a dismal and miserable state, or if they wanted to change. When most expressed a desire to change, he helped them create a vision of where they could be if they worked together as a team. He then explained that to attain their vision, they all needed to be humble and teachable and focus on what they could impact.

Chaser had to make some difficult decisions to transfer out individuals he knew would never embrace the vision or cooperate with the team. Over time, he earned the trust and respect of the rest of his team, including his department heads. By doing so, he gained the cooperation he needed from the commanding officer of the carrier and others onboard who could assist. Chaser frequently listened to his team and tried to remain humble and teachable enough to set aside his bias and ego and implement their suggestions when it made sense to do so.

Chaser's airwing removed the "We Suck" sign. Over time, with his guidance and leadership, they began to see that each of them brought something unique and important to the rest of the team, and they were stronger when they worked together. Within a few years, they turned things around and earned every top performance award available for safety, maintenance, and battle readiness.

For Chaser, the idea of leadership is an all-in proposition. If you can't commit to immersing yourself into the human aspect of an organization, you shouldn't be surprised when it never takes off.

"Virtually everyone wants to be inspired. If that essential element of life is lacking, your soul aches and you feel unhealthy and malnourished, almost as if you're dying inside. It's easy to get sidetracked by administrative tasks in a pressure-packed environment that operates at the speed of 'send.' The challenge for every leader is to ensure they are personally engaged with their team. Using a keyboard won't cut it. I can't remember a single time where I was impacted by a leader's virtual presence."

Chaser is now the executive director of the Tailhook Association. When asked why he went to work for a nonprofit organization after retiring from the Navy, he said, "Anyone who has been involved with flight operations on aircraft carriers, from pilots to aircrew to deck crew personnel, is automatically qualified to join the Tailhook Association. We have a long and proud reputation across many decades, and our membership includes some of the best pilots and crewmembers in the world, including aviators who fought in World War II, the Korean War, Vietnam, and the Iraqi wars. When I looked at my options after retirement, I wanted to stay connected with those who had inspired and impacted me over the years. The Tailhook Association has almost 9,000 members. Most are current or aspiring leaders, and I feel honored to be a part of this outstanding organization."

Chaser is motivated to ensure that the name Tailhook connotes a positive image in the minds of all who hear it. He feels it is vitally important to honor and respect the heroes who have risked everything to complete some of the most dangerous and daring missions in history.

Most importantly, by serving his country and leading others, Chaser discovered the importance of learning to love yourself by being humble and teachable.

TEN *PHILAUTIA* LEADERSHIP REVIEW POINTS

1. The First Neuron Secret is: The Principle of Prosperity: To prosper, you must love yourself by being humble and teachable.
2. This principle is about self-love as defined by the Greek word *philautia*.
3. *Philautia* is emotional, instinctual, and logical all rolled into one.
4. Embracing *philautia* requires creating an atmosphere of *eudaimonia*.

5. *Eudaimonia* is a Greek word that refers to a state of being happy, healthy, and prosperous.
6. Many leaders have learned that the true definition of leadership is love.
7. To improve our leadership abilities, we must be willing to undertake our own Hero's Journey.
8. We must also be ready to let go of the illusions that have previously plagued our journey.
9. To learn how to better love ourselves, and become better leaders, we must be humble and teachable.
10. This principle can be summed by these two words: *be humble*.

THREE STEPS TO *PHILAUTIA* LEADERSHIP

1. *Policy:* Leaders and teammates should be encouraged to be humble and teachable by spending one hour each week assuming the duties of one person on their team. For example, Herb Kelleher, founder of Southwest Airlines, often helped baggage handlers load luggage.
2. *Procedure:* The firm should pay for ongoing leadership training and third-party coaching to help leaders improve their team leadership knowledge, skills, and practices. Included should be an exercise for individuals to honestly evaluate themselves, recognize and accept character assets and deficiencies, and love themselves despite any shortcomings. Management by Objective (MBO) rewards should include items for how well leaders are teachable and readily adopt what they have learned in training and coaching programs.
3. *Practice:* Leaders should set aside one hour each week for one person to teach others on the team. For example, a sales rep might be encouraged to do a presentation on a customer case study to discuss the situations, problems, and solutions she and her team delivered. She should include the good and the bad aspects (areas of improvement) and ensure others are recognized for their contributions. This will reward the team for their success and inspire others to emulate the actions.

ONE *PHILAUTIA* LEADERSHIP EXERCISE

Our first exercise is short, but not necessarily easy. Take out a notepad or fire up your PC or iPad and answer the question below. Think about each numbered item for some time before writing your answer, and be as thorough as possible. You should write at least one paragraph for each number. If you skimp on this, the NSA will know and you'll receive an "F" for this exercise.

QUESTION: How would those whom you lead rate you as a leader in these seven areas?

1. Being humble and teachable
2. Encouraging playfulness and fun
3. Being generous
4. Having passion and purpose
5. Being courageous and committed
6. Exercising authority
7. Showing patience and wisdom

Life has its beginnings,
        each with its own
Special promises,
        each a door opening
To some new wonder,
Each a unique melody fashioned
        in our hearts,
Each a personal adventure
        even as at time's beginning
When darkness was dispelled
        and the sun and moon
Were first appointed to guard
        the heavens and lovingly
To guide the day and night.
Such beginnings are a renewal
        of our very being,
A sometimes fragile gift
        that must be tended and loved,
        nourished and understood,

Until all that can be, will be,

And life continues to be

      a joyful creation

Of promises and original melodies

      and endless new beginnings.

—*Dr. James Kavanaugh, from* Quiet Waters

CHAPTER 5

Playful Toto—Neuron Secret Two

FIGURE 5.1   Toto

Source: Getzion, Dreamstime.com.

> Toto played all day long, and Dorothy played with him, and loved him dearly.

—L. FRANK BAUM, *THE WONDERFUL WIZARD OF OZ* (FIGURE 5.1)

NEURON SECRET TWO

The Principle of Familiarity: Play to win by treating everyone like family.

Jo Dee Catlin Jacob was born into a Navy family in Annapolis, Maryland, home of the famous naval academy of the same name. Her father served as a diesel boat submariner during World War II. Jo Dee's high school record earned her entry into the prestigious Stanford University in Northern California. As a "Navy brat," she didn't quite fit in with her anti-war classmates and professors at Stanford. From her dorm room, she watched in horror as students smashed windows and burned down the ROTC building to protest the Vietnam War.

"I didn't share the anti-military opinions of my classmates," Jo Dee recalls. "Still, I never intended to pursue a long-term career in the Navy."

Jo Dee graduated with distinction in art history and then fought to find work in a struggling economy. "Everyone had trouble finding jobs," she said. "Even those who graduated at the top of their class couldn't get hired."

She accepted a position as a clerk in a local department store and supplemented her meager income by offering piano lessons. Every month, when she counted pennies to pay her rent, she watched a smiling friend parade by in a crisp Navy uniform.

"She was having a lot more fun than I was," Jo Dee said. "Finally, I said to myself, 'nuts to this! I'm joining the Navy.'"

Jo Dee figured she'd give Uncle Sam no more than two years of her life. She never imagined how demanding those first 24 months would be. Some of her friends shunned her for joining the military, and when she returned home on leave she faced curiosity and suspicion whenever she wore a uniform. In nearly every one of her duty stations, she was the lone woman in a sea of men. Lacking any female role models, she had to learn how to sink or swim on her own.

"I wasn't expecting a cakewalk," said Jo Dee, "but out of 15 different duty stations, I was the first or only woman in 12 of them. Even so, for every dinosaur I encountered, there were five egalitarian men who helped me succeed."

While she was stationed in Subic Bay, the Philippines, in 1976, one of those men, naval aviator Glenn Jacob, offered Jo Dee a ring. She said yes, and they are still happily married to this day.

Once Jo Dee's first two years in the Navy came and went, she signed on again, put her head down, and plowed through the next several years while working in ordnance, logistics, and international security.

Jo Dee thrived in the Navy for 27 years, and along the way learned several important lessons about leadership. She felt privileged that most of her career occurred before the age of mobile phones and the Internet.

"When you are eyeball to eyeball with your team," said Jo Dee, "you can be a much better leader. I worry that too many leaders today spend way too much time in front of screens instead of leading people on the front lines."

One of Jo Dee's early mentors was a captain named Stan Arthur. He was the chief of staff for operations at Headquarters U.S. Pacific Fleet, and later became Vice Chief of Naval Operations (VNCO). Jo Dee and Admiral Arthur remain friends to this day.

> "He was a wonderful man who had great faith in me and provided opportunities I couldn't even imagine," said Jo Dee.

Admiral Arthur accepted the post of Vice Chief of Naval Operations on July 6, 1992. While serving as the Navy's number two, he was the most senior naval aviator serving shortly after the infamous 1991 Tailhook Association sexual harassment situation. Arthur did what he thought was right and best in the wake of the incident, but Senator Dave Durenberger (R-Minnesota), disagreed. When President Bill Clinton nominated Arthur as the prospective Commander of the United States Pacific Command, the nomination was quickly withdrawn after Durenberger questioned Arthur's handling of the sexual harassment allegations raised by one of the senator's constituents.

Arthur set an example by remaining steadfast to his principles and exhibiting a high degree of integrity, even while many chose to throw stones. He elected to retire from the Navy in 1995, rather than allow the Pacific fleet command post to remain unfilled during the long Tailhook Association legal proceedings.

Jo Dee recalls having even more respect for Arthur after he chose to leave the career he loved rather than stand in the way of doing what he knew was right. While devastating to Arthur, the Tailhook incident reminds us of the need to ensure that we maintain proper boundaries around the "play" we allow our teams. *Ludus* love encourages us to instill levity, fun, and play into the mix to help relieve tension, foster better team bonding, and ensure a healthy balance, but we also need to provide clear limits.

Jo Dee recalls one boss who was not the best at setting proper limits, either with others or with himself. He apparently did not want women to serve in "his Navy" and so offered little respect, encouragement, or civility. His idea of "fun and play" was not a healthy one, and he was not willing to change.

> "The hostile environment that I experienced is a case study in bad leadership," said Jo Dee. "He encouraged and allowed filthy jokes, malicious office conduct, and blatant disrespect. Because of the way I was treated, and the way my hard work and ideas were dismissed, and the poor examples of leadership I was offered, my performance wobbled. I was thrilled to accept my next set of orders."

Jo Dee found the statement above to be a rare case, as most of her bosses and mentors were exceptional people with high moral standards, much like Admiral Arthur. Through 27 years in the Navy, Jo Dee worked for and with a host of excellent leaders. As in any career, she also met a few examples of the opposite. In her opinion, the difference is less about who we are on the outside, and more about who we strive to be on the inside.

> "Leadership really starts with people," said Jo Dee. "I don't think you can lead without having frequent interactions with people and without being kind, caring, and thoughtful. I try to treat people like expensive Waterford goblets that should be treasured. I think of them as vessels that deserve to be wrapped in velvet cases to be used again, and not just cups that are used once and then thrown away. I always place a Dixie Cup® on my desk to remind me of that."

Jo Dee learned that *ludus* love starts with being empathetic and caring about your people. While the ancients describe this form of love as mostly about fun and games, they also understood that it begins with viewing everyone as family. It requires seeing them as precious goblets and not as throwaway paper cups. *Ludus* love must include a healthy balance between serious work and stress-relieving recreation.

Jo Dee eventually attained the rank of captain and spent her final tour of duty commanding the naval station at Guam, a U.S. territory in the Pacific Ocean. Not long before airplanes flew into the World Trade Center buildings on 9/11, Jo Dee retired, otherwise she might have been at the Pentagon that very day. Instead, she stepped out of her military life after receiving a pivotal phone call. The voice on the line asked if she might be interested in leading a large nonprofit organization in San Diego, California, and spearheading their fundraising campaign.

"I never hesitated even though I didn't have fundraising experience. I was a top recruiter and I knew it would be easier to ask people for money than for their son or daughter," she said with a smile.

Jo Dee jumped in with both feet and accepted the positon as the Chief Executive Officer of Girl Scouts San Diego. At the time, the organization had 30,000 young girls, but like many nonprofits, gaining visibility and donations remained a difficult challenge. As the newly minted leader of one of the largest Girl Scout organizations in the country, Jo Dee needed to solve these difficult problems.

With 9/11 still fresh on everyone's mind, her Girl Scouts wanted to send cookies to active military serving overseas. Problem was, in the middle of a major anthrax scare, and given the expense and difficulty of sending anything by mail, this seemed impossible. Jo Dee used her military savvy to launch Operation Thin Mint®. She contacted a colleague in Singapore, Captain Jeff Wagner, and gained approval to ship boxes of cookies in bulk by way of commercial APL containers. Over the next fourteen years, the scouts shipped over 2.5 million boxes of cookies to tens of thousands of troops stationed overseas.

"The girls hand-wrote notes to sailors, soldiers, airmen, and marines, personally thanking them for their service," said Jo Dee. "This was great for the girls because it improved their writing skills along with their geography skills—they had to learn where the troops were located. It also taught them how to open their hearts and give to those who were giving so much to us."

This task, for Girl Scouts San Diego, entailed a lot of work, but Jo Dee and her team injected a lot of fun and laughter into the process. During hundreds of meetings across fourteen years, thousands of scouts shared moments of levity in a playful way while completing the hard work required to ensure mission success. During that time, Jo Dee and Girl Scouts San Diego gained notoriety and received numerous awards, including a national Silver Anvil Award for excellence from the Public Relations Society of America in 2003, a 2005 Nonprofit Leadership Fellowship from Harvard Business School, Lead San Diego Visionary Award for Graduate of the Year in 2015, and many others.

By 2017, Operation Thin Mint® had succeeded far beyond expectations. Not only did the service project put smiles on the faces of active military members around the world, but it also opened the eyes and wallets of hundreds of donors back home. When Jo Dee retired from Girl Scouts San Diego in 2016, the organization had 42,000 members and had increased Latina membership by over 3,500 girls. Under Jo Dee's leadership, the organization completed two successful capital campaigns to raise almost $8 million for new construction and camp enhancements. This is a testament to the fact that to receive, one first needs to give.

Today, Jo Dee is a past president of the San Diego Rotary Club—the fifth largest in the world. For her service to scouting, she received the Rotary International Cliff Dochterman Award. She fondly recalls her service in the Navy and with Girl Scouts San Diego, and the valuable lessons she learned across all those years. Jo Dee is using her experience as a nonprofit leader to teach classes on social entrepreneurship to undergraduates at the University of California San Diego Rady School of Management.

"I think a positive mental attitude is essential for leadership. Nobody wants to follow a negative person. We need to get up every morning and find something positive about the day, go to work with a smile, greet people kindly, make others feel good about themselves, and foster an environment of respect, hard work, and fun," said Jo Dee.

"Military leaders serve in some of the toughest environments in the world, where we're required to destroy things and kill the enemy. When we mess up, people die. But you can't let that turn you into an uncaring monster who's strictly focused on dangerous business. You can't expect others to do their best if they're always stressed and trying to meet your unrealistic expectations. As leaders, we need to find the right balance between hard work and recreation. Between serious business and lighthearted fun. Maintaining the right balance and a positive mental attitude can make all the difference in someone's quality of life and their desire to succeed."

LUDUS LOVE

Jo Dee Jacob's story underscores the Second Neuron Secret: *The Principle of Familiarity: play to win by treating everyone like family*.

The word familiarity has its roots in the Latin word *familia*, which means "family." Most of us are familiar with and therefore usually bond with our immediate family. Although we might squabble occasionally with our siblings and parents, most of us are far more motivated to help our brother or sister than a stranger. It's not that we lack any feelings for strangers, but we have built a level of familiarity and closeness with family members we love, so they will always take precedence. This is just human nature. This principle teaches us that we must treat others, especially those we are privileged to lead, as if they are close family.

Some of us have relatives we can't stand, but most of our family members mean the world to us. We need to treat everyone in our life, even those we don't like, with love and respect regardless of how they treat us. We can best accomplish this by creating an emotional bond that connects with others in a meaningful way. The following information and examples will us show how to do this effectively so we can create effective teams that work hard, have fun, and drive toward a common goal.

The Greeks called their playful form of love *ludus*. We most often see this kind of emotional fondness exhibited between young children because they are usually unconcerned about race, religion, social standing, political beliefs, or economic status. Like Dorothy's dog Toto, they just want to play and have fun. On the playground, everyone is family. This type of *ludus* love, unfortunately, unravels far too often and too soon as we grow up and are molded and shaped by society and parental figures who have lost their innocence.

Socrates once said, "Beware the barrenness of a busy life." Advances in technology make it nearly impossible to unplug from the daily grind. We can't seem to hide from a text or email or call. Some adults are so busy and stressed out that they have forgotten how to play and have fun with anyone, anywhere, anytime, and with complete abandon. They have become jaded, fearful, rigid, and perhaps even unhappy. Few people are truly "familiar" to them, including, in many cases, their own families. Brothers bicker with sisters, parents with children, spouses with each other, leaders with subordinates. They have abandoned their innocent *ludus* love and have become hardened souls who define themselves as black, white, red, blue, green, or brown.

Are you content with living in a shallow world where we distance ourselves with a text, post, or email? Or do you want to once again connect with your playful *ludus* heart and treat everyone like the family members you cherish?

From a neuroscience perspective, *ludus* love is emotional and appeals mostly to our emotional brain. As such, the best way to exhibit this type of love is through visual, audio, and tactile means rather than written words or spreadsheets. As leaders, we will not successfully encourage this type of emotional bond by displaying a PowerPoint slide in a team meeting with a graph depicting why teams that have fun are 50 percent more productive. Also, we know that promoting the release of oxytocin and dopamine increases trust, love, pleasure, and satisfaction. Too much stress inhibits the release of these positive chemicals. Encouraging an environment with a healthy mix of playful fun can ensure that the diabolical lord cortisol does not inflame vagus nerves—instead your teams are pumped up on joyful oxytocin and dopamine.

Said Dr. Zak, "Oxytocin and the chemicals with which it interacts can be harnessed to maximize teamwork."

THE FUN-LOVING DUTCH

Why are Dutch children the happiest in the world, according to a 2013 report released by UNICEF? The Netherlands has a reputation for being rather liberal and tolerant of a more progressive lifestyle, but at their core, the Dutch are actually somewhat conservative, especially when it comes to their home life. Parents view their children as individuals rather than "ego displays." They place more importance on the child's happiness than on things that will make the parents look good, like straight As or soccer championships. While Dutch children start preschool at the age of four, they don't do any heavy lifting, such as reading, writing, and arithmetic, until they are six.

The Dutch focus far more attention on play, fun, and healthy interactions than on flash cards, piano lessons, and spelling bees. While the French are consumed with quiet obedience, the Brits on sacrificing for your mates, and the Americans on earning a free ride to Stanford, the Dutch see far more benefit to noisy play, spontaneity, and fun.

Some suggest that although Dutch children may be happier, they grow up to be less productive and less mature. However, just the opposite is true. The Netherlands has ranked first on Legatum's list of happiest countries in the world for quite a few years in a row, and they're in great shape financially. Also, Dutch young adults have far fewer issues with teen pregnancy, drugs, alcohol, and "entitlement" attitudes.

Perhaps leaders in every country can learn valuable lessons from Dutch parents. By ensuring a healthy balance that fosters appropriate *ludus* fun, play, and comradery, rather than a maniacal focus on hard labor—as in a prison—leaders can help create happier and more productive team environments.

Ludus love also gives us the opportunity to consider our common welfare as a team. Life is meant to be fun and not constantly difficult or terrifying. We should not endeavor to be "lone wolves," but instead view ourselves as important members of a team, working together toward a greater good while also finding moments of levity and fun. In such an environment, we can free ourselves from the desire to manipulate or force unneeded change. For example, in a meeting where many of us are expressing opinions to determine an outcome or make important decisions, I may desperately believe that my viewpoint and recommendations are right and best, but I may also be completely wrong.

When I relax and turn over the outcome to forces beyond my understanding and control, whatever I perceive these to be, I am better able to listen and contribute as a team "family" member and not as a controlling autocrat. I can voice my thoughts once, listen objectively to the feedback and opinions of others, and be open to their ideas. If my team does not agree with me, rather than get angry or allow my sensitive ego to be offended, I can repeat my position—perhaps with better clarity and some modifications to address expressed concerns. This will ensure that my original statements and ideas were not misunderstood. Then, I can let go. Unless I am positive that the group's recommended course of action will run our ship aground, I can trust that perhaps I don't always have all the answers and the course suggested by others on my team will lead us to the buried treasure we seek.

Ludus love provides leaders with the opportunity to help members on their team define and enjoy their roles. While some organizations may encourage a "free for all" structure where roles and responsibilities are not clearly defined, this approach seldom works well as it's contrary to human nature. Some individuals thrive on chaos or get bored easily or want to have a hand in everything, but unless there are clear boundaries, teamwork is not possible. Most people have specific talents, which are usually based on what they like to do. We tend to focus on and become good at what we're passionate about. We tend to be passionate about something when it's fun and doesn't feel like work but instead like *ludus* play. One of the best ways to allow our teammates to focus on what they love to do, while also ensuring effective teamwork with other members, is to employ what I call the *Submarine Division*.

Aboard submarines, officers are assigned to run various divisions such as engineering, communications, and weapons. The Weapons Officer is called the "Weaps," and his team is responsible for the torpedoes, missiles, fire control (weapons) systems, and so on. The captain expects the Weaps to ensure that his team maintains the weapons and associated systems at peak operating efficiency. In a shooting war, which could happen at a moment's notice, if a Tomahawk missile fails to launch properly, it could cost lives. Even with the stakes this high, the best COs never micromanage or inject stress. They do just the opposite. They trust the Weaps, who in turn trusts his team. The torpedo men have their own space. It's called the torpedo room. A good Weaps allows his torpedo men to have fun while they work. They can play music, laugh, joke, and tell stories so long as doing so does not disrupt the work. If the space is keep clean and in top working order, and the systems are tested and repaired as needed, Weaps is a happy guy. In turn, the CO is all smiles and the enemy is in trouble.

When all is well in all departments, the crew is more relaxed and the captain can allow far more levity, fun, and play when appropriate.

CHALLENGES AND MISTAKES

People thrive on challenges. That's because a healthy challenge stimulates the release of "feel-good" oxytocin in our brains. Also, dopamine is released when we win, accomplish a goal, or complete a difficult task.

Recall that dopamine is a neurotransmitter involved with pain and pleasure. We feel pain when we lose and pleasure when we win. Encouraging healthy and fun competitive "challenge stress" in the work environment can boost oxytocin and dopamine levels and have everyone dancing in the aisles; or at least smiling in their cubes.

Said Dr. Zak, "During challenge stress, the brain directs the body to produce the fast-acting stress hormones epinephrine and adreno-corticotropin (ACTH). These produce hyper-focus and disconnect us from time."

One way I've injected challenge stress into the workplace is by creating a competitive Race Board. This is similar to the horse race boards you see at carnivals and fairs. Most white boards are magnetic, so we used pictures of funny-looking horses mounted by jockeys and glued them to magnets. We then created competitive teams who "raced" each other to accomplish certain goals. In our case, we were launching a large promotional campaign for a $1 billion division. We needed to create assets, prepare channel partners, and train sales teams. There were six product areas, and one team was responsible for each area, so we had six horses. We used Gantt charts to track our progress.

We huddled briefly every morning and compared each team's progress for the previous day. Horses were moved ahead for each Gantt chart step accomplished. We started each day with a healthy dose of laughter, fun, and team comradery as the horses trotted ahead toward the finish line. Smiles covered faces and determination filled eyes. Everyone was having fun, but they all wanted to win, so they worked even harder to see their red horse jump in front of the blue one.

Nothing worthwhile is accomplished without making mistakes, and during our race, individuals on some teams made a few. When this happened, horses were moved two steps backward; however, teams had the opportunity to regain those steps by later demonstrating how they had learned from the mistakes and had taken action to move even further ahead.

I bit my lip many times in meetings where domineering leaders berated others for making mistakes when they should have been doing the opposite. If someone repeats mishaps frequently, they should of course be reprimanded and perhaps even let go, but otherwise, the Edison Rule should apply.

Thomas Edison made 10,000 mistakes while inventing the lightbulb. That's how many times he failed to gain a glow. When asked about his "mistakes," he said, "I have not failed. I've just found 10,000 ways that won't work."

Jeff Bezos, CEO of Amazon, once said that a few big successes can compensate for dozens of failures and that he's made billions from the ashes of failures.[1]

Blasting someone personally for making a mistake is the biggest mistake a leader can make. You will close their spirit and stifle their passion and desire to innovate. A more productive approach is to discuss the mistake with the entire team in a fun yet productive way. I call this Blooper Brainstorming. Objective One in this exercise is to ensure honesty and openness on the part of the person who made the mistake. Objective Two is to make sure they are not ostracized or ridiculed by teammates. Objective Three is to encourage the team to find a fix for the mistake.

To accomplish this while practicing *ludus* love, I usually meet with the person (we will call him Bob) one-on-one to understand the mistake and quantify the consequences. Sometimes I find that Bob believes he has made a million-dollar blooper when it's really only worth a buck. Then, we all meet as a team. I inform everyone that Bob was brave enough to bring a mistake to our attention. He and I have analyzed this issue and determined it will cost us ten grand and two days' delay. Everyone is then encouraged to launch a brainstorming session to find ways to fix the mistake: together as a team.

PLAYFULNESS EQUALS PRODUCTIVITY

A new study from BrightHR, led by renowned psychologist Professor Sir Cary Cooper, found that almost 80 percent of millennial graduates believe fun at work is important. Companies that create a fun work environment lower sick days. Over 62 percent of employees with perfect attendance records also report having fun within the prior three months. Moreover, 58 percent of those who did not have fun at work were out sick for eleven or more days.

Another study conducted by the Social Market Foundation discovered that random individuals who received an injection of "fun" prior to completing a task averaged from 12 to 20 percent higher productivity. Proof that it pays to play.

THE PERFECT GAME

Randy Jones grew up in Orange County, California, where he played his first Little League baseball game at the age of seven. His coach noticed that Randy had a strong, accurate arm, and let him pitch for ten of the twelve games they played that summer. While learning the fundamentals of pitching, Randy soon fell in love with the game and sensed that this sport would become his passion and purpose in life. He dreamed of one day stepping onto the mound in Los Angeles stadium, with a throng of Dodgers fans cheering and shouting all around him, and then striking out batter after batter through an entire nine innings. No hits, no walks, no runs.

The perfect game.

"I learned that to achieve my dreams and succeed," said Randy, "I needed to fail. But I also learned that when I was faced with the possibility of failure, while shivering with fear on the mound, my love of the game and my teammates would be my silent coach. I could close my eyes and just remember that I was *playing* baseball. That I was having fun and sharing that fun with my team."

Randy received a baseball scholarship from Chapman University in Orange, California, where his coaches told him that to succeed, he needed to become mentally and physically tough.

"Baseball is a serious business," said Randy, "but it's also a fun game. Throughout my career, I always wanted to keep a healthy balance between the two."

Keeping that balance led to Randy's first big break. After graduating from college in 1972, the San Diego Padres drafted the burgeoning left-handed pitcher in the fifth round. He was assigned to the Texas minor league, where he shut down dozens of batters with a smattering of sizzling fastballs and hard-to-hit sinkers. Heads turned.

"When I got the call from the Padres I almost peed my pants. I was finally going to pitch in my first major league game. I was going to the Big Show."

Randy made his debut on June 16, 1973, but things didn't go quite the way he'd planned.

"I couldn't feel the ground under my feet," said Randy. "My adrenaline was surging, and I was so nervous that I almost lost my cookies. The first few guys I pitched to lit me up like a pinball machine. Then I closed my eyes, relaxed, and decided to just enjoy the rest of the game. My next pitch was to a guy named Willy Mays. I thought he'd light me up, too, but I struck him out."

Randy and his teammates lost that game three to two, but his confidence inched up a notch. He started to believe that he could compete at the big-league level. He proved it on the mound that year by winning seven of thirteen games as a rookie. Unfortunately, things didn't go so well the following year. During the 1974 season, Randy only won eight games and lost twenty-two. His earned run average (ERA)—the measure of a pitcher's success—was a bit high at 4.45. The best pitchers are usually under 3.0.

"I thought I was done for," said Randy. "I was sure that the Padres were going to send me back down to the Texas league and I'd have to start all over again. To keep that from happening, I decided to do two things: one, get some help from a pitching coach, and two, learn to relax even more and have some fun."

Randy recalled what he'd learned in college: that lots of failure usually precedes success, and that baseball, after all, was just a game.

"I learned that baseball, like any game or any profession, is a team sport. I can't and shouldn't try to go it alone. I realized that to be a winner, and to be a leader, I needed to first be a good teammate."

Randy discovered what nearly all great performers and leaders discover: You're only as good as your team.

"I decided to spend more time with my 25 teammates," said Randy, "really getting to know them and having fun both on and off the field. When I did this, I started thinking of them as not just teammates, but as family. Then something miraculous happened. We really started caring about each other, and that showed up on the field. I practiced harder and tried harder because I didn't want to let those guys down. And they also went the extra mile to help me get a win instead of a loss. I was a groundball pitcher, so I had to rely on them to field the balls and get outs. That's what teamwork is all about."

With the help of his teammates, Randy turned things around. In 1975, he won 20 games with a respectable 2.24 ERA and earned *The Sporting News* Comeback Player of the Year award. The following year, he won 22 games with a 2.74 ERA and won the National League Cy Young award—the most coveted in baseball for a starting pitcher. Randy also earned a selection as the left-handed pitcher on *The Sporting News* National League All-Star teams in 1975 and 1976.

To this day, Randy holds a record that no pitcher has yet broken: sixteen wins and only three losses at the All-Star break (midseason).

"I owe my success to my teammates," said Randy. "Without their friendship and support, I would not have won all those games. They played their hearts out for me, and I played mine out for them. We all loved this game, and loved playing for each other. We also had a lot of fun, and never forgot that to win, you also need to *play*."

LUDUS TEAMS

Without knowing it, Randy discovered the secret to success found in the first Neuron Leadership Principle: ***play to win by treating everyone like family***. This is best done by understanding what Greek *ludus* love is all about. In Greek and in Latin, *ludus* refers to fun, games, and sports. The ancient Greeks described *ludus* in terms of the early stages of falling in love with something or someone, when we might have attraction, excitement, heart flutters, teasing, flirting, and euphoria. They also described *ludus* as the love of a good challenge, especially when playing to win.

Many psychologists today agree that playfulness and fun are required ingredients to enjoy a long-term relationship or having success in a professional endeavor. We must stoke the fires of our childlike innocence and wonder to keep our flames of passion alive. This is true for both personal and professional relationships and situations.

> "When another teammate made an error by missing an easy groundball," said Randy, "because I'd taken the time to get to know him as a friend and not just another baseball player, I wanted to help bail him out. I was even more motivated to strike the next guy out so that my teammate wouldn't feel so bad about the error."

The game of baseball is stressful. There's very little time off during a six-month season that requires playing 162 games, most of them back-to-back. One day you're in San Diego and the next you're in New York. Still, Randy's fondest memories of his decade in baseball were about the fun, levity, and laughter he enjoyed with his teammates.

> "You know what I missed the most about baseball after I retired in 1983?" said Randy. "It wasn't the thrill of winning, even though that was great. It wasn't all the travel because we weren't doing any sightseeing. It wasn't even the money, although that was also nice. It was the camaraderie with my guys. I literally had two families, one at home with my wife and kids and one with the 24 guys I played with. I love my family at home with all my heart, but I also loved my family at the ballpark. I really miss those guys."

What can team leaders learn from Randy, as well as the ancient Greeks?

Three important things:

First, that being a team leader starts with a lesson derived from the old saying: "There ain't no 'I' in team." In fact, when we replace "I" with "we," *illness* becomes *wellness*. One of the things I recommend in team meetings is to refrain from using the word "I." Often, our egos propel us to do a little bragging. We want our peers, subordinates, and superiors to recognize our accomplishments. Others might praise themselves and make us a bit jealous when admiration is showered upon them. It's a difficult thing to do, but as leaders, we must set the example by using the word "we" as often as possible.

Even if it was "me" that did most of the work, I will still use "we" to describe the accomplishment. "We, together as a team, exceeded our monthly goal." I also do my best to praise examples of great teamwork. I might say, "John and Mary deserve recognition for the way they performed as a team to complete three important tasks that helped us achieve our goals."

Second, I need to ensure that my team is afforded frequent opportunities to bond and vent. We often hear about execs taking employees on a team-building exercise, perhaps once a year. These can be highly effective, and I strongly recommend them, but I also suggest doing more than just one annual event. For example, I often schedule "burger Fridays" with my teams. Every Friday at lunch, we wheel out a grill or call for catering or go to a local burger joint, together as a team. We chomp on burgers, whether beef or veggie, and joke, laugh, and bond. This ensures that at least once per week we keep the fires of our *ludus* love for one another burning bright. If we care about each other, we'll be more motivated to perform at our best because we won't want to let each other down.

"One of the events that impacted me the most," said Randy Jones, "was when one of my teammates got cut. That devastated me. I'll never forget seeing him sitting on the bench with his head buried in his hands. When he looked up at me, with tears streaming down his face, and his eyes locked with mine, my heart sank. It really hit me hard. I felt like I'd just lost a part of my family. After that day, I was even more motivated to play harder so that no one else got cut. I loved those guys, and I didn't want to see any of them get hurt like that."

Third, I need to always strive to be an example of *ludus* love in my daily affairs. My team, and virtually all others I interact with in life, will be far more impacted by what I do than what I say. I must always remember that I'm a mentor and a friend.

Randy Jones said, "Ray Kroc owned the San Diego Padres when I was a pitcher. He was also the owner of McDonalds. He once told me that if I was willing to work hard, I could accomplish anything I wanted. But he also said that to get to where I wanted to be, I needed to love the game, love my God-given gifts, and love my teammates. To this day, I've never forgotten that."

TEN *LUDUS* LEADERSHIP REVIEW POINTS

1. The Greeks used the word *ludus* to describe a playful type of love.
2. This type of love is often exhibited between close family members and children while playing.
3. *Ludus* love is also seen between adults when socializing, playing, or competing in a sport.
4. For leaders, *ludus* represents the second Neuron Principle: *The Principle of Familiarity: Play to win by treating everyone like family*.
5. Military commanders, especially those leading small teams, often encourage fun and recreation to diffuse tensions, inspire a more close-knit unit, and instill loyalty and flexibility.
6. Leaders should embody and foster *ludus* love. This creates a team environment where people have an affectionate familiarity with each other and care enough about each other to perform at their best so as not to let down anyone else on the team.
7. *Ludus* love is emotional and appeals mostly to our emotional brain.
8. The best way to exhibit this type of love is through visual, audio, and tactile means rather than written words.
9. The dog Toto in *The Wonderful Wizard of Oz* provides a good metaphoric representation and embodiment of this principle.
10. This principle can be summed by these two words: ***be playful.***

THREE STEPS TO *LUDUS* LEADERSHIP

1. *Policy*: Leaders should be required to set aside at least one to two hours per week for social and fun activities for team members and should not frequently require subordinates to work late.
2. *Procedure*: Leaders should set aside at least two hours per month to play games or sponsor a fun activity with their teams. For example,

gather in a conference room, turn off all mobile phones, no PCs allowed, and take out a board game or play cards.

3. *Practice*: Leaders should create friendly team competitive activities that instill a fun and challenging element into the workplace, such as a horse race leaderboard or other playful ways that track progress toward team goals in a competitive way.

ONE *LUDUS* LEADERSHIP EXERCISE

To better ingrain the principle of *ludus* love, let's all do the following at least once per month in our personal lives: Turn off everything electronic. No mobile phones, no WiFi, no televisions or radios, no microwaves, and no cheating. Pop some stovetop popcorn and take out an old-fashioned board game like Monopoly® or Clue®. Encourage the entire family to set aside at least one night together to have *ludus* fun and play. You'll laugh and bond in ways that will strengthen you as a family and keep you all close and "in love" for life. Teenagers may complain about how unfair it is to turn off their vital appendage and give up texting for a night. After the first hour, while laughing and having fun, they'll thank you. One night out of thirty is not asking too much. Help your family instill this healthy habit into their lives. You, and they, will be glad you did.

Now do the same thing with those on your professional team. For one day or night, even if just during lunch, turn off and tune out. Allow your team to play, have fun, and bond over a board game or other social activity. This will be one of the best things you can do for them as a *"ludus* leader."

Laughing Down Lonely Canyons

Fear corrodes my dreams tonight and mist has greyed my bills,
Mountains seem too tall to climb, December winds are chill.
There's no comfort on the earth, I am a child abandoned.
    Till I feel your hand in mine
    And laugh down lonely canyons.
Snow has best the trees in grief, my summer dreams are dead,
Flowers are but ghostly stalks, the clouds drift dull as lead.

There's no solace in the sky, I am a child abandoned,

       Till we chase the dancing moon

       And laugh down lonely canyons.

Birds have all gone south too soon and frogs refuse to sing,

Deer lie hidden in the woods, the trout asleep till spring.

There's no wisdom in the wind, I am a child abandoned,

       Till we race across the fields

       And laugh down lonely canyons.

—*Dr. James Kavanaugh, from* Laughing Down Lonely
Canyons

CHAPTER 6

Generous Tin Woodsman—Neuron Secret Three

FIGURE 6.1   Tin Woodsman

Source: Anna Velichkovsky, Dreamstime.com.

> I shall take the heart, for brains do not make one happy, and happiness is the best thing in the world.
>
> —TIN WOODSMAN (FIGURE 6.1) IN *THE WONDERFUL WIZARD OF OZ*

NEURON SECRET THREE

The Principle of Generosity: Give not to receive, but only to fill your heart with joy

Lance De Jong is a Vice President of North American Sales for Oracle. He concurs that it is important for leaders to care for the members of their team, and a good way to do that is to generously offer your time and wisdom as a mentor. He recalls, earlier in his career, being mentored by a man named John who informed Lance that if he wanted to be mentored, he had to abide by three rules. One, Lance had to bring the questions to John. This forced Lance to do his homework and come prepared with questions for his mentor. Two, Lance had to honor and respect the time commitment. They would never cancel or reschedule unless a life-threatening situation forced them to do so. Three, Lance needed to be a river and not a reservoir. He had to agree to pass on what he'd learned from John to someone else.

"In my first lesson with John," Lance said. "He challenged me to do my homework and write down and memorize my primary six core values. What did I stand for? What defined me? I thought I knew, but John taught me how to dig deeper and really understand who I was."

John's mentorship helped Lance formulate his three pillars of leadership. Of most importance is trust, which forms the backbone of everything he does. Lance defines the second pillar with one word: serve. His philosophy is to flip an organizational chart upside down and determine how he can add value to his direct reports and their teams. In his opinion, if he is not finding ways to help his team, he is not doing his job effectively. The third pillar is caring.

"You must find a way to show your people that you genuinely care about them," said Lance. "It can't be phony. It must be authentic."

Lance believes that effective leaders should constantly ask themselves three important questions. First, are the people you are leading following you, and how do you know? Second, is your team growing personally and professionally, and how do you know? And third, are the people you are leading succeeding, and how do you know?

"There's a big difference between a manager and a leader," said Lance. "If I were a CEO, I'd strive to nurture leaders, not managers."

Lance reported to a manager, we'll call him Fred, who had a military background. While Lance knows that the military can and has produced some great leaders, a few have emerged as more managers than leaders, and Fred fell into this category. He was an invasive micromanager who managed by spreadsheets and made Lance feel untrusted. When challenged, Fred got defensive, raised his voice, and demanded respect. Rather than argue with Fred, Lance instead tried to understand. He recognized that Fred did not feel safe, so Lance said, "I respect you, and I'm glad you brought this up." He then endeavored to earn Fred's trust while not compromising his own principles or acting like a doormat. During this experience, Lance learned a valuable lesson about "leading up."

Lance advises aspiring leaders to do as he did while being mentored by John. First, understand what you are deeply passionate about and what you are *not* passionate about. How do you believe your talents will help you excel, and in what areas? Also, set clear and attainable goals that will help you stretch and gain confidence.

"I think it's important to turn aspiring leaders into leaders of leaders," said Lance. "Leading is all about relationships, not tasks. You must have someone's permission to lead them. Others will follow you if they believe you can help transform them into what they want to become."

Vision and inspiration are two key components that Lance feels are vital to help your team transform. You must impart a clear vision that incorporates a worthwhile overarching passion and purpose beyond only profits. Then, inspire others to reach for those stars. Team diversity is also important, along with open communication and healthy arguments.

"A team with 'five Lances' is not a good thing," said Lance. "I much prefer a diverse team where everyone has different strengths, personalities, and opinions. The sum of our parts makes us greater as a whole."

Lance believes that as a society we are starving for strong, effective, and inspirational leadership. We have the opportunity to lead in almost every aspect of our lives. Leadership is not something that is gifted to us, it is something we can choose to learn and to earn. We become leaders not by stepping on others as we climb the ladder to success, but by the choices we make and how we treat others with generosity, caring, and respect.

AGAPE LOVE

Lance's insights help set the stage for the Third Neuron Secret: ***The Principle of Generosity: give not to receive, but only to fill your heart with joy.***

Other authors, experts, and sages often refer to this principle as *Reciprocity*. They cite studies wherein someone gives something to someone else, which usually results in the other party feeling obligated to reciprocate. For example, researchers found that when a waiter or waitress offers a single mint along with the restaurant bill, tips increase by 3 percent. However, when two mints are offered, tips quadruple to 14 percent. Even more astonishing, when that same waitress offers only one mint, but then pauses, turns back and offers an "extra special mint" for customers, tips increase by 23 percent.

From this perspective, Reciprocity obviously works, but it's also a bit selfish. We're not giving because it's the right thing to do, we're giving because we want something in return, like a bigger tip. However, there's another side to this coin. Reciprocity also stands for the mantra that "for every action, there is an equal and opposite reaction." Does this mean that if we offer kindness to someone their reaction will be just the opposite, as in animosity? Actually, no. Reciprocity refers to a *direction* that is opposite, not an action.

By reflecting anger, hatred, intolerance, ignorance, bigotry, misery, fear, or any negative emotion, thought, or feeling, we receive an equal measure of this in return. However, if we give love, understanding, patience, kindness, tranquility, tenderness, or positive emotions, thoughts, or feelings, we receive a like measure in return. This is only true if what we give is genuine and if we have no expectations of reciprocation. For that reason, we should think of this as the *Principle of Generosity* and *not* Reciprocity.

This principle aligns with the Greek word *agape*, which refers to a selfless, unconditional type of love for everyone and everything. *Agape* love extends to all humankind, whether family or complete strangers. Proof of the relationship between the words *agape* and generosity can be found in the modern word *charity*, which is a derivative of the Latin word *caritas*—a later translation of *agape*.

Agape love appeals mostly to our emotional brain, therefore it is best expressed through visual, aural, or tactile means rather than through written words or numbers. As leaders, we must exhibit this type of love by stepping out of our office and managing by "walking around." Even if we're a die-hard introvert, and *especially* if we are, we need to get out of our comfort zone and engage with our team. We cannot exhibit this form of love by burying our noses in a computer screen. Set aside at least fifteen minutes each day to visit with as many people on your team as possible. Smile and ask them how they're doing. Point to a picture of their family and ask a few questions, such as "what's your daughter's name?" Get visual and appeal to their emotional brain by showing them a picture of your family. Doing so will build trust, which will increase their oxytocin levels.

"Stress inhibits the release of oxytocin," said Dr. Paul Zak. "Leaders who are more generous, open, vulnerable, and approachable increase the likelihood of oxytocin release. In return, that person will be more motivated to perform for that leader. Conversely, screaming, intimidation, or force will lower oxytocin. Those tactics may work short term, but almost never long term. Workers will become jaded, unmotivated, and may eventually leave."

Modern neuroscience also validates that when we are generous and grateful, we can increase dopamine and serotonin production—in ourselves and others—and improve our feelings of contentment and desire to perform.

Dr. Zak said, "Oxytocin works by activating a brain network that makes us more empathetic."

If we treat others nicely we will increase their oxytocin level. They will feel good and want to treat us nicely in return. This is what many refer to as reciprocity. However, it is not effective if the generosity offered is not genuine. Our brains are highly receptive. Most people can smell a fake. Picture a sleazy used car salesperson. When this happens, cortisol is triggered along with norepinephrine. The cortisol lowers oxytocin and therefore trust while the norepinephrine triggers an adrenaline fight or flight response.

In work environments, giving praise when justly due for positive actions is an excellent way to exhibit *agape* love. The giving must be genuine and void of expectations or manipulative motives. It's also best when it occurs not long after the employee's action. Dr. Zak calls this *Ovation* and notes that it "can cause the direct release of the neurotransmitter dopamine in the brain." He also said that "dopamine's effect is most powerful when Ovation is unexpected, tangible, and personal." He cautions against focusing on money as a reward as it's not very personal. A Boston Consulting Group survey found that recognition is the most important thing people want, while higher salary is number eight on the list.[1]

Many leading firms now place *agape* love, in the form of mutual compassion, at the top of their company culture list. Google studies indicate that top-performing managers "express interest in and concern for team members' success and personal well-being."[2] In 2015, Amazon CEO Jeff Bezos responded to a *New York Times* article that gave the company negative marks for caring about employees. He said, "… any such lack of empathy needs to be zero" and asked employees to email him directly if they experienced a lack of empathy in their work environment.[3]

Compassion equals cash. A 2012 Towers Watson Global Workforce Study on 32,000 workers from almost thirty countries validated that exhibiting compassion was at the top of the "must do" list to increase engagement.[4] Employees who work for genuinely compassionate and empathetic leaders are 67 percent more engaged, and they value this attribute more than money or benefits.

To increase engagement, retention, and profitability, our goal as leaders should be to embody *agape* love to set the right example for our team. Also, empower other leaders to do the same by encouraging the right culture and rewarding the right behaviors. Finally, enlist (hire) leaders who exhibit a spirit of unconditional *agape* love.

REALISTIC EXPECTATIONS

How can we love unconditionally when we live in a conditional world? Everything in our life is defined by conditions. We can keep our job if we perform adequately. We can keep our home if we pay our mortgage. We can advance our career if we work hard and leverage our professional relationships. We can have loving relationships if we nurture them. How then does the term "unconditional" have relevance when our lives are filled with all these conditions?

We must leave our expectations at the door.

The term unconditional love is an oxymoron. It's redundant. If we love, *truly love*, it should always be unconditional. Achieving this requires loving and receiving love without expectations. In fact, when it comes to love, the word "expectation" is synonymous with the word "condition."

During our childhood years, most of us learned from well-meaning parents, teachers, coaches, pastors, or other authoritarian figures. They taught us the concept of "pain and gain." If we did something wrong, we felt pain. If we did something right, we "gained" a reward. Many of us unwittingly began to equate "gain" with love. If we did what Mom or Dad wanted, they smiled and showered us with praise and admiration. They bought us ice cream. They loved us. Naturally, we drew a straight line from performance to love. Is it any wonder that so many of us began to feel that love must be earned?

Of course, for most, our parents showered us with unconditional love and validated this often in word and deed. However, there were many times when indications of love were preceded by a positive action on our part. We got a pat on the head when we did something right. Those in positions of authority gave us a treat or a whack based solely on our ability to either please or anger them: a rap on the knuckles or a candy bar. We felt hated or loved. We developed expectations and "love" became conditional. Now, we must remove the shackles of our past and learn how to give from a heart filled with *agape*.

C.S. Lewis described *agape* as "gift love," which he called the highest form of love. Unfortunately, studies show that this type of love has declined dramatically over the past several decades. Apparently, our desire and capacity to love each other and give unconditionally is on the decline. How can we regain this lost art, which is vital to our very survival?

Through generosity. We must learn *how* to give again.

There's a quote in the Bible (John 15:13) that says: "Greater love hath no one than this, that he lay down his life for his friends." Those who use this verse in their teachings typically refer to "life" as "death." They imply that the greatest way for us to exhibit love for someone else is to "die" for them. I interpret this verse quite differently. I don't believe John was referring to death. He plainly said "life."

What is life? Think about that word for a moment. How do we define life? Most of us might say, "it's what we do every day." If so, what is "every day?" The simple answer is: every day is twenty-four hours. Therefore, life is the equivalent of time. For without time, we have no life. From that perspective, we can see that what John was really saying is: "Greater love hath no one than this, that he lay down his *time* for his friends."

Our *time* for our friends, not our *death*.

Ask yourself this tough question: how much *time* did you lay down today for anyone besides yourself? How much *time* did you dedicate to your family or loved ones? How much *time* did you give to your friends or colleagues or team? How much *time* did you donate to perfect strangers? Each and every minute of our day is precious. How much love did you show anyone else today by generously giving them your *time*?

If you want to incorporate *agape* into your life, and you should if you want to have a life worth living, then you must be generous enough to lay down your life—your *time*—for others. This is a tough ask in a busy world with deadlines and demands, but if we remain sequestered between the walls of our closed-off mind, we will live a life devoid of meaning or true happiness. We will die depleted, decrepit, despised, and devoid of any humanity. If that is your goal in life, forget about the word *agape*. Stay selfish with your time and give it to no one.

If your desire, however, is to live a life filled with passion, purpose, and unconditional love, then embrace the principle of generosity and give of your *time* freely. Throwing a few bucks at a charity won't cut it. Find something that fills your heart with a burning desire and your eyes with misted love. Volunteer your time, your passion, your love, and your life to that cause, charity, mission, or purpose. Give it your time. Give it your life. Give it your love.

"The greatest gift you can give someone is your time," said Gordon England, former deputy secretary of defense. "Time is precious to everyone. It's not renewable. I believe that the most effective leaders are the ones who spend time with their people."

In team leadership environments, *agape* love allows us to create and foster an atmosphere of cooperation and support. If we care about each other as people, we are apt to be more generous and sharing and open to change, especially when stress is high and resources are low. By giving of our expertise and *time* to others, without any expectations of reciprocity, we instill trust and respect. If others are giving unconditionally to us, it's nearly impossible to not be motivated to give back to them. We trust that they have our back, and they trust that we have theirs. This is called "foxhole" trust.

In tight military units, most especially in Navy SEAL teams, initial training focuses on building foxhole trust. For these units to operate efficiently, each teammate must feel that everyone else on the team will take a bullet for them, literally. They call this "having your six," which means they are watching your back at the six o'clock position (as if you were standing in the middle of a clock). Teams in these environments operate at a high level of efficiency not simply because they are ordered to do so by a control freak with a bullhorn. They do so because they love each other unconditionally. They live by a moral code that none would ever consider violating. They know they do not have to face hardships or the enemy alone. They can close their eyes and sleep in a foxhole because they trust that another teammate is wide awake with their finger near a trigger.

Jordan Goldrich is a Master Certified Corporate Executive Coach and executive consultant for CUSTOMatrix in San Diego, California. He partners with senior leaders to produce results in complex, competitive, and rapidly changing environments by creating aligned, empowered teams and workgroups. He helps executives inspire trust, loyalty, and commitment by understanding and articulating their purpose and passion while demonstrating integrity, humility, and courage. Jordan also specializes in working with valued executives, who may be considered as abrasive by their employees, to change the unintended impact of their style by refining their "Warrior Spirit." He has a diverse background as a Chief Operations Officer and a Center for Creative Leadership executive coach.

Said Jordan, "The greatest warriors in the world, which include U.S. Navy SEALs, Marine Raiders, and other Special Operations forces, are successful because they create a team culture wherein everyone feels they are part of the 'tribe.' They are committed to the mission; everyone's back is covered, and their duty is to serve humbly."

THE CARING COMMANDER

John Robert (Bob) Wood grew up as an "Army brat." His father was a career officer in the infantry and encouraged Bob to apply for the United States Military Academy at West Point, New York. He was accepted in 1968 and graduated in 1972. He served in various units and then earned a Masters of Business Administration (MBA) degree from the University of Chicago. The Army then asked him to return to West Point to teach courses in economics and finance.

Three years later, Bob became a White House Fellow in the Reagan National Security Council before transferring to Germany. He also served for four years in a variety of Army field artillery staff jobs. He returned to the United States in 1990 to assume command of an artillery battalion at Fort Bragg, North Carolina. Shortly afterwards, all hell broke loose.

When Iraq invaded Kuwait in 1990, Bob commanded one of the initial units to deploy and face Saddam Hussein's forces head on in Operations Desert Shield and Desert Storm. These two complex operations required months of preparation and remarkable execution in combat logistics by his team. Bob discovered that inspiring his soldiers to commit the time and effort needed to meet the demands of these tough and dangerous missions required a generous and caring attitude.

"When I graduated from West Point and assumed the role of an officer and a leader," said Bob, "one of the first things my father told me was to 'take care of my people.' I never forgot that. Caring is not the same thing as coddling. It means honestly paying attention to and having an interest in the needs of your team. You need to know what concerns and motivates them. In the Army, you have both the family side and the soldier side of the coin, and you need to help your team maintain a proper balance between the two."

Bob believes that it's vitally important for leaders to understand the complete breadth of what it takes to support and care for your troops. Building strong units requires building strong individuals. A weak link in the chain can break your entire team. Sometimes you need to replace the link, but more often you need to help the link become stronger.

"You need to adopt a caring and generous attitude," said Bob. "If you're not willing to give every person on your team what they need to succeed, including understanding and support for them personally and for their family, then it's almost impossible to ask them to give you their all."

Bob also believes that few will give you their "all" unless they trust you; and trust is earned, not given. In his opinion, it only takes an instant to lose your team's trust. You must demonstrate that you care about them every day, and you must be willing to stand up for them when it's the right thing to do, even if you're risking your career.

"I think it's vital not to set up anyone on your team to fail," said Bob. "Whenever a new commander reported to me for duty, I always wanted to help him succeed. I'd give him a few small tasks to complete and then get out of his way. By planning, executing, and succeeding, he learned how to lead his new team and earn their trust and confidence. My father told me early on to always take care of my people, and I hope I did him proud."

John Robert Wood was promoted to Deputy Commander of the U.S. Joint Forces Command and earned the rank of Lieutenant General (Three-Star) prior to his retirement from the Army in January 2009. He was later recruited by AFCEA International to serve as Executive Vice President for National Security and Defense.

TEN *AGAPE* LEADERSHIP REVIEW POINTS

1. The Third Neuron Secret is the Neuron Principle of Generosity: give not to receive, but only to fill your heart with joy.
2. *Agape* is emotional and is best expressed through visual, aural, and tactile means rather than through copy, graphs, or numbers.
3. Adopting this principle requires an understanding of, and desire to live by, the ancient Greek form of love called *agape*.
4. *Agape* love refers to unconditional love, which requires loving without expectations. We must love the people we lead and serve as an example of how they should love each other.
5. Teams can learn from tight military units that foster foxhole trust, wherein each teammate can rely on others unconditionally.
6. Our mission as leaders requires knowledge, courage, dedication, and, above all, generous and unconditional love.
7. We must treat team members like a close family of brothers and sisters who alongside us equally risk careers and livelihoods and reputations.
8. We must show our love by laying down our life—our time—for those whom we lead.
9. The Tin Woodsman in *The Wonderful Wizard of Oz* provides a good metaphoric representation and embodiment of this principle.
10. This principle can be summed by these two words: *be generous*.

THREE STEPS TO *AGAPE* LEADERSHIP

1. *Policy:* Leaders should be privately evaluated by their teams at least once per quarter. The evaluation should contain the typical business aspects, but should also include evaluative criteria related to the leader's personality, likability, demeanor, and trustworthiness. While these aspects may not seem "businesslike," studies show that

teams are far more productive when they admire, like, and trust their leaders—especially those who exhibit "unconditional love" and generosity for their team members.

2. *Procedure:* Leaders should set aside at least one hour per month to show unconditional love and generosity to each team member by offering praise and mentorship. This should include suggestions for improvement, offered in a positive rather than negative way, as well as recognition for accomplishments—which should not strictly relate to business but also include the person's ability to function well with other team members.

3. *Practice:* Leaders should create an atmosphere of unconditional love and generosity by sharing one uplifting and inspiring story about a team member, customer, and so on, with the entire team each week (an example of this can be found in The Neuron 3-Act Play chapter). This can serve to reinforce the organization's commitment to a higher purpose and demonstrate a desire to reward selfless and generous behavior.

ONE *AGAPE* LEADERSHIP EXERCISE

For this exercise, you will first need to create a journal and then do the following:

1. Write down the full name of everyone on your team. This includes everyone you lead and everyone who helps you accomplish your professional goals.

2. Under each name, create a list of everything you want to know about them. This should include their background—personal and professional—and their family member names. What is their favorite pastime? Sports team? TV show? Book or author? Food? Restaurant? Place to visit on vacation? Other questions?

3. Also under each name, create three columns. Label one Motivators and the second column Fears. Label the third column Desires. *Do not* label this "Goals."

4. Meet with each person one-to-one, whenever you have at least 30 minutes uninterrupted. Devote your *entire* attention to them. *Do not* answer your phone, reply to an email, and so on. Show them that

they matter, you care, and you truly want to know more about them. Open with your own *ludus* fun stories and information about yourself to make them feel comfortable, and then start asking questions from number two above. Once they are open to talking, ask them questions from number three above.

 a. For Motivators, try to understand what their real passions are—what truly motivates them personally and professionally.

 b. For Fears, this is tougher as they may not want to reveal any. You might "ask around" this question by getting them to describe one of their most terrifying experiences.

 c. For Desires, help them to be more open and tell you what they really want in life. What drives them? What are their passions? Why did they choose their current profession? Where do they want to go in life?

5. Armed with the above knowledge, use the web or mobile app at www .neuronleaders.com to determine their *Neuron Personality Profile*. If they feel comfortable enough, some individuals may answer these questions on their own and let you know what profile they selected. If not, you can use the answers to the questions you asked and make an educated guess. Usually, once you have spent some time observing someone, their profile type will become obvious.

6. Now that you better understand your teammates, you can use the *Neuron Personality Profiler*™ app (www.neuronleaders.com) to determine optimal messaging, approaches, Do's and Don'ts, and so on, to better communicate, motivate, and inspire these individuals.

7. Having set the right example, encourage your team to do all the above with each other.

> There is quiet water
> > In the center of your soul,
> Where a son or daughter
> > Can be taught what no man knows.
> There's a fragrant garden
> > In the center of your soul,
> Where the weak can harden
> > And the narrow mind can grow.
> There's a rolling river

In the center of your soul,
An eternal giver
With a rich and endless flow.
There's a land of muses
In the center of your soul,
Where the rich are losers
And the poor are free to go.
So remain with me, then,
To pursue another goal
And to find your freedom
In the center of your soul.

—*Dr. James Kavanaugh, from* Quiet Waters

CHAPTER 7

Our Beliefs

FIGURE 7.1   Core Values

Source: Ivelinr, Dreamstime.com.

> When your values are clear to you, making decisions becomes easier.
>
> —ROY E. DISNEY

Before we explore the next two secrets, we need to first understand and clarify our core values (Figure 7.1) and beliefs. Philosopher and poet Dr. James Kavanaugh once said, "At the root of all our actions and opinions lie our belief systems, most of which we well may have inherited. If they remain frozen beyond change or examination, personal development remains stagnant."

Our beliefs often have a direct connection to our reactions. If we grew up in a troubled household, where perhaps one or both of our parents was difficult, insensitive, angry, manipulative, controlling, and so on, we may recognize these attributes when they are exhibited by our subordinates, boss, customers, or professional colleagues, and therefore those same attributes may trigger reactions like those of our childhood. This is a typical Pavlov's dog reaction.

If one or more of our parents drank heavily, or even if their parents were alcoholics or addicts, their unacceptable behaviors might have been prevalent or passed down through generations. Thus, we may have developed perfectly acceptable defense mechanisms to deal with these behaviors that served us well as children. However, those "traditions" that we developed years or even decades ago are probably no longer needed and may be detrimental to our current relationships and professional life.

Leaders who wish to inspire productivity in others must intimately know and live by their core beliefs and values. This chapter helps us shed beliefs from our past that may be holding us back from becoming better leaders by refining our core values.

A good friend of mine, we'll call him Matt, spent nearly three-fourths of his time traveling for his leadership job. He hated his boss for making him spend so much time away from his family three out of every four weeks of the month, but he felt he had no choice. His belief system told him he needed the income to provide for his family and to be respected by others. Turns out his wife and children didn't care if they lived in a trailer park. They just wanted Dad home at night to read them stories, laugh at dinner, watch them blow out birthday candles, or attend their recital or big game.

Matt blamed his boss for all his misery until he finally realized that his boss was not the problem. His own beliefs were responsible for forcing him to remain a slave to a society that really didn't care what he did. His neighbors were unconcerned about the size of his house or what he built in his backyard. His friends and subordinates had no opinions about what he drove to work or wore on his wrist. However, they all had concerns about his constant displays of anger, depression, and fatigue. He finally mustered the courage to approach his boss and ask for a different position. He knew he'd have to take a pay cut and a demotion. He'd have to trim his lifestyle and swallow his pride, but he'd gain a much higher measure of joy with his family and have the time to pursue his passions and purpose.

As it turned out, this higher measure of joy shined through every time Matt engaged with a customer, which made a huge difference in his ability to close sales. He quickly shot past all his quotas and wound up making more money than he had previously, and with far less stress. He also discovered his true purpose in life: to bring joy to others through his gift of caring and empathy. Shedding our illusionary beliefs is not easy. We must first become aware of what we believe, and how those beliefs may be holding us back.

EXERCISE

Let's take a moment to honestly list our ten most prevalent beliefs. They may be that men should work and women should tend to chores. Or that women should work and men tend to the yard. Perhaps we have strong religious beliefs, gained in childhood that we now question. Maybe some-one long ago forced us to accept his or her definition of a deity—or that one does not exist. Does our heritage or nationality force us to believe something? Do we hate others because they don't share our political or societal beliefs? Do we always believe we are right and everyone else must therefore be wrong? Or that we're wrong so they must be right?

Do we believe we are undeserving, unworthy, untrustworthy, incompetent, ugly, unintelligent, or something else shoved down our throats by our parents or bullies in our past? Do we think we are better than everyone else or more deserving? Do we fear that we'd be embarrassed or ridiculed if we lost our job? Do we believe we have no option but to accept a bad situation in life? Do we feel that it's all someone else's fault and we have no responsibility or culpability when things go wrong? Do we think there's nothing we can do to make our situation better (and if so, why are we reading this book)?

Go well below the surface and don't be afraid to dredge up the truths and write them down. No one else needs to see your answers. Forget about what anyone else may think or say about your responses. This is between you and you, so don't hold back.

To complete this exercise, bring up a notes app on your mobile device, or use a sheet of paper, a notebook, or a document on your computer to create your list now.

Have you completed your list? If not, please do so now before continuing.

Take a look at your list. A *hard* look. Peer deep inside those corners of your soul, open the doors to those hidden rooms, and pull out the old furniture. Don't skimp on this exercise, it's vital to your leadership journey. When you're satisfied that you've painted an honest picture of your true beliefs, go back to your list and delete anything and everything you no longer want to believe. This courageous step will be hard to do, but you must do this if you want to stop living a life that is less than you deserve.

Face your fears, let go of your past, and free yourself from the shackles that society, subordinates, customers, parents, friends, siblings, children, priests, pastors, colleagues, and bosses have clasped about your hands and heart. Stop letting their expectations, their beliefs, their desires, and their guilt trips force you to believe things you no longer want to believe. This is *your* life, not theirs.

Today, and every day going forward, believe what is right and best for you, not them. Shed those beliefs that no longer take you forward, that hold you back from the peace, serenity, happiness, rewards, fearlessness, success, and the ultimate joy you deserve. To be sure they never haunt you again, completely obliterate the false beliefs of your past and remove them from your life forever. *Do this now.* Do this completely. Do this and feel the weight of the world lift from your shoulders. Feel yourself become free to be who you are, who you were meant to be, and who you should be. Today, right now, in this moment, you are on your way to becoming the leader of your own life.

CORE BELIEFS

What should be left on your list are your core beliefs. Most of us will have a short list. If you have not deleted any beliefs, take another hard look at your list. Be as honest as you can and rid yourself of the dogmas or debilitations of your past and of other people's thinking. Narrow your list to only a few important, truthful, and meaningful beliefs. Perhaps it is your belief in a God, or in no God at all. Maybe it's your devotion and love for your family or your responsibility to nurture and protect them. Maybe it is an altruistic or philanthropic endeavor or simply a desire to have a life filled with happiness, freedom, and joy.

If you cannot imagine a life without these core beliefs, they should remain. However, if deleting a belief from your list will not change who you are fundamentally, or keep you from fulfilling your dreams and your purpose for being, imagine how you'd feel after eliminating those unhealthy or unneeded beliefs and moving on without them.

Our true values reflect our true selves. They are not imposed upon us by external sources. When we know our true values, we know and trust ourselves and our actions because our values dictate our thoughts and beliefs. We reveal our beliefs through our interactions with others. Our rigid, long-held, and deep-rooted beliefs stem from teachings, judgments, and unfounded fears, not from our truth. Remaining unwilling or unable to admit we may be wrong, or that our past beliefs may be false or inappropriate, or staying intransigent to healthy change, will forever lock us into a life of misery and pain and keep us from becoming the best leaders—the best people—we were meant to be.

REVIEW QUESTIONS

- Do I now have a better and clearer understanding of my true beliefs?
- In what way have the beliefs of my past kept me from having the life I truly want?
- How have I felt like a victim in my professional life?
- Have I used my feelings of being victimized as an excuse for my own bad behaviors?
- Do I feel that I am inferior or superior to others, including my subordinates, and if so, why?
- Do I believe that I am more or less deserving than others, including my subordinates?
- Is it possible that I might someday be able to better understand and empathize with others?
- Do I set unrealistic expectations for others and continue to expect different outcomes?

I left my traditions
On the far side of a foggy hill,
And I will stay away

Until I can return in sunshine,

Rescued from them,

Free to choose

Which are really mine.

—Dr. James Kavanaugh, from Sunshine Days
and Foggy Nights

CHAPTER **8**

Passionate Wizard—Neuron Secret Four

FIGURE 8.1   The Wizard of Oz

Source: Anna Velichkovsky, Dreamstime.com.

Who are you, and why do you seek me?

—THE WIZARD OF OZ (FIGURE 8.1)

NEURON SECRET FOUR

The Neuron Principle of Passion: Without passion and purpose, you are a ship without a rudder.

Do our dreams speak to us? If so, are they evil sirens bent on luring us toward the rocks of doom? Or benevolent oracles offering a portent of our future? Maybe they're only random brain impulses devoid of any prognostication or meaning at all. Then again, perhaps they are the trumpets of our soul, alerting us to a change in the melody that guides our hearts.

Several years ago, on a fateful Saturday in June, the images that filled my head when sleep finally came were not the surreal or disconnected wanderings found in a typical dreamscape. They seemed as vivid and tangible as real life. I can remember each second of my nightmare in horrifying detail. Every time I recall this story, I shudder with fear, and my throat tightens.

In my dream, a bitter wind woke me from a deep sleep. I opened my eyes to the glint of the morning sun as it brushed away the night. Glimmers of violet rested atop distant hills and revealed the gray rectangles of scattered houses on the horizon. I sat up, tugged at the collar of my Navy pea coat, and tried in vain to cover my neck.

Dogs barked and roosters crowed. A frigid gust tossed dry leaves into the air and transformed them into spiraling paper airplanes. The fresh scent of the morning dew awakened my senses. I squinted toward the remaining darkness as I sat on the side of a grassy hill. Below me, more than a football field away, a row of tract homes lined a quiet street. I turned my head. Above me, a tall fence ran across the top of the hill and stretched for hundreds of yards in both directions. I could not see what lay beyond.

I felt movement near my leg and glanced down. Blond curls covered the edges of a worn jacket. My wife, Sarah, opened her blue eyes. She stared up at me and smiled. My heart melted, and I was filled with joy. Then my heart sank, and I felt only agony.

I knew why we were here. Why we sat under God's sky on this cold and damp earth. Why we struggled to stay warm in our dingy clothes. I knew why my stomach remained empty, along with my pockets. Why I had no roof over my head and little hope in my heart.

We were homeless and just trying to survive.

We were nowhere because we had nowhere to be.

The sun crested on the horizon. Dashes of crimson yellow illuminated four figures in a yard at the bottom of the hill. A man and three Doberman Pinschers. The dogs barked as they lifted their noses in our direction. One caught our scent and charged up the hill. The other two followed close behind.

My heart thudded. I jumped to my feet and beckoned for Sarah to stand. I pointed toward the fence at the top of the hill. She squeezed my hand and ran. I sprinted in the opposite direction and started yelling. I prayed that the dogs would take the bait and come after me.

All three dogs raced toward me as I ran. My lungs heaved and my muscles burned. The dogs yelped as they drew closer. Barks echoed off the silent hillside like rifle shots on a battlefield. I instinctively recoiled as distant memories filled my head. The angry howls grew louder and sent a shiver down my spine. My breath misted in the wind as I dashed up the hill.

Leaves crackled under the pounding of paws.

The lead dog was nearly on me.

I could almost touch the tall fence.

I forced my legs to move faster, but as a Doberman Pinscher bit at my feet, I knew I'd never make it.

I stopped and turned to face my enemy. The lead Doberman leaped into the air. Long fangs glistened in the morning sun. I raised my right arm in defense. Large incisors bit into my flesh. A dozen pointed knives stabbed through my skin. Stinging pain filled my head. I screamed and rolled onto the ground.

The Doberman clamped down harder. The two other dogs howled as they raced toward me. Only seconds remained before all three might tear me to pieces. The pain in my arm was unbearable, but also familiar. I'd felt this agony before, in a distant land fighting a distant enemy. My mind battled the panic that swelled inside my chest. I closed my eyes and tried to relax. The dog loosened his grip but did not let go.

As the other dogs drew near, I knew I had only moments to act.

I grabbed a nearby rock and smacked it against the side of the Doberman's head. He grunted and opened his jaw wide enough for me to break free. I turned and scrambled up the hill. The three dogs nipped at my heels as I climbed over the fence. I heaved myself onto the hard ground. The Dobermans jumped and barked, but the fence was too high. They could not follow.

I removed my coat and gingerly rolled up my sleeve. My wound oozed but it did not gush. I knew I'd been lucky. The Doberman had not punctured an artery. I tore off part of my sleeve and wrapped the torn flesh. I donned my coat and ran toward where I'd seen Sarah climb the fence.

I found her there, frightened and hiding in the bushes. Together, we ran down a winding road until we found a large country home with a long driveway. Near the house sat a white Ford pickup truck with a cover over the back. I peeled away the cover, and we climbed in behind the cab. I pulled the cover over our heads. We curled up together, shivering, starving, and scared. Drained and wounded, I finally fell asleep.

Hours later, a bright light made me open my eyes. The cover over the back of the pickup had been removed. Sarah also opened her eyes. We looked at each other, and then upward toward the sky. When my vision finally cleared, I saw four faces peering down at me. A man, a woman, and two young girls. Panic gripped my heart. We'd been caught. We were trespassing, and they had every right to call the police and have us arrested. I had no idea what might happen next, but I feared the worst.

The mid-fifties man was plump and balding. He glanced at my Navy pea coat. "Are you a veteran?"

I nodded but could not find the will to speak.

He motioned with his hand. "Follow me."

Given no choice, Sarah and I climbed out of the truck. The man and woman walked toward the house. The two girls ran ahead and opened the front door. Starving and defeated, Sarah and I followed.

Once inside, I waited for the ugly hand of fate to punish us. I waited for the man to grab his phone and call the police. I waited for the woman to scold us for trespassing on their land. None of these things happened. Instead, the two children beckoned for us to join them in the kitchen. We followed and sat at their table.

"I'm Fred," the man said. "This is my wife, Karen, and my two daughters, Jill and Kaitlin. Thank you for your service. Now let's get you two something to eat and a warm bed."

Karen approached and rested a loving hand on Sarah's shoulder. Jill and Kaitlin stepped near and wrapped their small arms around me. I lowered my head and sobbed into my hands.

I awoke from my dream, sat up in bed, and cried until morning brushed away the shadows. As the tears touched my cheeks, conviction touched my soul. I knew then that I had been given one last mission to complete before I left this earth. I knew it was time to leave my petty worries and fears behind and serve more than my selfish pride. I knew what my purpose in life must be. To decline this mission to pursue money or fame or the petty pleasures of life would leave me tossed against the rocks in an empty vessel devoid of love.

The next day, a harsh summer sun hammered the city of San Diego, California, and turned once-green lawns into dry and brittle dirt. Despite the heat, I shivered as I sat on the patio of an American Legion facility and recalled my dream. The meaty scent of grilled hamburgers caught a ride on the breeze and taunted my nose. A large television, mounted on the wall, displayed a San Diego Padres baseball game. The crowd at the game cheered as the pitcher threw a strike. On the next pitch, the guy on the mound offered the opposing team an easy home run. A few dozen veterans, seated all around me, groaned in unison.

A young Marine to my right leaned over and said, "I should have stayed in Afghanistan."

He was sitting in a wheelchair. He didn't have any legs. He smiled and held out a hand. "I'm Jimmy."

We shook. His grip was firm and his smile engaging.

"I'm Bill," I said, "but everyone calls me B.C."

"I know who you are," Jimmy said. "I read your book, *Red November*. Loved it."

"Thanks. Are you an avid reader?"

Jimmy nodded. "You know what they say about being in a combat zone. It's two percent sheer terror and 98 percent sheer boredom."

I nodded again. "I was a Navy diver. Waiting around for the next mission is always the hardest part."

Jimmy wheeled a bit closer. "Reading helps. Calms you down a bit. Helps you fight better. You word jockeys probably don't even realize how many lives you're saving."

Jimmy's comment hit me like a blow from Evander Holyfield. I was reminded of my responsibility to use my writing talents to do more than just entertain or inform. I had a responsibility to help others by making a difference and inspiring change.

That afternoon, I met with two veteran colleagues, Ken Greenawald and Tony Stewart. I had served with Ken aboard my first submarine, the USS *Haddo* (SSN-604). Ken had been a sonarman, much like "Jonesy" in the movie *The Hunt for Red October*. He was now a technical expert in the medical field. I had met Tony at the American Legion. He was also a former submariner and an American Legion base commander.

Now a civilian, he was a Veteran of the Year recipient and served as the administrative director for the U.S. Navy SEAL training command.

We sat on the patio and shared the usual comments about sports, politics, and world events. Guys aren't the best at going beyond skin deep. We keep things bottled up. Our egos can't risk showing the world too much of our souls. Moved by my dream and what Jimmy had said, I let down my guard and opened my mouth, along with my heart.

"I want to do something for veterans," I said.

"I'm a veteran," Ken said. "Why don't you get me a cheeseburger?"

I smiled. "After I get you a burger, I want to find a better way to help veterans, their families, and our troops."

Tony leaned forward. His face turned serious. "I'm in. I've been thinking about this for a long time."

Ken sat up straight. "I'm in, too. What can we do?"

We tossed around ideas, debated a few, and landed on one. We'd start a nonprofit called the *Us4Warriors Foundation* and find unique ways to help 100 percent of veterans and their families, and not just one or two segments. We knew that thousands suffered from posttraumatic stress disorder, depression, or alcoholism. Many were struggling with transitioning from military to civilian life. We didn't want to just "give them a fish" and "feed them for a day" but instead help them through difficult situations and then empower them to become better leaders of their own lives and within their communities. We knew that they possessed unique training, experience, insights, and leadership skills, and we wanted to help them leverage these qualities. We also wanted to help their families, especially children who'd lost a parent in combat.

Four years later, the Us4Warriors Foundation was honored as San Diego county's veteran's nonprofit of the year.

Over the past three decades, I've had the privilege of serving as a senior executive for several organizations. I launched four start-ups and successfully sold three, helped build companies and teams from scratch, consulted for multibillion-dollar firms, and coached dozens of executives and teams on sales, marketing, management, and team leadership skills.

Along the way, I heard the whispers of my life's purpose call to my heart, but the disjointed tune never coalesced into a clear melody. Not until I had that nightmare. Not until I was granted the privilege of living one night in the shoes of the hopeless. And not until that family took me in and showered me with love.

EROS LOVE

My personal story above about finding passion and purpose underlines the Fourth Neuron Secret: *The Neuron Principle of Passion: Without passion and purpose, you are a ship without a rudder.*

This principle is related to the Greek form of love called *eros*, which is about passion, romance, and a love of life and work. Although this may sound emotional, looking at *eros* from a neuropsychological perspective validates that it is instinctual and carries overtones of curiosity and caution.

The mythological Greek god of love, known as Eros, was the son of Aphrodite and either Ares or Hermes. No one really knows because, apparently, Aphrodite got around. In some Greek myths, Eros was portrayed as a child of Chaos, a primordial god whose name describes his personality quite well.

As you may recall, Eros, also known as Cupid, was the little guy with the bow and arrows, that when shot into your heart could make you fall in love with the first person you saw. Perhaps that's why the world's divorce rate is so high. Cupid keeps missing and shooting the wrong people.

The ancient Greeks tell us that after Eros fell for the beautiful Psyche, her jealous sister tricked Psyche into betraying him. Thereafter, crushed and filled with sorrow, Psyche wandered the earth in search of the bow-and-arrow guy but never found him. She failed to look in the local pubs, one can surmise.

Finally, Psyche prevailed upon Aphrodite for help. A fan of *ludus* playful love, Aphrodite invented a bunch of "fun" tests for Psyche that when successfully passed would lead her back to Eros. Psyche's love allowed her to pass the tests, rejoin with Eros, and become immortal. They gave birth to a daughter named Hedone.

When Hedone grew up, she became the goddess of pleasure, delight, enjoyment, and as the name implies, hedonism. Leaders might wonder how Eros and his family, or the Greek form of love derived from this god, embody a Neuron Leadership Principle. The connection is passion.

All too often, as leaders, we become so business-like, so rigid, so stressed, so focused on the bottom line, that we forget how to have pleasure in our professions. We fail to instill any form of excitement, passion, purpose, or abandonment in our troops. Then we ask ourselves why they're not delighted to work until midnight to complete a project.

In modern times, the Greek word *erotas* translates into "intimate love." In ancient times, Plato thought of *eros* as a feeling one might initially have for someone that also entails admiration for that person's inner beauty. Taken to a higher degree, this can lead to an appreciation of all things beautiful. Plato refrained from discussing *eros* as sexual love, which led to the term "platonic love."

In Plato's *Symposium*, a famous ancient dissertation on the topic, he intimates that *eros* love can help one's soul better understand, recognize, and remember beauty, which can serve as a cognizant steppingstone toward an understanding of spiritual truths.

The ancients both feared and desired *eros* love. They described it as passion and perhaps even madness derived from "love's arrows." They explained "love at first sight" as the piercing of the heart by these arrows, which later blossomed into a passion, longing, or even agonizing and painful ache.

Many fairy tales and adventure stories that little girls and boys love to read and someday experience begin with *eros* love and ends with "they lived happily ever after."

Obviously, the writers of these tales never had teenagers.

In Frank L. Baum's *The Wonderful Wizard of Oz*, the Tin Woodsman, Lion, and Scarecrow all believed they were flawed in some way. Their individual passion and purpose in life became their quest to find the Wizard, who they believed could grant them what they lacked. Once they met the "Great and Terrible" Oz, they discovered that he wasn't so terrible after all and that none of them lacked a heart, brains, or courage, they just thought they did. By showing compassion, Oz helped each of them attain their initial desires but then inspired them to raise their sights even higher.

> "... and remember, my sentimental friend, that a heart is not judged by how much you love, but by how much you are loved by others."
>
> —*The Wonderful Wizard of Oz*

CURIOS AND CONSCIOUS

Eros teaches us to be passionate and curious, but also balanced and moderate. We should be curious enough and attractive enough to others that they will risk opening their doors wide enough to show us their honest and true selves. We should do likewise, but cautiously. Until we have developed a more trusting relationship with someone, we should not open our doors so wide that we risk serious harm if the other person turns out to be "dangerous."

For those in sales or marketing, this principle is powerful. All too often, in our initial engagements, we want to flood customers with a long list of value propositions. The *eros* principle teaches us that customers have difficulty changing their course of direction, and attraction is far more powerful than promotion. Also, it requires a strong element of curiosity. If we're not curious, we can't be attracted enough to something or someone to eventually become passionate. That curiosity can be stimulated by something interesting, novel, and relevant. For marketers, on your websites and in your collateral, try delivering just enough information to stimulate your customers' curiosity and desire to engage with you to find out more.

For leaders, to motivate your team to follow you or make changes, they must be attracted to you as a leader. Does your style appeal or repel? Be courageous enough to lower your guard and let others see your true self and encourage others to do the same via your example. Foster curiosity about yourself, your vision for change, and your environment. For example, you might share a few snippets of interesting, new, and relevant information about a market niche you're exploring. Raise your team's curiosity and then encourage them to discover more on their own. In this way, you will attract them to this endeavor and help them feel like explorers forging an exciting path toward the X on the map.

From a neuroscience perspective, we know that trust is a critical factor in improving performance and job satisfaction. According to the 2015 Society for Human Resources Management Employee Job Satisfaction and Engagement Survey, trust exhibited between senior management and employees was the second most important contributor to job satisfaction.[1] Google's Project Aristotle study conducted on 180 teams discovered that the highest performing teams had a culture of trust.[2]

Eros love entails fostering team trust as well as narrowing your organizational, departmental, team, and personal focus down to a single, clear, and compelling purpose borne of passion. This purpose needs to be less about business and more about a greater good. The Conscious

Capitalism movement outlines four key tenets organizations can use for this:

Higher purpose: Also known as the "mission"—the purpose of the company beyond making a profit or dominating a market position. A compelling sense of purpose can create a high level of engagement by the stakeholders and generate tremendous organizational energy.

Stakeholder orientation: Explicitly managed for the good of all stakeholders including customers, employees, investors, suppliers, and the larger communities in which the business participates. By creating value for all stakeholders, the whole system advances.

Conscious leadership: Management is driven by service to the firm's higher purpose and focuses on delivering value to the stakeholders. Conscious leaders adopt a holistic worldview that goes well beyond the limitations of traditional business. Enterprises and individuals are part of a complex, interdependent, and evolving system with multiple constituencies.

Conscious culture is captured by the acronym TACTILE:

T = trust

A = authenticity

C = caring

T = transparency

I = integrity

L = learning

E = empowerment

A conscious culture is very tangible to stakeholders and outside observers.

In the fourth quarter of 2016, Whole Foods Market reported record earnings of $3.5 billion with almost 8 percent EBITDA and a return on invested capital of 13 percent. They returned $44 million in quarterly dividends to shareholders.

John Mackey, co-founder and co-CEO, said that the company had made measurable progress toward attaining industry-leading sales per gross square foot and healthy returns on invested capital, despite being a difficult year for food retailers in general. The firm's higher purpose statement is posted on their website and twice uses the word "love."

Whole Foods is a Conscious Capitalism company. Recall that extensive studies validate that public companies operating by the four tenets noted above outperform their counterparts on Wall Street by a factor of 11 to one. To be profitable, the best firms still focus on profits but even more so on a greater good. They open their eyes and hearts and become guided by a passion and purpose that transcends money and accolades.

Aristotle was a famous philosopher, but he was also adept in biology. His *Ethos* ethical beliefs were based on psychological theories about human nature. He believed that humans were biologically wired to be rational, virtuous, social, and happiness-oriented. Do you as a leader align your policies, rules, procedures, and culture with natural human tendencies? Or do you create built-in conflict by forcing square pegs into round holes?

Richard Ryan and Edward Deci created what is known as the Self-Determination Theory, which is based on Aristotle's humanistic philosophies. Their model suggests that employees will work harder and perform better for leaders when given tasks that are meaningful and serve a higher, moral purpose. Does your organization take the high ground by striving to serve a higher purpose beyond only profits?

PASSION, VISION, AND MISSION

Lenny Alugas is a senior vice president at Western Union. He grew up in New Orleans, earned an engineering degree, and was later recruited by Hewlett-Packard as a pre-sales engineer. Seventeen years later, Lenny was running a $160 million business unit with 600 employees. While there, he became a big fan of HP's leadership development programs and philosophies.

"HP had a well-defined and excellent set of core values," said Lenny. "They believed in an open-door policy with their leaders and encouraged managers to walk around and observe their environment. They had a strong desire to create effective teams where people could thrive."

Lenny recalls that HP considers their number one passion to be customers and employees. Even today, on the HP "About Us" web page, the company leads with a quote from Dave Packard about the necessity of people working together toward common objectives.

Under Shared Values, HP lists passion for customers, trust and respect for others, and achieving results through teamwork as vital to success. They also indicate that a commitment to employees and leadership skills are top corporate objectives. These philosophies are apparently working. HP is consistently listed by *Forbes* as one of the top 10 technology firms in the world.

"When you received a pay raise at HP, they gave you a print-out with all the information on it," said Lenny. "That wasn't good enough for my boss, Paul Hansen. He always hand-wrote a personal note on that paper to congratulate me and thank me for my hard work. That meant a lot to me. Twenty-five years later, I still have copies of those notes."

Lenny enjoyed his time at HP, but after many years decided to explore the world of a "start-up." He joined Veritas in the early nineties and helped drive the company toward success and an acquisition 12 years later by Symantec. At one point, Lenny was managing a $4 billion software maintenance renewal business with several hundred employees.

"Symantec also had some excellent leaders," said Lenny. "I enjoyed working for our CEO, Steve Bennett, who came from General Electric. He had an incredible leadership philosophy. I resonated with his beliefs that leaders should communicate the firm's mission, strategy, and goals clearly, and ensure employees are inspired to attain them. Also, he felt it was important to develop personal character at every level."

Lenny also praised Bennett's philosophies that good leaders need to have the courage to make decisions and teach their team members how to do the same. Bennett indicated that it was vitally important to treat employees as if they were valuable investments. He encouraged his direct reports to keep at least 30 to 40 percent of their time free so they could invest time in their people.

"I learned several valuable lessons from the leaders I worked for at HP and Symantec," said Lenny. "Most importantly, I learned that it's vital to develop a strategy, mission, and vision that align with your passion and purpose, and then communicate those clearly and effectively to your entire team. Then, inspire your team to work together to achieve the vision."

Lynelle Lynch is the president of Bellus Academy in San Diego, California. The academy is one of the largest and most successful beautician, spa, and training schools in the United States. Said Lynelle, "On their first day at the academy, we ask students to write down their passion, purpose, and goals. Many of them say they want to bring joy and beauty to others and perhaps someday own their own spa or salon. To help them attain their goals, we offer some of the best beautician and spa training, but we also teach them business, marketing, sales, and entrepreneurial skills."

When students graduate from Bellus, the academy helps them find jobs by uniquely connecting them with spas, barbershops, and salons around the world. Lynelle also believes in supporting the military and giving back to the community. The school accepts military assistance funding, offers complimentary services to the military and discounts to veterans, and frequently sponsors outreach programs to offer free haircuts and services to the homeless.

THE PASSIONATE LEADER

Anthony "Tony" Stewart hailed from a small town in Kansas. U.S. Representative Bob Dole, also from a small town in Kansas, became a strong influence when Tony was growing up. He still remembers Dole's quote that we should be "doers and not stewers." That mantra propelled Tony to pursue a career as a radio announcer at a local radio station while attending college. He'd been gifted with a smooth, soft baritone that earned him an award for his radio performances at the age of 19. During his first few years in college, Tony had also been cursed with a rebellious spirit that got him in a little trouble with the law upon occasion.

Tony finally decided to turn his life around by joining the Navy in April 1987. He originally thought he'd be a journalist in Uncle Sam's canoe club, but that opportunity evaporated not long after he completed boot camp. Instead, he opted for a yeoman rating aboard nuclear submarines.

"At first I thought a yeoman was just a glorified secretary," said Tony. "I almost turned the job down because I didn't think it would be challenging enough for me. When I found out what a yeoman really does, and what submarines really do, I got excited."

Tony completed submarine school in Groton, Connecticut, and was transferred to a submarine in construction in Newport News, Virginia.

While waiting for the boat to be built, he reported to a support squadron in Norfolk, Virginia, where he gained a lot of knowledge about submarine administrative operations by rotating through a variety of assignments. He learned that a yeoman's job entails everything from human resources to operations management to legal support and handling highly classified information. That's when he became passionate about his work.

"During that first year with the squadron," said Tony, "a master chief took me under his wing and gave me lots of opportunities to learn a variety of tasks. I was eager so I asked a lot of questions. Over time, I eventually learned most of the answers, and then other people started asking *me* the questions. That master chief kindled a desire to 'own the process' that I've carried with me throughout my career."

Due to a delay in the construction of Tony's originally assigned sub, he was transferred to another boat in Bremerton, Washington. The USS *Flying Fish* (SSN 673), a *Sturgeon*-class sub, was returning to the fleet after an overhaul. Reporting aboard was a culture shock and a lesson in humility for Tony. Despite being junior in rank, he had earned a reputation at the support squadron for being the guy with all the answers, so he quickly became the brunt of some unrealistic expectations from his crew and initially some undue harassment from his leader due to unfounded rumors that Tony thought he knew more than others.

Like all submariners, Tony was also overwhelmed by the requirement to qualify and earn his submarine warfare designator, which submariners call "dolphins." Tony was faced with the significant challenge of earning the respect of others while embedding himself as a valuable member of an important team. He decided that allowing the stress to control his tongue would only make matters worse, so he instead chose to gain the crew's trust by endeavoring to be a good teammate and offering help wherever possible.

Tony is a strong believer that great leaders are built and not born. He advises exercising your leadership muscle over time, most especially by observing and asking questions.

"When I was aspiring to become a leader," said Tony, "I observed the actions of other leaders, most especially the commanding officers on my submarines. The most successful ones were knowledgeable and confident, of course, but they were also passionate and relayed that passion to their crew. They loved what they did and loved their guys."

Tony recalls two contrasting COs on two different boats. He described one as a "hammer" and the other as a "rake." The hammer was more task-oriented and often used a "push" leadership style wherein he was more apt to dictate his will and force compliance. He did not seek to be a coach or mentor, but instead delegated that responsibility to his junior officers and chiefs. He hammered his crew toward the goals he desired, and although he was moderately effective, and eventually rose through the ranks, he probably did not inspire many along the way.

The other CO was more relational in style. He was like a rake in that he cultivated performance rather than force compliance. Tony was stationed aboard a ballistic missile submarine with this CO where complex and sometimes dangerous drills and maneuvers were commonplace. Split-second decisions were required, and one wrong move could be disastrous. The CO ordered battle station drills that required maintaining accurate depth, speed, and course settings. Tony recalls that while some COs seemed tense or rigid on the bridge during these types of drills, this CO was as "cool as a cucumber" while remaining attentive to his crew.

"Instead of barking orders like other COs might," said Tony, "this guy finessed everyone into being leaders in their own right. He inspired us to work together as a team and support each other. He showed a genuine concern for everyone on the boat and led with confidence, strength, passion, and caring. We wanted to perform for him because we respected him, and that loyalty helped us achieve several unit awards for our efforts."

Tony rode the boats for 20 years, retired as a chief petty officer, and is now the administrative director for BUD/S—the Navy SEAL training command—on Coronado Island in San Diego, California. Tony served as a Southern California district commander for the American Legion and was selected as a San Diego County Veteran of the Year. His experience aboard submarines, combined with his own research on the topic, helped him devise six core principles of leadership.

One, you must pledge to become a student of leadership. Longevity does not make a leader. You need to observe and learn from other great leaders to become one yourself. Two, connect with others. Leaders create leaders, and we need to foster close relationships with mentors and aspiring leaders on our team. Three, articulate a clear vision, passion, and purpose for your team.

Four, simplify things for your team. Break down complex steps into achievable, smaller ones and ensure everyone remains focused on the goals while completing the tasks. Five, be genuine and sincere. Two-way communication is important. A leader should not do all the talking.

"I always try to wrap up any conversation I have with my team with one question: 'Is there anything I can do for you?' When I ask this question, I really mean it. This helps me find ways to help them and remove any barriers to their success. One of my most important jobs as a leader is to remove my team's roadblocks."

The sixth principle is reward achievement. When Tony Stewart and I co-founded the Us4Warriors Foundation, along with Ken Greenawald, I knew that Tony's leadership skills made him the best choice to be the CEO. He eagerly grabbed that ring, and through his efforts, knowledge, and connections, the foundation flourished. Over time, we grew to 11 directors and 250 volunteers, as well as dozens of associates and advisors.

I recall several meetings where Tony called a few people to the front of the room. He then rang a ship's bell, handed them a certificate of accomplishment, and praised them for their hard work and achievements on behalf of the foundation. I watched the faces of these volunteers radiate with pride. Broad smiles stretched from cheek to cheek, and tears filled their eyes. I could see that these individuals were inspired and motivated to achieve even more. They were not being paid a dime, yet I knew that they would willingly follow Tony to hell and back. In my opinion, this is the mark of an inspirational team leader.

I'm convinced that Tony achieved the loyalty and dedication of hundreds of volunteers and successful partnerships with outstanding veterans support groups like the American Legion, because he focused first on defining a clear and compelling commander's intent. Together, our team created three core principles—our passion and purpose—that helped the Us4Warriors Foundation become San Diego County's number one veteran's nonprofit in 2016. They are:

We are dedicated to helping the whole veteran—100 percent of veterans in every way rather than a small selection in limited ways.

We are focused on the mission and not the money—the foundation is almost all volunteer. No directors are paid, and no one wastes a dime. All donations are put to work where they are needed most.

We are passionate about creating leaders—we don't just feed veterans a "fish for a day." We also help veterans and their families thrive as leaders of their own lives through our five core programs.

"You must have a sense of passion and purpose to be a great leader," said Tony. "Sometimes that passion is something grand. Other times it's as simple as helping others. At all times, it is not achievable without the help of others. No leader is an island. We can't achieve anything great alone. When I look back on every worthwhile goal I've ever achieved, I don't think about the goal. I think about the people who sacrificed and helped us attain that goal. I think about the fact that we did it together, as a team."

One of Tony's most important goals is helping every individual on his team find their own personal passion and purpose in life. He seeks to know what motivates and inspires them. He then finds ways to align their personal passions to those of the organization. This ensures buy-in to the vision and commander's intent, as well as sustained dedication. Tony recognizes that keeping the flames of passion alive is difficult at times. People can get tired or burned out. They can forget about the "why" that drove them initially. Great leaders find ways to stoke the coals and keep the home fires burning bright by continuously and creatively reminding their teams about the vision. They use success stories, personal recognition, award ceremonies, and "pep rallies" to constantly reignite passion and purpose.

"When we conclude a board meeting for the Us4Warriors Foundation," said Tony. "I ask each board member to sound off by using one word to describe how they feel. I listen closely to the word they chose because it helps me understand where they are right now. Then, as I always do, especially if the word they chose was not upbeat, I ask them what I can do for them."

Even when Tony's plate is completely full, he always asks me what he can do for me. This is one of the best examples of *eros* love that I have ever witnessed from one of the best leaders I have ever known.

FLYING HIGH ON PASSION

Sangita Woerner grew up in a traditional Asian Indian household. Both of her parents were first generation and immigrated to America before she was born. Sangita's mother was a stay-at-home mom and her father worked for Ford Motor Company throughout his career. He advised her that the two most reliable career paths were engineering or accounting. She decided to pursue the latter.

After graduating from college with an accounting degree, Sangita eventually discovered marketing and worked her way up the ladder to a vice president of marketing position at Starbucks. She then became the vice president of marketing for Alaska Airlines, where she empowered, motivated, and guided her team toward success. Aspiring leaders at Alaska Airlines often speak of Sangita with admiration as they try to emulate her leadership style and approach.

Sangita advises her team, as well as up-and-coming leaders, to focus on what's important. Almost every leader can be challenged by dozens of problems, tasks, and distractions daily. Discerning which ones to focus on at any given time takes practice, patience, and an open mind.

"I think it's critical to listen to your team, colleagues, customers, and mentors. Their input can help you determine proper priorities and make informed decisions."

Sangita recalls being encouraged by a mentor to refrain from focusing only on results and to spend more time turning her head from side to side. He advised her that she was not spending enough time building relationships and ensuring that she was in step with her team on the journey toward their goals.

"He said that I couldn't end up on the finish line alone. I needed to run the race alongside my team and colleagues. By fostering closer relationships, I'd be rewarded with diverse perspectives and insights and perhaps more efficient paths to reach our goals. Every person can bring something unique and special to the table because we all have different backgrounds, expertise, and viewpoints.

"A leader can accomplish far more with the help and support of an empowered and impassioned team," said Sangita. "While it's important to remain focused on a grand vision, sometimes it's just as important to focus on what you and your team can accomplish on a smaller scale every day."

REBOOT

Maurice Wilson was born and raised in Chicago, Illinois, and at the age of 23, he decided to join the Navy. He entered boot camp in 1973, near the end of the Vietnam War. Up to that point, Wilson had felt like a ship without a rudder. He had not yet determined his life's passion or course. During boot camp, he met an African American master chief who had served in the Navy for more than two decades. As an African American himself, Wilson was inspired by the master chief's example. His eyes were drawn to the ribbons, pendants, and stripes on the chief's uniform, but even more so to the chief's genuine kindness and energetic confidence.

"He was everything I envisioned a leader should be," said Maurice. "He had a passion and purpose to serve his country and help others to do the same. I feel fortunate that, at least for a time, he became a mentor and motivator for me to perform at my best so I could eventually become a master chief as well."

Twenty-two years later, Maurice did indeed add that second star to his uniform as a master chief. Then he "ran out of gas." He hadn't formulated a vision beyond that goal, so he decided to retire. Listless and uncertain about life beyond the Navy, he became "an aircraft carrier without a rudder." Maurice spent the next eight years floundering and wondering. He wanted to serve, to achieve, to give his heart and energy to something, but didn't know what that "something" might be.

He started working for the Urban League, a community-based organization, in San Diego, California, but found difficulty "fitting in" due to his military mindset, which had defined his demeanor for half of his life. Struggling but motivated, Maurice went back to school. He had an interest in behavior-based education, so he focused his energies in that direction. That's when he met Ronnie Foman. They became instant friends and together joined the Call of Duty Endowment, a nonprofit founded by Bobby Kotick that's dedicated to helping unemployed veterans find jobs.

While helping Bobby launch the Endowment, Maurice and Ronnie met with dozens of transitioning veterans and started asking questions. They learned that most were still unemployed because they were "fish out of water." Most had learned valuable skills, managed hundreds or thousands of people and millions of dollars in budgets and assets, and had worked in high-demand and high-stress environments. In many cases, they were highly qualified for almost any civilian job in their area of expertise, but lacked the confidence and knowledge to seamlessly transition from the military into a civilian career.

"They didn't know how to recalibrate their lives," said Maurice. "In the military, they'd had a clear vision and were following their passion and purpose. Now they were on the street without a uniform, without a job, and without a direction in life."

Maurice watched many of them spiral downward. They lost even more confidence and hope and became depressed. Some became so distraught that they took their own lives. They became one of the "22" veterans on average who commit suicide every day. Maurice decided it was time to make a difference.

"I asked Ronnie, 'what's going on here and how do we fix it?' We agreed that these veterans needed a 'mental reboot.' They had been conditioned by the military to think and act a certain way. They had come from a structured environment with a different mindset and now needed to reorient their brains and lives. It's like someone moving from a small town in Alaska where it's cold and unpopulated to Phoenix, Arizona, where it's hot and crowded. These veterans needed help to adjust to the contrasts."

Inspired by a new passion and purpose to help veterans transition, Maurice and Ronnie founded National Veterans Transition, Inc., a nonprofit they nicknamed Reboot. Their charter is to assist veterans in adjusting to civilian life and securing meaningful employment through best-practice performance social solutions and techniques. They accomplish this by offering early-stage cognitive-behavioral educational intervention to help their fellow veterans "reboot" from military programming. They show veterans how to develop a successful reentry plan and, most importantly, help them discover their new passion and purpose in life.

"Most of the veterans we work with have been so dedicated to and consumed by their military duties that they've never had the opportunity to understand their own personal mission in life," said Maurice. "We help them find that, determine the best career path to align with it, and translate it into an effective resume. We also help them gain the confidence they need to interview with companies and show them why they're the best candidate for the job."

To date, Reboot has helped almost 2,000 veterans boost their confidence and transition effectively. Selected veterans attend a three-week workshop where they are mentored by experts in social and career transitional requirements. They're also taught universal principles of cognitive science from two of the best authorities in the United States—The Pacific Institute and Operation Legacy.

I had the privilege of attending a Reboot graduation ceremony in San Diego, where I watched several of the Reboot graduates speak about their experience. Many of them welled up with tears when they spoke about where they had been just a few weeks earlier as compared to where they were now. They talked about walking through the doors of Reboot on that first day with their heads and spirits in the gutter. They had been uncertain, afraid, depressed, and lost. The instructors at Reboot taught them how to manage their positive and negative thoughts, unlock their potential, and gain the desire and confidence needed to accomplish any goal they desired.

"It's truly fulfilling to be a part of helping someone change their lives," said Maurice. "Virtually everyone who walks out of here does so with their heads held high and a bright smile on their face. They step in front of recruiters and hiring managers with a newfound purpose and confidence, get multiple offers from companies, and go on to become some of the best leaders these firms have. If I were an employer, I'd actively seek to hire veterans. Almost all of them are disciplined, smart, hard-working, loyal, and passionate."

Quite a few employers agree with Maurice. Many of them now have several recruiters who are dedicated to hiring transitioning veterans, and for good reason. They've seen the latest research from Gallup and other research firms. They know that around two-thirds of employees are disengaged and "checked out." Just the opposite is true for most veterans. Veterans have spent years in situations where it was impossible to be checked out, even for a few minutes. Lives could be lost if someone took their eye off the ball. Handling stress and pushing yourself beyond limits was a way of life. Being in the military taught them how to naturally gravitate toward the best leaders and learn how to become leaders themselves. For a civilian employer, these veterans can help bring a vibrant spark to almost any team. Once they embrace a firm's passion and purpose, most will enthusiastically volunteer to "take the point" and "carry the flag," and inspire others to do the same.

For more information on Reboot, or to contribute to their cause, please visit www.nvtsi.org/.

TEN *EROS* LEADERSHIP REVIEW POINTS

1. The Fourth Neuron Secret is the Neuron Principle of Passion: without passion and purpose, you are a ship without a rudder.

2. *Eros* is instinctual in nature and appeals to our instinctual R-Complex brain.
3. Adopting this principle requires an understanding of, and desire to live by, the ancient Greek form of love called *eros*.
4. *Eros* is about passion, romance, and a love of life and work.
5. The *eros* principle teaches us that attraction is far more powerful than promotion and requires a strong element of curiosity.
6. *Eros* love entails narrowing your organizational, departmental, team, and personal focus down to a single, clear, and compelling purpose.
7. The tenets of Conscious Capitalism embody the *eros* principle of focusing on passion and purpose more than just profit.
8. Team leaders need to select team members with great care and ensure they will embrace the firm's passion and purpose.
9. The Wizard in *The Wonderful Wizard of Oz* provides a good metaphorical representation and embodiment of this principle.
10. This principle can be summed up with these two words: *be passionate*.

THREE STEPS TO *EROS* LEADERSHIP

1. *Policy:* Leaders should meet with each team member quarterly to review the firm's mission, passion, and purpose and inspire buy-in on the part of each member. Also, to review the member's personal passion and purpose in life and discuss how this aligns with the firm's goals.
2. *Procedure:* Every organization should consider the benefits of adhering to the tenets of Conscious Capitalism, and align these to the firm's mission, passion, and purpose. Executives should consider becoming involved with this organization, and create and frequently review metrics to ensure progress toward achieving the Conscious Capitalism tenets.
3. *Practice:* Leaders should strive to continuously communicate the firm's core tenets, mission, passion, and purpose. Also, to frequently share stories—such as customer success stories—that embody these principles and inspire employees to improve productivity. The Neuron 3-Act Play chapter discusses how to accomplish this.

ONE *EROS* LEADERSHIP EXERCISE

For this exercise, you will need to dig deep to discover three important things:

1. What are you most personally passionate about in life?
2. What is the passion and purpose that drives your organization?
3. What is the passion and purpose that drives every member of your team?

For number one, this should expand beyond your profession and encompass your entire life. For example, I revealed in this chapter how I had come to know, without doubt, my life's passion and purpose. You may already know the answer to this question intimately. If so, write it down. If you are religious or spiritual, you might consider meditating and praying on this. If you are not, consider quieting your mind, looking deep within, and allowing your inner passion to reveal itself. Once you know what fills your heart with a glow, waters your eyes, and drives you forward each day, write it down.

For number two, your organization may already have a mission statement, which in many cases outlines the professional purpose of the firm. This is a good starting point, but might not go deep enough. Your firm or department or small team needs a clear passion and purpose that can change lives or even the world as we know it. The people in your organization will be more motivated if they believe that what they do each day can make a difference beyond quarterly profits. For example, I was asked to complete an executive leadership consulting project for a multimillion-dollar consumer electronics firm on an emergency consulting basis. The former team had left, and I needed to build a new one from scratch. While I had previously launched a consumer electronics division from zero to almost $30 million within two years, I had not done so in this industry. In fact, this sector was completely foreign to me.

The company manufactures electronic cigarettes, or "vape" hardware as it's called. These devices were cutting edge and sophisticated, with advanced microprocessors. The users were typically technical, younger, and "hipper" with a propensity toward nose rings and tattoos. My first inclination was that I was not the best fit for this project as I could not align with any passion and purpose that might drive this type of company. When I set aside my prejudices and misperceptions and took a closer look, I found something that opened my eyes … and my heart.

I learned that the U.S. tobacco industry was trying to discredit the vaping industry and had encouraged the FDA to impose regulations that were orders of magnitude more restrictive than those found in Europe. They were downplaying the fact that vaping was 90 percent safer than smoking cigarettes and highly effective at helping smokers to quit. The flashbulb went off, and I worked with my team to create a compelling passion and purpose statement that we could all get behind: *We save lives*.

This mantra became our driving force and propelled us forward each day to excel at delivering the best quality, performance, and enjoyment on the market. Why? Because we knew that if we delivered joy with every vape "cloud," we had the opportunity to save a life. If someone loved our products so much that they could quit smoking forever, then perhaps we could stand proud because we helped them have a longer life.

What's the passion and purpose of your organization, division, or professional endeavor? Discover it, discuss it, write it down, and then use it to inspire performance.

For number three, meet with each member of your team to determine their personal and professional passion and purpose. What drives them to get up and come in to work or brings them joy in other areas of their life? What are their dreams and aspirations? This should be more than just "we want a new car or a new house or a big raise." This should be far more personal. It may be difficult to coax some people into opening up and revealing their deeper desires, but your goal is to gain their trust over time so that eventually they will. In this way, you can help them to personally want to help your organization succeed because you can show them how they also achieve their goals.

It's time to clothe my dreams in reality,
To move beyond jealousy and possession,
isolation and imprisonment,
To confront boredom and loneliness,
sadness and lovelessness,

To make known my secret needs and reveal my
hidden yearnings,
To risk self-exposure as the only path to final
freedom,
To surround myself with the energy flowing from
the earth's core,
The passion of rivers and resilience of trees,
And thus, to clothe my dreams in reality!

—*Dr. James Kavanaugh, from* Quiet Waters

CHAPTER 9

Courageous Lion—Neuron Secret Five

FIGURE 9.1   Courageous Lion

Source: Anna Velichkovsky, Dreamstime.com.

> You have plenty of courage, I am sure. All you need is confidence in yourself.
>
> —THE WIZARD OF OZ TO THE COWARDLY LION (FIGURE 9.1)

NEURON SECRET FIVE

The Principle of Courage: It takes courage to have integrity and to be accountable

King George VI, whose real name was Albert, ruled England from 1936 until his death in 1952. Most Brits laughed when he assumed the throne. They wondered how he had succeeded his brother, Edward VIII, who was far more handsome, charismatic, and understandable. Albert had been plagued with a serious speech impediment that Edward chided him about constantly.

Edward appeared to be the lion, full of fortitude and blessed with a fluent tongue, while Albert assumed the role of a reclusive sheep, destined to live in his brother's shadow. Underneath Edward's façade, however, lurked an undisciplined jackal. He was sometimes a bit hedonistic and politically immature. In contrast, Albert held his head high and exhibited dignity and determination. Had his brother Edward not abdicated the throne in 1936, to marry Wallis Simpson, the Nazis might have conquered Britain.

Albert assumed the throne, but his impediment was so bad that he couldn't even pronounce the letter "k," a decidedly bad thing for a guy whose first name had just become "King." His constant stammering mocked him whenever he opened his mouth and served as a terrifying reminder of his shortcomings. How could he possibly hope to lead if he couldn't inform and inspire the masses? It seemed that his debilitation would not allow him to shed his sheep's skin to become the lion that England desperately needed.

This problem was exacerbated by the invention of the wireless radio. English subjects sat in their living rooms, cocked an ear toward their radios, and waited patiently for their king to speak. Much to Albert's dismay, he could speak to millions, but he could not pre-record the broadcasts. This meant he had to endure his ultimate agony: speaking live into a microphone while stuttering and stammering incessantly.

Even worse, Albert knew that the Nazis were also listening to his broadcasts. Lord Haw-Haw, during his *Germany Calling* radio shows, often joked about England's "stammering King."

Albert could have let his disability define him, own him, and keep him from becoming a great leader. He could have allowed fear and a lack of confidence to deprive the world of a king that changed history. Instead, he found the courage to not only gain more control over his tongue, but to also turn his deficit into a valuable asset. By facing the microphone to muddle through a long speech, Albert offered inspiration to the fearful and the downtrodden. His example of courage become the flag they charged behind, the banner of their defiance against Nazi tyranny, and their symbol of the hope to prevail against impossible odds.

To accomplish this feat, Albert enlisted the help of Lionel Logue, an Australian speech therapist, who taught the stuttering king how to slow down and dictate clearly. Logue did so by employing what the ancients would have referred to as *philia* love. He did not force, harass, or embarrass Albert into submission, but he did "call him on his crap." He refused to let Albert make excuses or shun the hard work necessary to succeed.

After months of frustrating and difficult practice, Albert never became fully cured of his impediment, but he did become proficient enough to deliver his clear and understandable vision of a bright and glorious future for all of England.

On September 3, 1939, Albert was called upon to deliver one of the most important speeches in history. He dressed in his naval uniform and approached the desk at Buckingham Palace. Although his throat tightened with fear, he looked deep into the eyes of his teacher and found the courage to remove his jacket, open a window, and step toward the microphone.

Logue stared into Albert's eyes and reminded the king to forget and to focus. Forget about everyone else and focus only on the importance of the message and the love of his country and its citizens. While announcing a declaration of war on Germany, Albert's delivery was clear, understandable, and majestic. He had found the will and the way to remove his sheep's wool jacket and open wide the window to his brave lion soul. He and Logue eventually became good friends and remained so until Albert's death on February 6, 1952.

While alive, Albert did not know he was a lion. He never imagined that he'd be anything more than a sheep, let alone find the fortitude and ability to lead an entire nation. By delivering *philia* "tough love," Logue had helped Albert to see his true potential and become the lion leader he was meant to be.

PHILIA LOVE

Philia is the Greek word for love that involves an abiding friendship, which is a key element of the Fifth Neuron Secret: *The Principle of Courage: It takes courage to have integrity and to be accountable.*

Like *eros*, this principle may sound emotional, but it's actually more instinctual. The ancient Greeks understood well that courageous veterans who have fought and bled together on the battlefield readily share this type of love. Loyal comrades who have experienced adversity together and protected each other from harm often develop a close brotherly or sisterly love that is underscored by trust and respect.

We've all heard stories of bravery on the battlefield, and perhaps we've wondered how these men and women found the courage to risk life and limb to face great dangers. Maybe we've wondered if we had the "chops" to accomplish something great or accomplish anything at all. Maybe we've thought of ourselves as too timid to lead or just brave enough to rise to middle management but not much further.

You can become a courageous lion that others trust and respect by first finding your heart, embracing your passions, and being brave enough to empathize with and care about those whom you lead. To do this, you must act with conviction, and above all, with unwavering integrity. You must also continuously demonstrate the courage to make difficult decisions.

Plato once said that "courage is knowing what not to fear." What most leaders fear most when making difficult decisions is the uncertainty of the outcome. It's easy to focus on worst-case scenarios that may never happen. It's harder to disengage our fight or flight instincts and quantify the consequences. What we often discover is that the worst-case possibility is highly unlikely and not as bad as we thought.

This famous quote is attributed to Alexander the Great: "I would not fear a pack of lions led by a sheep, but I would always fear a flock of sheep led by a lion." This means that a great leader with the courage of a lion can lead an army to victory, whereas an army of lions led by a sheep may be destined for failure.

Although some of us are intimidated by strong personalities or in awe of great leaders, others are just the opposite. Their mettle is like iron, and raw strength runs through them like lava through the guts of a volcano. They have an abundance of lion's blood and can't understand how anyone could be a sheep. If that's you, hopefully this chapter will offer some enlightenment to help you realize that leading by force or intimidation is only temporarily effective and can have disastrous long-term effects.

Leaders should seek not to create a farm filled with sheep so they can feel like the "Great and Terrible Oz," but instead build a team of lion leaders. If an army of sheep led by a courageous lion can win battles, imagine what a team of lions led by a lion can do.

The Greeks viewed *philia* as a special form of friendship that requires shared goodwill. Aristotle believed that we can only offer that goodwill to others provided we adhere to three conditions: First, we must be useful in some way to each other. Second, we must maintain a respectful and pleasant demeanor. And third, we must be rational and virtuous.

Relationships based on these three foundational elements ensure mutual benefit, integrity, dependability, and trust. Plato believed that *philia* transcended a surface-level form of friendship wherein two people learn to love each other by tearing down the walls that divide them. He felt that *philia* love could only be achieved if it came to life after an initial *eros* type of love. This may sound romantic, but recall that *eros* is really about passion and curiosity. In a platonic relationship, as with a leader and a subordinate or peer, the optimal course is to first ensure a shared passion and purpose, which is born of *eros*. Then, over time, transform this passion into a lower level of mutual understanding and respect that incorporates a shared philosophy and a deeper understanding of each other and common beliefs.

While two individuals may never be completely in sync in terms of shared beliefs, as they may have differing opinions about religion, politics, or world events, they can often mutually align with an organization's mission and overarching beliefs. If they are not aligned, then a *philia* form of love may not be possible.

Moreover, this type of love requires the courage to speak freely. In military environments, for example, an enlisted sergeant may say, "Permission to speak freely, sir." When permission is granted, the officer allows the sergeant an opportunity to offer a form of *philia* love. The sergeant needs to be brave enough to offer it, and the officer needs to be courageous enough to hear it.

Perhaps the sergeant is questioning an order. The officer may have commanded that his soldiers change the way they were planning to charge a certain hill. The sergeant, who may actually have more battlefield experience than the officer, has been granted the opportunity to "speak freely" and inform his leader about the risks of charging the hill using the new approach. If the officer wants to be a good leader, he needs to set aside his ego and listen closely to his sergeant's opinion. He needs to have enough courage to allow the sergeant to "call him on his crap" and express his concerns. Not doing so could cost lives.

Once fully informed, the officer must have the guts to consider his sergeant's opinion and also consider making appropriate changes if the information received is sound. Alternatively, a good leader must also have enough courage to reject his sergeant's input if he or she is absolutely convinced that it will impede the ability to achieve the objective or may have catastrophic consequences. Sometimes rejection is harder than acceptance because it requires potentially hurting someone's feelings. Gently but firmly explaining to your sergeant why his objections to the changes are not rational may take more gumption than simply doing it his way, even if you're certain that his plan will end in failure.

Socrates felt it was important for all of us to think for ourselves rather than sleepwalk through our lives or act like cattle that blindly follow the cow in front of us to the slaughterhouse. He believed in strong moral character and would have died before he willingly compromised his principles. As a leader, do you encourage independent thinking and praise people who may disagree with you, but do so because they're following their conscience? Do you allow team members "permission to speak freely" and give them critical feedback? Do you encourage "whistle-blowers" or do you try to cover up mistakes?

Philia love requires that a leader, for a time, become and act as an equal with the members of his or her team. We need to share as equals and learn from each other while understanding and appreciating our value to each other. This form of love, and the related neuron principle, also reminds us that we need to be brave enough to ask for help when we need it.

As leaders, we may often believe we need to show our teams and our superiors that we're strong and smart enough to do everything on our own without help. We may think that asking for help is a sign of weakness or inability. Just the opposite is true. We often have a great deal of help at our disposal, and a smart leader is courageous enough to trust others to contribute their unique value and skills to the success of the mission.

If the last few paragraphs are touching a nerve, rather than run from the pain of exploring this topic, I encourage you to do the opposite. Become a courageous lion and face your discomfort head on. For example, the next time to you lead a team meeting, especially where the topic relates to change, you may want to consider doing the following:

1. *Listen, don't talk.* Impart the goal, vision, or "commander's intent." Do so with as few words as possible and offer no opinions about how to achieve the goals. Then, remain silent except to ask an occasional question to guide the discussion or clarify the information offered. Plutarch, an ancient Greek biographer, offered this advice: "Know how to listen and you will profit even from those who talk badly."

2. *Inspire simplicity and humility.* Allow your team to disagree with you and each other. Healthy arguments are healthy. However, keep your team on focus and on point. Do so by asking questions such as, "By going off on this tangent, are we staying focused on our objectives?" This will remind everyone to stay the course, but it will also allow someone to explain why the tangent may be related to a particular goal.

3. *Encourage equal participation.* Remember that team meetings offer excellent opportunities to foster deeper *philia* team relationships built on love, trust, and open communication. Encourage all teammates to speak their mind and contribute. When someone who is more introverted remains silent, ask them what they think. When someone who is more extroverted is dominating the discussion, you might say, "John, thank you for your passionate opinion. I'd also like to hear more from Linda."

4. *Foster trust. Philia* love is instinctual. Our instinctual brain is fear-based and pushes us to make decisions based on avoidance of pain, harm, or loss. As a consultant, I've participated in dozens of team meetings where leaders have steered their team toward change management decisions based on their personal instinctual beliefs. These individuals were convinced that the sky was falling and that erecting a massive dome was the right course of action. Good leaders diminish fear-based, decision making by asking their teams to quantify the consequences (how to do this is covered in the Neuron Decision Making chapter). This engages the logical brain and quite often shows why the sky is not falling. The numbers indicate that, worst case, a small cloud might rain, so spending months and millions building a giant dome is a bad idea.

The other side of the *philia* coin also requires large doses of courage. We must be prepared to "call others on their crap." That is, not offer too much help and admonish them when it becomes obvious that their course of action may be leading them off the proverbial cliff. While it's important to trust enough to delegate to others and then get out of their way, some individuals may be reluctant to relinquish any control. Others with strong control tendencies may like to delegate a bit too much. They may tend to feel empowered by dumping many of their responsibilities on others. To avoid either scenario, leaders should consider three actions:

1. Remind your team that they are a team and are equals in that respect. While one member might get most of the accolades for "scoring the touchdowns," he or she can't run a single yard if others on the team don't block properly.
2. No one should do for others what they can do for themselves. We might think that we're doing someone a favor by constantly completing their tasks or covering for their mistakes. This does them and us a great disservice. Eventually, we become disgruntled, and they fail to grow because their path is too easy. Some leaders may tend to "do it themselves" to attain perfection rather than delegate anything, while others delegate everything. The true purpose of a leader is to set expectations ("commander's intent"), empower and encourage, step aside, remove roadblocks, review, and assist as needed.
3. Ensure clear boundaries, roles, and responsibilities. Make sure that everyone on the team is aware of their boundaries and understands the requirements of tending to their own areas. While it's encouraged to ask for help when needed, it's discouraged to constantly expect others to clean your bathroom.

THE COURAGEOUS GENERAL

Judith A. Fedder's father was a career Army warrant officer, so when Judy was a young girl, she and her family moved frequently. When they finally did settle down, and Judy was growing up in a small Michigan town, she never imagined that she'd follow in her father's footsteps and join the military. She aspired to be a medical professional. That changed in the middle of her sophomore year while attending Michigan State University.

"I wanted to belong to something greater, to do more with my life," said Judy, "so I joined the Reserve Officers' Training Corps (ROTC). But instead of going Army, I chose the Air Force."

Judy was too short to be a pilot but wanted to be close to the action, so she decided on a career path in aircraft maintenance. In her first few years as a junior officer, Judy had to adjust to being a woman in a world dominated by men. It was challenging to find the courage to speak her mind and stand up for herself. She finally decided to get out of her comfort zone and find her leadership voice. She got that opportunity in the early eighties.

"One Memorial Day weekend during the Cold War," said Judy, "tensions increased in the Middle East so we were ordered on Friday to prepare all of our aircraft for immediate operations by Monday morning. This was a huge task that included loading live missiles, adding extra fuel tanks, completing repairs, and running through hundreds of checklists. I was a green lieutenant in charge of 300 airmen, so I was nervous but decided it was now or never. I had to find the guts to get out of my comfort zone and step up and be the leader of my team."

By being brave enough to take a risk, Judy discovered an inner strength that served her well throughout her career in the Air Force. She also learned how to impact and inspire her team to follow her organization's vision and mission directives, which she translated into a "commander's intent." Later in her career, she faced a similar situation wherein she had to rally and motivate over 9,000 technicians, airmen, and civilian contractors to support several important missions.

"I had to find a way to appeal to their intrinsic values and to their sense of service," said Judy. "I did that by finding a common denominator; an understanding of what linked us all together as a team. I started with that core foundation and went from there."

Judy understood early on that leading a team takes courage, but it also requires inspiring courage and commitment from your people. She found that by effectively and clearly communicating a sense of purpose and urgency, and by painting the bigger picture that made the team feel as if they were a part of something grand, she could inspire loyalty and passion. This approach imbued her team with the courage and drive needed to accomplish the mission.

"I always make sure that credit goes downhill," said Judy. "People will work ten times harder for praise than for money. As leaders, we need to be 'good finders' by paying close attention to what our people do, and immediately recognizing them for extra effort and ingenuity."

Judy recalls that the Air Force employed various personality tests for their personnel, which helped leaders better understand individual traits, motivators, and fears.

"I always took the time to listen to individuals on my team," Judy said. "I also tried to set aside my personal bias and be open to criticism or different points of view. In our case, as my teams literally got their hands dirty maintaining aircraft every day, lives could be lost by ignoring their input."

Judy also discovered that leaders must inspire courage in their team by being a good example and by listening and praising others when they take risks or accomplish difficult tasks.

Judith Fedder retired from the Air Force as a lieutenant general (three star) after 35 years of service. During her career, she was awarded a Distinguished Service Medal with oak leaf cluster, Defense Superior Service Medal, Legion of Merit with oak leaf cluster, Meritorious Service Medal with four oak leaf clusters, a Joint Service Commendation Medal with oak leaf cluster, an Air Force Commendation Medal, and an Air Force Achievement Medal.

ONCE A MARINE

Major Glenn Ferguson, USMC (Ret), served in the U.S. military for over 24 years, extending through three wars: World War II, the Korean War, and the Vietnam War.

Glenn's father had served as a gunnery sergeant in the Marine Corps during World War I. Following in his father's footsteps, Glenn enlisted in the Marine Corps on November 13, 1939. Leaving his family and friends behind in Harvey, Illinois, he reported to the Marine Corps Recruit Depot (MCRD) in San Diego, California.

"The year following boot camp," said Glenn, "I saw a plane flying over North Island and decided that I was going to become an aviator."

Determined to live his dream, on the following Monday, Glenn applied for Naval Officer Training with the goal of becoming an aviator. The Navy granted Glenn's request for admittance into the Naval Academy Prep School in July 1940. He spent a year at sea aboard the battleship USS *Tennessee* (BB 43) before being transferred to the Prep School in Norfolk, Virginia. His determination to become an aviator motivated Glenn to study and work hard.

Glenn's efforts and fortitude earned him the opportunity to undergo flight training, and he received his "wings" on March 3, 1944. He then got orders to the dive-bombing training unit in Jacksonville, Florida. During the last year of the war, Glenn flew in the Pacific theater and trained for the inevitable invasion of Japan. The atom bomb negated the need for the invasion and eventually created a surplus of pilots.

Glenn was one of the lucky aviators who survived the force reduction for pilots after World War II. In 1952, he was transferred to the Heavier than Air Marine Observation VMO 6 Squadron in South Korea. Converting from fixed wing to helicopters, Glenn become an evac pilot in South Korea, and evacuating the wounded became his primary mission.

One day Glenn saw his squadron doctor stowing a box of small brandy bottles in the infirmary. Glenn remembered that pilots in World War I were issued bottles of brandy upon their return after a combat mission. It was not an uncommon practice for flight surgeons to offer medicinal brandy to settle the pilots' nerves, and this convention had carried over into the Korean War.

"Why don't you give the extra bottles to me, and I'll take them up to our friends on the line," Glenn asked the doctor. The squadron doctor nodded and mentioned that there was plenty of extra brandy in the Officer's Club, and it might be possible to obtain a few cases. Glenn found the booze, and his logistical prowess became a big hit with the Forward Air Controllers (FACs). He soon earned the moniker of "Booze Runner," and superiors overlooked the operation as they knew it lifted the spirits of the men on the forward line. However, they did not overlook the flight risks.

"The ops officer was furious with me for flying in the black moonless night because of the danger of not being able to rely on instrumentation," said Glenn.

Despite the risks, Glenn continued the operation for the remainder of his tour. He felt strongly that the single most essential weapon a leader can offer his teammates is *esprit de corps*. Higher moral and camaraderie often translate into lower casualties.

After his time in Korea, Major Glenn Ferguson also flew dangerous missions during the Vietnam War, and then he eventually retired. He still proudly serves the Marine Corps to this day. His concern for the degradation of our schools in training students in the elements of honor, courage, and commitment inspired him to initiate a youth leadership program run by the Flying Leatherneck Historical Foundation (FLHF) located on the Marine Corps Air Station (MCAS) in San Diego, California. The program is a collaboration between Dr. DeRoche, who heads the leadership program at the University of San Diego (USD), and the FLHF. Middle school children are rewarded by competing in an essay contest on the topic of leadership that emphasizes honor, courage, and commitment.

"By the time most students reach college," said Major Ferguson, "it may be too late to instill in them the attributes that are essential for leadership. Our program helps to teach young kids these important principles and encourages them to excel by offering a writing competition on the topic. The last young man to win was very impacted by the experience. His father mentioned that he could see a profound change in his son's attitude toward education. His father was amazed at how he was suddenly interested in learning, reading, and applying himself. He was eventually placed into the Gifted and Talented Education (GATE) cluster. I'm really honored to have the opportunity to help these kids learn valuable life lessons about leadership and courage."

FINAL THOUGHTS

The Fifth Neuron Secret is about the courage to be honest and open with ourselves and others, and to hold each other accountable. The ancient Greeks called this *philia*, which represents a brotherly or sisterly type of love. This is when we get to call each other on our crap but in a "tough love" respectful way. The best way to ingrain this into our daily lives is by seeking help from others. We can and should form networks of trusted friends, colleagues, advisors, and mentors to help us along our journey.

I have done this by joining a small group of like minds and spirits that meets every other week to share our most inner secrets, dreams, desires, frustrations, problems, joys, and more. Over many years, we have grown to love and trust each other implicitly, and we are now very open to being "called on our crap." In fact, we welcome it. We don't want to be coddled. Instead, we ask to be told the truth, no matter how painful. We recognize that facing that truth is difficult but also necessary if we are to make progress toward our goal to become better leaders.

Some people attend church groups, professional organizations, networking groups, 12-step programs, self-help book clubs, and more.

I mentioned earlier that Dr. James Kavanaugh wrote a book called *Search* that inspired a movement and workshops by the same name. When Kavanaugh died, this movement waned, but there may still be some active groups. You can research this on your own at www.jameskavanaugh.org.

Whatever type of support group you choose, it's important to remember that when someone does call us on our crap, our "fight or flight" instinctual brain will kick into gear. Our initial instinct will be to either fight the guy or run away and cry. Neither of these are appropriate responses. We need to engage our emotional and logical brains, uncurl our fists, turn our open palms upward, and thank the person who told us that we sometimes act like a jerk. We need to remember that they are simply pointing out facts that will help us see ourselves and our actions more clearly.

Likewise, when we admonish someone, we need to do so with empathy and compassion. Our motives should be pure and prompted from a heart filled with love. Our only objective should be to help the other person learn and grow.

Since this principle is instinctual, writing someone an email or letter is not the best approach to demonstrate *philia* love. It is best to meet with them in person. I try not to meet with someone in my office and, if I do, I come around from my desk and sit next to them, not across from them. I need to act like a friend, not a boss.

I realize that this sounds counter to most of the leadership guidance the big guys spout, but other writers or consultants may not understand that to appeal to someone's instinctual brain, they must trust you. They must feel that you are on their side, not on the other side of the river. This part of our brain does not react well to a logical email or PowerPoint slides. We could point to facts and figures and show them charts to prove that we are right and they are wrong, say that they should be a better employee and do it our way, but this approach is usually doomed to failure.

We are better off using visual and audio aids whenever possible. A whiteboard can be the visual, and our soft and calm voice the audio. We need to be collaborative rather than confrontational.

A courageous lion leader can win a battle with an army of sheep, but rarely will he or she win an entire war. The best leaders cultivate a team of lions by never asking someone to do what they would not do themselves. They lead by example and encourage others to do the same by exhibiting courage, integrity, and accountability.

TEN *PHILIA* LEADERSHIP REVIEW POINTS

1. The Fifth Neuron Secret is: *The Principle of Courage: It takes courage to have integrity and to be accountable.*
2. This principle relates to the Greek form of love called *philia*, which is an abiding friendship exhibited between brothers and sisters, colleagues, and close friends.
3. This type of love requires the courage to speak and act freely when appropriate between peers, subordinates, and superiors without fear of ridicule or reprimands.
4. This principle is instinctual and appeals to the R-Complex instinctual brain. It requires a level of integrity and trust between all members of a team.
5. To embrace this form of love, leaders must listen rather than do all the talking, inspire simplicity and humility, encourage equal participation, and foster an environment of integrity and accountability.
6. Leaders should also remind team members that all are equals, no one should do for others what they can do for themselves, and everyone should maintain clear and respectful boundaries and roles.
7. The courageous Lion in *The Wonderful Wizard of Oz* provides a good metaphoric representation and embodiment of this principle.
8. For leaders, it takes more courage to be an example of compassion, understanding, and patience than to be an uncaring, whip-cracking, task-oriented bully.
9. When we lack courage, it's because our instinctual brain is in control and is blanketing our life with fear. Usually these fears are unfounded and can be vanquished by engaging our logical brain to quantify the consequences.
10. This principle can be summed by these two words: *be courageous*.

THREE STEPS TO *PHILIA* LEADERSHIP

1. *Policy:* Leaders should work with upper management to create detailed, clear, and flexible job descriptions and expectations for each team role.
2. *Procedure:* Leaders should meet weekly with team members to review roles, expectations, problems, concerns, roadblocks, and the resources needed to function in their role. Also, to politely admonish when appropriate.

3. *Practice:* Leaders should be trained, by internal or outsourced coaching experts, to act as coaches and mentors for others on their team. Also, leaders should be coached on how to be courageous enough to offer and accept critical input and differing opinions.

ONE *PHILIA* LEADERSHIP EXERCISE

For this exercise, let's answer the following questions:

- How do I typically act when I'm faced with a fearful situation?
- What situations or circumstances usually cause the most fear?
- How do I allow my fears to influence my decisions?
- Do I dominate discussions and meetings, or do I listen attentively to my team?
- Do I encourage equal participation among all members of my team?
- Do I have the courage to empower and let go, or do I constantly micro-manage?
- Am I too timid to speak up in meetings or discussions so my opinion can be heard?
- Do I try to force my will and opinion on others, or am I open to other points of view?
- Am I a "control freak" who overworks my team to get results in order to make myself look good?
- Am I too easygoing and afraid to set proper boundaries or stand up for my team?
- Do I exhibit unwavering integrity in all my affairs?
- Do I have the courage to hold myself and others accountable?
- What new habits will I form, starting today, to ingrain *philia* love into my life?

> There is no failure for one unafraid to be himself,
> No defeat for one who does what he can without
>   sacrificing the private rhythm of his being,
> A rhythm created over centuries and shared
>   with life itself.
> Failure is only a chance to begin again,
> Defeat but a gentle warning to walk another road,

Loneliness an invitation to find a new friend.

A life built on sand and avarice is the victim

of every earthquake or avalanche,

Every rise and fall of Dow Jones or a robot's dictation.

Wrap yourself in your own feeble being,

Warm yourself with your own fragile heart,

Defend yourself in peace and silence, and do battle

with smiles and shrugs

And an awareness of eternal change.

Patience and humility are your impermeable armor,

Love and prayer your impregnable protection.

Your worst adversary is crippled with everyman's fears,

The most severe critic but a raconteur of his own story.

How can there be failure when the ocean still rolls

toward the land?

And the night still embraces strong and weak alike

with love?

The morning will come with its soft light

to offer you a childhood again,

And the wind will sing the gentle rhythm that makes

of each day a new adventure.

—Dr. James Kavanaugh, from Quiet Waters

CHAPTER 10

Our Needs

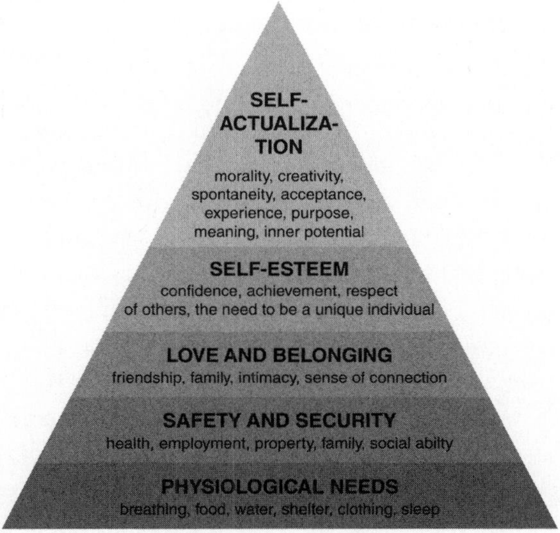

FIGURE 10.1   Self-Actualization Pyramid

Source: Elenaphoto21, Dreamstime.com.

> I do think a carpenter needs a good hammer to bang in
> the nail.
>
> —Oliver Reed

Before moving on to explore the next two secrets, we need to first spend some time determining and examining our personal and professional needs (Figure 10.1). In this chapter, we will affirm that it's our right and our responsibility—not someone else's—to determine our true purpose in life and have our needs met. All of us have needs, personally and professionally, to enjoy a happy, healthy, and productive life. These needs must be understood and met in an appropriate way.

To determine our most important needs, let's reflect on our shortened list of beliefs. These beliefs, and their underlying values, dictate our needs. For example, if our belief is that it's our responsibility to nurture and care for our families, one of our needs may be income. That means we probably need a job or business. But what kind of job? If our list of beliefs does not include the need for superficial, ego-gratifying luxuries (as fun and desirable as these may be), then do we really need that high-paying yet highly stressful career that keeps us away from home six months out of the year? Do we really need that brand-new Mercedes, or does that desire stem from an antiquated and unhealthy belief that our neighbors and friends will think less of us if we drive a Prius?

This viewpoint may seem contrary to the "you can have it all" philosophies espoused by many other self-help books or programs. These authors or well-meaning advisors may say we must all set lofty goals and focus on pictures of the fancy house or car we desire. If we do so, the universe will magically make them appear just as we imagined. This may be true, but how often have we focused on the "desire of our hearts" only to discover that it was not at all what we really wanted—or needed? Perhaps we fixated on that big house by convincing ourselves we needed it to provide for our families. Years later, the "universe" or God or hard work or whatever we believe in miraculously granted us our wish.

As we stood in our mansion with the spiral staircase and manicured lawn and massive pool, we patted ourselves on the back for attaining our "dream." It all came true, just as we envisioned, yet we were not smiling. Our grand house was empty because our spouse divorced us and took the kids. We worked so hard that we forgot about them. The medical report in our pocket said we have only six months to live. We stressed so hard we failed to take care of ourselves, and a fatal illness caught us unaware.

How often have we heard "be careful what you wish for"?

Maybe it is better not to wish or pray for specific outcomes, lest our limited knowledge of the future prevent us from fulfilling the destiny we are meant to have. Perhaps we should ask only for the wisdom to discern what is right and best for us today—each day—that will lead us to a life filled with joy and abundance.

ANCIENT TAR

In ancient times, the Sumerians used the word *NAM.TAR* to depict one's fate. NAMTAR was a minor god who dwelled in the underworld and brought forth evil, pestilence, and disease that Sumerians thought of as the "fate of the gods." More importantly, NAMTAR acted as a herald or messenger of fates beyond one's control.

Today, we often bemoan our fate and wonder why bad things happen to good people … like us. We question what we did to "deserve this fate." We forget that we probably asked for it when we prayed for, hoped for, or asked the universe for an outcome.

We wanted to be healthier, so why did we get sick? *To develop an immunity.* We wanted to be richer, so why did we get hammered in the stock market? *To teach us how to invest better.* We wanted to reach that goal at work, so why did our team fail? *So we'd learn how to work better and smarter as a team and succeed in the future.*

Be careful what you wish for. If you're not prepared to take the bad as a stepping-stone to reach the good, then be content where you are. If you're not content where you are, the Sumerians used another word called *TAR.*

This word means destiny. It literally means to cut or break, as in altering one's direction. *TAR* describes a predetermined course that can be altered by what we do … or think. For the Sumerians, *TAR* began in the heavens with the pre-ordained path of the planets and arrangement of the universe. However, one's *TAR* can only be altered by changing what *can* and *should be* changed.

Perhaps this is what inspired the saying by Reinhold Niebuhr:

Grant me the serenity to accept the things I cannot change,

Courage to change the things I can,

And wisdom to know the difference.

EXERCISE

For this exercise, we're going to list our top 10 needs. You don't need to be overly specific, but you do need to be clear. For example, you might say, "I need an adequate income that ensures I can provide for my family, reduce financial stress, and ensure we are happy and healthy." Examine your beliefs and your values, think about what's most important in life, and write down your top ten needs now.

To complete this exercise, bring up a notes app on your mobile device, or use a sheet of paper, a notebook, or a document on your computer to create your list now.

Have you completed your list? If not, please do so before continuing.

Now reexamine your list and delete those needs that do not speak directly to your heart. Trust your heart, your feelings, your gut, your instincts, your emotions. Close your eyes and visualize your life without a need you have listed. Can you live without it? If your heart does not glow when you think about a specific need, ask yourself honestly just how important it really is. You may replace a need or two with others you hadn't thought of earlier. Take your time. It's not important to have a minimum number of needs, perhaps you only have one, but it is important to understand your need or needs before continuing your journey. Only when you are absolutely convinced that the needs you have listed are essential, and reflect your true heart, should you move on to the next chapter.

CHAPTER 11

Authoritative Wizard—Neuron Secret Six

FIGURE 11.1   The Wizard of Oz

Source: Anna Velichkovsky, Dreamstime.com.

I am Oz, the Great and Terrible.

—*THE WONDERFUL WIZARD OF OZ* (FIGURE 11.1)

NEURON SECRET SIX

The Principle of Authority: Tough love leaders are authoritative mentors, not authoritarian dictators.

155

Not long before Tom Flanagan graduated from college and received his commission as a naval officer, he met Admiral Hyman G. Rickover—the "father" of the Submarine Nuclear Navy. Tom stood in the top 25 of his class of nearly 900, so Rickover tried to recruit him for submarine duty. Tom had his sights set on being a Navy SEAL, so he declined. Rickover upped the ante by guaranteeing Tom a Navy-paid opportunity to earn a master's degree in engineering at the Massachusetts Institute of Technology (MIT). Tom took the deal, got his degree, and reported for submarine duty aboard the USS *Whale* (SSN 638). The CO of the sub assigned Tom to the communications division, which consisted of six petty officers and a master chief.

"I was the guy in charge of communications, but I must admit that I was new at communicating orders and managing a division," said Tom. "I had just come from MIT and I had been given authority, but I hadn't yet earned it. I knew that I would never earn it if I didn't learn how to connect with my team and speak their language. Fortunately for me, the master chief took me under his wing. He also ensured that the team knew that I was now in charge."

Tom learned how to better translate his thinking and "commander's intent" into easily understood directives by observing the master chief, his CO, and other officers on the boat. He improved his leadership skills by exhibiting confidence, compassion, and the ability to listen, but also by adjusting his communication style. Over time, he earned more trust and respect from his team, and later took charge of the largest division on the submarine in engineering. He was then transferred to the USS *Memphis* (SSN 691) but harbored plans to serve one final year of his obligation and then leave the Navy. Not long after getting married, an unexpected series of events changed the entire direction of his career:

> The *Memphis* was in new construction, and I was counting the days to my discharge from the Navy when we received an unclassified message. They were looking for a volunteer to help lead a new cruise missile program in Italy. I was bored at work so I volunteered, got accepted, and then had to clear it with my new bride.

Tom's wife gave him a green light, so he packed his bags and flew to Naples to work on a classified project called Outlaw Shark. The program entailed launching a cruise missile from a nuclear submarine with targeting information provided beyond the sub's sensors via satellite. Tom spent the next few months on what later became the Tomahawk cruise missile program.

Launching cruise missiles from a submarine was not new. The Navy had previously equipped subs with *Regulus* nuclear turbojet missiles after World War II. The USS *Tunny* (SS 282) launched the first *Regulus* in 1953, and was later joined by four other submarines. These five subs became America's first nuclear-deterrent strike force and completed 40 patrols before being replaced by newer fleet ballistic missile subs.

In 1976, when Tom got involved with operation Outlaw Shark, the Navy had decided to integrate several new technologies from intelligence sources and "big data" satellites, mid-range computers, and new cruise missile platforms. The new missiles would be smaller, lighter, and faster. They would also fly farther and would be extremely accurate, going well beyond the range of a submarine's sensors.

By Christmas, Tom and his teammates had solved a lot of technical issues, but they were just getting started. Tom had promised his wife that he'd be home for the holidays. Then he got a call from the local Submarine Group (SUBGRU) 8 admiral.

"They wanted someone to brief Admiral Stansfield Turner, who ran the Sixth Fleet, on operation Outlaw Shark," said Tom. "There were only two of us who could do that, so we drew straws. Damned if I didn't get the short one."

Instead of flying home to see his wife, Tom spent the next few days preparing his presentation, which he later gave to Turner. He then joined his wife and after the holidays returned to Naples to finish the project. Three months passed before he received another call from Submarine Atlantic (SUBLANT) command in Norfolk, Virginia.

"They wanted me to brief a bunch more officers," said Tom. "One of them was Admiral Isaac Kidd, the guy in charge of the entire Atlantic fleet. I was within two months of leaving the Navy, and it was a Saturday morning when I got the call to be in Norfolk immediately. Needless to say, I wasn't pleased with the unexpected request."

Tom recalled his experience as a junior officer and thought about how his CO and other senior officers had helped him improve his communication style. He decided that instead of trying to show off and impress the admiral with his technical prowess, he'd instead simplify his presentation so it could be easily understood.

"One thing I learned on my first submarine was how to communicate well," said Tom. "Sometimes when we have authority, we don't do a great job of explaining to others what we want them to do, and we often fail to keep the message simple and concise. My message was simple: technology was about to revolutionize modern warfare. Back in 1977: my team and I were painting a vision of drones and cruise missiles as they might be used twenty or thirty years in the future."

Tom briefed the Commander of Submarine Atlantic (COMSUB-LANT)—a three-star admiral—who reported to Admiral Kidd. Then Kidd walked in and Tom spent another 25 minutes briefing him. Kidd stood up, smiled, shook Tom's hand, and then turned to COMSUBLANT and said, "It's on."

After ADM Kidd left, COMSUBLANT said to Tom: "Congratulations, you are going to brief the president of the United States."

Tom's jaw dropped. He learned that Admiral Rickover had scheduled a briefing on the latest nuclear submarine capabilities for President Jimmy Carter. As Carter was the only president in history to have qualified on submarines when he was a naval officer, he had an interest in the newest technologies.

Carter arrived in Norfolk, Virginia, to tour the USS *Los Angeles* (SSN 688). ADM Kidd had convinced ADM Rickover to have Tom brief the president while he was aboard. Rickover agreed, but allotted only 15 minutes.

Tom met with President Carter in the control room and began his briefing. Carter was very interested, stopped Tom, and asked that his wife, Rosalynn, also hear the presentation. When she walked over, Tom continued his talk.

"The president asked a lot of questions about the program," said Tom. "He was genuinely interested and frequently asked me what I thought. He really wanted to know my opinion. For me, that was an excellent example of authoritative leadership. Here was the president of the United States making a junior lieutenant feel empowered while asking intelligent questions so he could be informed enough to make decisions."

For President Carter's briefing, Rickover had given Tom a hard stop at only 15 minutes. At 30 minutes, Tom saw Rickover standing on his toes behind the president and Rosalynn. He was tapping his watch. He did not look happy. Rickover was widely known throughout the Navy as an authoritarian leader. His controlling style had proved effective at ensuring a safe nuclear submarine force, but it had also created occasional difficult situations for junior officers.

Tom did his best to balance the demands of the two leaders. He knew that the effective use of the Tomahawk program could potentially one day save lives, and it was important that the leader of the United States have a full understanding of the system's capabilities. He continued with the briefing for a while longer to ensure that the most important information was imparted, and then said, "Mr. President, I think we have exceeded our allotted briefing time."

Carter glanced at Rickover and then nodded.

During a Town Hall Meeting on October 9, 1980, President Carter remarked that when he had become president there was no long-range cruise missile program, and now the United States had a very good one.

A decade later, during the first Iraq War in 1990, two nuclear attack submarines launched a barrage of Tomahawk cruise missiles on Iraqi communications centers, tanks, and the Zaafaraniya nuclear fabrication plant. One senior Defense Department official commented that the Iraqi plant was "a perfect candidate for a strike by cruise missiles because of the need for pinpoint accuracy and because Baghdad is so heavily defended."

Experts estimate that dozens and perhaps even hundreds of lives were saved by having the ability to implement initial strikes on targets with accuracy from distant stealth positions.

"I never forgot my briefing with President Carter," said Tom. "In less than one hour, I observed a man with the weight of the world on his shoulders. He was genuinely interested in what a young lieutenant had to say about an important new technology. Today, whenever I think I have too much on my shoulders, I remember that briefing and it helps me place my situation into proper perspective."

Tom's experience with the Tomahawk program and his briefing with President Carter helped him learn several valuable lessons:

1. Take control of your career. If you are bored or if your job is growing stale, get out of your comfort zone and volunteer for something new.
2. Sometimes in life you will pull the short straw. You may get an unexpected call on the weekend that could change your life. It's okay

to get angry, but then get over it. Sometimes opening new doors in life requires enduring a little discomfort, but that pain might just lead to a career-changing meeting with the president of the United States.

3. Great leaders don't force their opinions or their authority on anyone. They invest appropriate time to gain their team's input and trust. They ensure that others are a part of creating ideas and making decisions so they will be motivated to take ownership. They also relinquish authority by delegating and empowering.

"Prior to giving all those Tomahawk program briefings, not once did an admiral or officer require that I first do a dry run or presentation preview," said Tom. "They empowered me and trusted me."

Tom Flanagan retired from the Navy after nearly 25 years of service. He later became Chief Information Officer (CIO) for MCI, a global communications giant. He was also CIO and Senior Vice President for Amgen, the world's largest biotechnology company, where in 2008 he earned recognition as a Top Ten Global CIO Leader and Innovator. In 2010, Tom was selected to the CIO Hall of Fame and is now a vice president at IBM.

STORGE LOVE

Tom Flannigan's experience serves as an introduction to the Sixth Neuron Secret: *The Principle of Authority: Tough love leaders are authoritative mentors, not authoritarian dictators.*

The ancient Greeks practiced a form of love called *storge*, most often found in the authoritative relationship between parents and children. This form of love underlines the Principle of Authority. The ancients would have believed the actions of "helicopter parents" to be humorous and sad. In the Greeks' view, a parent shows the opposite of love by shielding a child from pain or effort. These two essential elements of life sharpen swords and teach our offspring the painful lessons they need to face a difficult and harsh world.

For leaders, we may frequently be required to act like a parent with those whom we lead in that we are given the authority to hire, fire, and direct. Understanding this Neuron Principle and the logical neuropsychology that dictates how we respond to authoritative figures will help us improve our ability to set proper boundaries, instill trust, and deliver "tough love."

We learned earlier that Dutch children are the happiest, and perhaps the most well-adjusted, in the world. One might think this is so because the Dutch, being more liberal, are less authoritarian and disciplinarian. In a few scenarios, this is true, but in most it is not. Most Dutch parents have mastered the delicate balance between stifling domination and benign neglect. They refer to this as being authoritative rather than authoritarian.

The best leaders understand the difference between these two words. Authoritarian favors complete obedience or subjection to authority rather than individual freedom exercised within appropriate boundaries. Authoritative means having an air of authority, usually supported by a demeanor of confidence and underscored by knowledge and experience. To be authoritative, the best leaders also know that it's important to gain the enthusiastic support of your team. They must be committed and willing to do whatever it takes to follow the commander's intent. This requires removing yourself as the authoritative figure.

That last statement may seem counterintuitive, but recall that teams are far more motivated to achieve a higher passion and purpose than to simply follow an order or line their pockets ... or yours. To achieve a *storge* form of authority, it's important to point your team toward a higher passion and purpose and make that the "authoritative figure."

Years ago, in a movie titled *Knute Rockne: All American*, Ronald Reagan played the part of a Notre Dame college star football player, George Gipp, nicknamed Gipper. In one scene, when Gipper fell ill and was on his deathbed, he asked his coach, Knute Rockne, to make him a promise.

Gipper said to Rockne that when the team was up against difficult odds and the boys were being defeated, he should go out there and tell them to give it their all and win one just for the Gipper. That line became so famous that Reagan later used it to help him win a presidential election. This is an example of using a higher purpose, or passion, as the authoritative figure or goal that motivates a team to "give it their all."

In most thrillers, famous writers usually employ a plot device called "the MacGuffin." It's a term made up by Alfred Hitchcock for his 1935 movie, *The 39 Steps*. It's the objective, desire, or item that most of the characters want. For example, in the original 1977 *Star Wars* movie, everyone wanted the plans for the Death Star. The Empire wanted them back, and the Rebellion wanted to use them to find a weakness. The antagonist, Darth Vader, and the protagonist, Luke Skywalker, were pitted against each other and stopped at nothing to find "the MacGuffin" plans. Both used this goal to invoke authority and gain the undying cooperation of their respective teams.

Leaders are wise to do the same by first understanding and clearly communicating a higher purpose and passion that drives their organization and teams. Name it, visualize it, clearly portray it, and create a MacGuffin to symbolize it. For example: saving lives by encouraging the use of electronic cigarettes. The MacGuffin could be the attainment of one million units sold of a new e-cigarette device designed to help smokers quit their habit. We might use a poster showing a near-death smoker on one side contrasted by a healthy and happy vaper on the other side. Above the two figures, we might place the headline: 1M SAVED.

Now, in company meetings, we can leverage the "authoritative goal" displayed on our MacGuffin poster. As a team leader, we can point to the picture and say, "Let's do the following so we can make our next campaign a huge success. Let's save one more life for the Gipper."

Some leaders might find the statement above a bit corny or illogical, but remember that our brains are more motivated by emotional and instinctual triggers than logical ones, so maybe this approach isn't so corny after all.

In The Netherlands, discipline is based more on an authoritative *storge* form of love than on strict obedience. The Dutch believe in teaching children how to adopt socially appropriate attitudes and behaviors. Dutch children respect their elders, but do not automatically defer to them as they would in France, Britain, or Asia. They are expected to be helpful and friendly with grandparents, for example, but are not required to be blindly obedient. They are not willfully disobedient, but they *are* taught to speak their minds. Dutch parents believe that it's important for their children to stand up for themselves. Learning how to voice a sound argument is a valuable life skill. Being a doormat is not.

Storge love admonishes us to set good examples for others to follow. We must earn respect, not demand it. Likewise, Dutch parents seek to be good examples for their children. They use two common expressions to illustrate this: "Parenting is practicing what you preach" and "What the old cock crows, the young cock learns."

Storge love requires clear, firm, and polite communication. Children in most Western countries have learned how to argue with their parents when told to do something, like take out the trash. If they argue long and loud enough, parents may eventually throw up their arms in frustration and give up. Dutch parents have learned that "no" is a complete sentence. Their child-rearing experts recommend *telling* rather than *asking*. Saying "will you please take out the trash?" may seem more polite and correct. It may *feel* like a better way to teach children how to be kind and courteous, but it's not the best leadership approach. In The Netherlands, parents don't ask, they tell. They will say in a polite but firm tone, "please take out the trash." This removes any options or arguments. By asking, you give your child a choice. What if their answer is, "No, I will not take out the trash"? Now you are backed into a corner.

Likewise, as leaders, to be a good example and exhibit a *storge* form of love, we must politely direct rather than timidly ask. Again, this should not be done in a dictatorial, harsh manner, but instead by using a courteous but firm voice. The best way to do this without sounding like a tyrant is to phrase it in the right way by indicating the desired expectations in relation to the firm's stated vision, and the need for your subordinate's help to exceed the expectations. For example, you might say, "I need your help to complete this project by Friday so we can save another life. What help do you need from me or others on the team to do this?"

In this way, we have "told" the person what needs to be done but phrased it within the context of needing their help so as not to let us or the team down. We then asked how we or others could help them. When they state their needs, we can offer encouragement by letting them know that we trust and believe in them and their ability to accomplish the goal. This is called the Pygmalion effect, wherein the confidence level of previously average-performing employees is boosted, resulting in higher performance to meet the socially stated goal.

The U.S. Navy and Israeli Defense Forces conducted studies years ago and validated the Pygmalion effect. They determined that between 12 and 17 percent of average performers gained a significant boost up to the superior level when this approach was used. The opposite is also true, and has been referred to as the Golem effect, named after a clay creature in ancient Jewish mythology that was given life.[1] Recall Captain Jo Dee Jacob's story about her abusive boss that made her feel inferior? Her desire to perform also wobbled.

The Dutch do a good job of avoiding the Golem effect by delivering discipline that does not entail forcing children to bend to wills. It is not about bullying, power struggles, constant spying or monitoring, or imposing threats. It does not require yelling, screaming, demeaning, or shouting. Instead, Dutch parents gain cooperation by delivering praise for good behavior and setting proper but loving boundaries to limit unacceptable or harmful behaviors.

Leaders who practice *storge* love, in like measure, understand that balance is the key. Subordinates should be given ample rope and autonomy. They should not be micromanaged or spied upon. They should be trusted to act like adults and do their jobs correctly and effectively. However, when the end of the rope is reached, a polite but firm yank is acceptable and required.

Leaders should clearly communicate where the rope ends. It's not appropriate to yank someone's chain when they did not even know they had one. Double standards are not allowed. If a boundary is set for one, it must be set for all. A favored employee should not be allowed to come in every other day with a hangover while everyone else risks being fired. *Storge* love means setting proper examples. As leaders *we* should not come in every other day with a hangover and expect our employees to be model citizens.

Open communication in other areas is also important. Employees should be kept well informed about all aspects, aspirations, and attainments of the firm, the marketing, and the competition. They should also be told about all the awful stuff. Lying and hiding will diminish trust and lower oxytocin and productivity levels. Recent research studies verify that only about 40 percent of employees say they are well informed about their organization's strategies, tactics, and goals.[2] If workers don't know what their firm's goals are, how can they align them to their personal goals?

To some, being open is akin to being vulnerable or losing control. These individuals tend to control others and information flow to feel safe and secure. We may fear that relinquishing any control or information will cause us or our organization harm in some way. This is our instinctual brain talking to us. It sits upon our shoulder like an annoying little devil and whispers things in our ear like "don't tell them anything, they'll leak it on the Internet and scare off customers," or "better keep an eagle eye on that guy because he'll never do the job well enough." Generally, these are unfounded fears. That little devil is lying to us. We need to flick him off our shoulder and let go of our unrealistic expectations of perfection. We need to delegate and allow others the dignity to perform assigned tasks to the best of their ability. Our job is to point toward the MacGuffin poster and ensure everyone is marching in the same direction. We can then let go and trust that if we are all focused on the same higher purpose, even if we take different paths to get there, we will reach our goal together.

From a neuroscience perspective, *storge* love is logical and is best expressed with numbers, facts, figures, graphs, charts, and other analytical data and information. Our demeanor when demonstrating this form of love should be calm, authoritative, and knowledgeable. When we practice this principle correctly, we can raise serotonin and GABA in the brains of those we lead, which both have a calming effect. In high-stress situations, where cool heads need to prevail, leaders should engage their logical brain so they can remain calm and collected. Teams will more readily follow leaders who act rationally and who have demonstrated a thorough understanding of the situation. Also, they have thought several "chess moves" ahead and will make sound, intelligent decisions.

An authoritative leader is a wise and rational leader. Teams have confidence in these leaders and will more readily follow instructions and overcome fear to accomplish the "commander's intent." They will remain calm and confident because their mirror neurons will help them emulate the attitude, demeanor, and actions of their leader.

LOSE THE LADDER

A U.S. Navy SEAL team is commanded by a Navy Commander (O-5 rank) and comprised of eight operational platoons with 16 operators in each. Platoons usually operate as eight-man squads, four-man fire teams, or two-man sniper/reconnaissance teams. Operators report up to a senior enlisted man or officer, but regardless of rank, there is no "ladder." No one is trying to climb over anyone else, and everyone is empowered to act within their envelope of authority.

Team operators work in tandem to complete the mission objectives, which are clearly communicated as the "commander's intent." Most civilian organizations would do well to lose their ladders. They incentivize employees to climb up to manager, then director, then vice president.

Titles stroke egos, and everybody wants a higher one along with more pay. Unfortunately, a "bottom-up" or "top-down" hierarchical structure is usually not very effective in today's fast-paced environments.

The executive coaches at CUSTOMatrix, a successful leadership consulting firm in San Diego, California, cite that one of the most common problems their clients iterate is the inability to be agile. They are getting eaten alive by competitors because their structure prevents fast decision making and action. If an employee is required to gain permission from a "boss" who also needs permission from another "boss," and both are busy or traveling or slow, decisions take forever and opportunities are missed or threats are allowed to escalate.

Dr. Paul Zak said, "High performance teams anticipate each others' moves and respond effectively without having to articulate what they are doing. These teams integrate new information deftly in order to reach a known objective. High-performance teams are also generative, improvising new solutions. For this to happen, though, team members have to trust each other."

Small teams are best, which is why SEALs usually operate in teams of eight. Studies show that individual performance degrades when teams expand beyond six to 12, depending upon the objectives and environment.[3]

COMMANDER'S INTENT

Former U.S. Navy SEAL Lieutenant Jason Booher, now the CEO of consulting firm Northwest Harbor Solutions, learned a lot about authoritative team leadership during his 23 years on the teams. He joined the Navy as an enlisted seaman at the age of 19. After enduring a year of the world's most demanding military training, he spent his career risking his life to complete dangerous missions in third-world countries as part of an elite team of warriors.

Like all SEALs, he often used a "briefback," which is a detailed briefing and mission plan starting with the objective and working backward to the start. This plan might include deploying from an aircraft, Zodiac, or attack submarine. The plan ensures that everyone on the team knows where their rope begins and ends.

Said Jason, "It's critical for a mission commander to outline the 'commander's intent' and clearly communicate that to everyone on the team.

The leader's intent must be commonly understood so it can be carried out effectively."

If you haven't figured it out by now, when translated into the corporate world, the 'commander's intent" is like an executive's passionate vision, departmental or project goal, or quarterly objective. Delivering this correctly requires an understanding of *storge* love.

As Jason explains, "SEAL teams excel in extremely complex and high-risk environments because we ensure common understanding in a defined 'commander's intent,' and then empower aligned decision making at the lowest level possible. Corporate leaders can also drive agility and performance in their companies by better aligning their people and teams to their mission."

It may seem that Jason and others who have operated in close-knit units, such as SEAL teams, have a unique perspective unadaptable by corporate executives or others in commercial leadership positions. In some respects, this may be true, but common ground can be found by adopting and using *storge* love.

Leaders, like SEAL commanders, need to politely direct, not ask. They need to do so in clear and uncertain terms. They need to outline the objective, the "commander's intent," and communicate the rewards for success and consequences for failure. Then, they need to empower and let go. Micromanaging is not an option. They need to trust, reasonably monitor, gently guide when needed, and occasionally yank a chain when limits are reached. They must set good examples, be fair and consistent with every member of the team, and do so out of a genuine love for everyone on the team. All of this may seem unattainable, but that's only true if your heart is cold and closed. Conversely, if it is open and full of compassion for those you lead, if you genuinely know and care about everyone on your team, then *storge* love is not only possible, it is inevitable.

CHIEF EVERYTHING OFFICER

Eric Casazza's grandfather, Vice Admiral Eugene P. Wilkinson, commanded one of the submarines that launched Navy SEAL teams into action. In fact, he was the first captain to command the Navy's first nuclear submarine, the USS *Nautilus* (SSN-571) and worked closely with Admiral Hyman G. Rickover to pioneer the nuclear submarine

Navy. Eric concurs that properly and clearly communicating your organization's passion and vision is critical to great leadership.

"A great leader helps his or her team visualize where they can be by creating an extremely detailed picture of the future," said Eric. "With input from my team, I do this for our entire company and then have them translate that into something similar for each practice area."

Eric is the CEO of FMT, an IT consulting firm in San Diego, California, with almost 80 employees. He also sits on the board of Saint Vincent de Paul Village, which offers shelter and care to the homeless. Eric launched his career with Andersen Consulting and later became a senior consultant for Deloitte Consulting.

"At the young age of twenty-three, I was managing teams of 150 or more people," said Eric. "Many of them were older than me, which was a huge leadership challenge."

Eric later joined AMN Healthcare Services, Inc., a $400 million healthcare staffing firm in Del Mar, California. Under the direction of CEO Susan Salka, over the next 11 years, AMN blossomed into a $1.3 billion company. During that time, Susan became one of Eric's most remembered mentors.

"Susan is charismatic, smart, and decisive," Eric said. "She is a great listener and knows how to communicate her vision extremely well, and then get out of the way. She is authoritative but also passionately invested in her people. She makes you feel important, wants to know about you personally, what your aspirations are, and all about your family."

Obviously, Susan Salka uses an authoritative rather than an authoritarian leadership approach to clarify her company's passion and purpose and then allows her team to take charge. Leaders like Susan and Eric understand that it often takes more guts to empower than it does to micromanage. They are excellent examples of *storge* love, in that they truly care about those they lead, empower them to succeed, and then step aside and trust. The best leaders know how to set proper and loving boundaries and politely *tell* rather than *ask*.

"I need to exhibit a lot of patience to help my team learn and grow," said Eric. "I also need to be humble and set good examples. I believe the title CEO really means Chief Everything Officer in that I need to be willing to roll up my sleeves and wash dishes or whatever it takes to get the job done."

COMMAND AUTHORITY

Charles Michel's father was an Army artillery officer during the Cold War. Like most military brats, Chuck moved a lot from base to base so it was hard to form long-term relationships. He initially wanted to follow his father's path and pursue a career in the Army. To that end, he joined the Army Junior ROTC program while in high school. During a "career night" event at his school, dozens of companies and military recruiters set up tables in the gymnasium. Chuck shuffled past most, spent some time at the Army and Navy table, and then by happenstance started talking with a Coast Guard petty officer.

"I asked him if the Coast Guard was a part of the military," said Chuck. "I admit that I didn't even know if it was. The petty officer said 'of course it is.' I asked if they had officers, and he then told me about the Coast Guard Academy, which is a lot like West Point."

Chuck chose the Coast Guard and packed his bags. A few years later, at the age of 22, he graduated near the top of his class. On board his first ship, he learned a valuable lesson about leadership and authority.

"My first ship was a Coast Guard cutter out of Saint Petersburg, Florida," said Chuck. "Two other ensigns from my class of 1985 joined me onboard. We had a crew of 75, and our primary job involved drug-running interdiction in the Caribbean. When I met Captain Jake Jacoby, he had a scruffy gray beard and salty demeanor, and I thought he looked like a cross between Ernest Hemingway and Black Beard the pirate."

Underway, Jacoby "handed the keys" to Chuck for the first time as the Officer of the Deck (OOD) on the bridge. They had received orders to board a suspect vessel and search for drugs. Slightly nervous, Chuck issued orders to maneuver the ship into position and commence small boat operations. The seas had turned rough with six-foot swells hammering against the sea painter towing the small boat. Thirty feet below the bridge, Chuck watched the small boat rock and bounce on the surging waves as the interdiction crew struggled to climb aboard.

"Captain Jacoby scratched his beard, turned toward me and recommended that I loosen the stern line to stop the small boat from jerking back and forth so much," said Chuck. "I radioed the deck crew and told them that the captain had ordered them to loosen the line. They followed the order, and the boat calmed down enough to allow the crew to board so we could complete the mission. Later, Jacoby pulled me aside and asked me one question: 'Who is charge on this bridge?' I said that he was. He said, 'No, I am not. You assumed complete authority when you became the OOD. You do not say to the crew that I gave an order. You are the one giving the order, is that understood?'"

Chuck nodded and swallowed hard. He had learned a valuable lesson that day he never forgot. Leaders must delegate, and when they do, they must have complete trust. They must step aside and allow those empowered to make decisions and give the orders. They can and should then become mentors, and as such can and should offer advice, such as "loosen the line," but they should not actually give the orders to their crew.

More importantly, Chuck learned that when given authority, a leader must assume command completely and with confidence.

"It's a lot like riding a horse," said Chuck. "Once you're in the saddle, you're in command. The horse will not follow your lead if he senses that you're not in control."

Chuck also learned a valuable lesson in humility. He was reminded that even though he had graduated at the top of his class and had a high degree of theoretical knowledge, he was still a junior officer. Cracking a book is far different from operating on the high seas in a stressful situation where people might be injured or even killed. Chuck learned that "crusty old" seadogs had a lot of real-world experience to offer that could be invaluable.

When Chuck was promoted to higher ranks, he remembered the words and actions of his CO that day. He recalled the right way to delegate, step aside, trust, and advise. He refrained from allowing his fear of losing control to cause him to micromanage his junior officers.

Jacoby continued to mentor Chuck and taught him a host of other valuable lessons that helped him throughout his career. Chuck swallowed his pride, became humble enough to be teachable, and took Jacoby's guidance to heart. His willingness and attitude helped him progress through the ranks and assume the reigns of his current position as vice commandant—the number two ranking officer in the Coast Guard.

Chuck bottled his views on leadership and condensed them into a powerful presentation that he uses as a reference to help guide his officers and enlisted personnel through their careers. He sees leadership development as consisting of four separate but integrated phases, each containing three key ingredients. The four phases are peer-to-peer leadership, field operations, command or HQ operations, and senior leadership that might entail political interaction. Under the peer-to-peer phase, Chuck outlines the three keys as being fair and above reproach, being decisive, and remaining calm under pressure.

For the more advanced phases, Chuck's three keys are to know your stuff, delegate without fear, and maintain a "big picture" view. Chuck doesn't see leadership as either relationship- or task-oriented, but believes it to be more situational, based on the people you are leading and the situation you're dealing with. He also feels that it's vital to understand each person on your team and know what motivates and inspires them to perform at their best. He does not see authority as a license to bully or coerce, but as a responsibility to educate, inspire, and set a worthy example.

"Leadership has never been more important than it is right now," said Chuck. "Motivating and directing people today demands the highest level of skill, dedication, and courage."

AUTHORITY, RESPONSIBILITY, ACCOUNTABILITY

Mike Petters grew up on an orange farm in Florida. His family also raised cattle so Mike started driving a tractor when he was 10 years old. By the time Mike turned 15, he was given his first opportunity to lead when his father placed him in charge of a three-person orange tree spraying crew.

"Everyone on the team was twice my age," said Mike, "so I learned early on how to be responsible but also to be respectful of others who had more experience than I did."

His father served as an officer in the Army National Guard and frequently expressed his gratitude for being born in a free country. He encouraged Mike and his five siblings to serve in the military, and all of them did. One joined the Navy, three went Air Force, and one sister selected the Army. She eventually earned the rank of two-star general.

Mike chose the Navy and received an appointment to the United States Naval Academy at Annapolis, Maryland. When he graduated, Admiral Rickover recruited him for the Nuclear Submarine Navy. Mike completed his training and reported for duty aboard the USS *George Bancroft* (SSBN 643), a nuclear fleet ballistic missile "boomer" submarine. He initially led two engineering divisions and was later given responsibility for the communications division. As a green ensign, Mike worked hard to prove himself and qualify as a submariner so he could earn his golden "dolphins" pin. Operating in the tight confines of a "425-foot-long tube" quickly changed his entire perspective about teamwork.

"Teamwork on a submarine is vital," said Mike. "Everyone has clearly defined areas of responsibility, accountability, and authority, but we need to operate as an efficient, close-knit team. If we fail to do that, we place everyone on board at great risk."

While serving aboard the *Bancroft*, Mike also learned that being authoritative is vastly different from being authoritarian. Many of the enlisted men in his division, especially the "crusty old chief petty officers," had a great deal more experience and working knowledge than Mike. He knew that forcing his will on his team by being a domineering authoritarian would not work. They might do what he demanded, but begrudgingly. Adopting an authoritarian approach might also create an environment of mistrust and disengagement that could unravel the fabric of teamwork that's vital to the survival of all submariners.

Mike earned the respect of his team by treating them as equals. While he was granted the authority to be the "boss" of this team, he noticed that other officers who treated their guys with respect and trust, and empowered them to do their jobs, were far more successful.

"As their division officer, I could have ordered my team around," said Mike. "Some junior officers did that, but it rarely worked. The officers who inspired others to take full responsibility and be accountable were far more successful. In my opinion, this is what authority is all about. You need to lead your team by example and earn their respect rather than force them to follow you."

Mike was working 20-hour days until the CO called him into his stateroom.

My CO talked to me about my performance and said I was doing a great job, but that I was killing myself. He told me that it was important to enjoy the job I was doing and to not think so much about the next one. He emphasized that it wasn't the rank or the title on the door that was important, it was about making the most out of each job and being the kind of leader that makes everyone around them better.

I was startled when he said this but it served to re-center my views about what was important. I've reflected on my CO's words again and again throughout my career. In fact, I often tell people to not chase titles but to make their current job the very best one they've ever had, and in doing so, success will usually follow.

After serving five years in the Navy, Mike and his wife, Nancy, decided that it would be better for their family if he left the military. Mike continued to serve his country by joining the Naval Reserves and by becoming an employee at Newport News Shipbuilding. Many years later, he became the president and chief executive officer of Huntington Ingalls Industries—a Fortune 500 public company and the world's largest military shipbuilder with $7 billion in revenue and 37,000 employees.

"That discussion with my CO helped me to understand that I needed to determine what I was passionate about and that there were many ways I could fulfill my passion and purpose in life," said Mike. "Anyone who works at Huntington Ingalls can impact hundreds of thousands of lives worldwide, as we build the Navy's capital ships, aircraft carriers, submarines, destroyers, and amphibious warships. We're also involved in a wide array of government services and even do work for the U.S. Army, the United States Post Office, and our country's court systems. Today, Huntington Ingalls Industries is the largest industrial employer in Virginia and the largest employer in Mississippi."

Thanks to the leadership style exhibited by his CO on the *Bancroft*, Mike learned how to be an authoritative mentor rather than a domineering authoritarian. Now, when he meets with employees on his team, he asks them how a career at Huntington Ingalls aligns with their life's goals.

"When someone comes into my office to talk about their career path," said Mike, "I ask them about where they are and where they want to be. If, for example, their ambition is to be a director, I say 'director of what?' I try to mentor them by saying that a title means little if your job does not inspire you, and it won't inspire you if it's leading you away from your true aspirations. Gaining authority does not automatically gain you happiness."

Mike advises his team that if they're not fulfilled and thrilled by their current position, they will not be inspired to do their best work. If they don't give it their all, they'll have a difficult time convincing anyone in authority to promote them to director or any other position they desire. Mike also believes it's important for those in authority to create an environment where people are set up for success and appreciated, recognized, and empowered.

"Leaders can either set their teams up for success or for failure," said Mike. "One of the best ways to ensure success is to create leaders and not managers; to teach people that a position of authority is a privilege that is earned by showing others in authority who you are and what you're made of."

Mike also cautions aspiring leaders to refrain from adopting a "lone wolf" attitude rather than being a part of a team. Highly ambitious individuals may be tempted to "go it alone" so they can earn all the credit for a successful outcome. Even worse, they may try to dominate the limelight by stealing credit from others. Employing these tactics may sometimes result in short-term accolades, but rarely do they ensure long-term recognition or success. Moreover, these behaviors may result in mistrust and alienation from teammates, which could cause irreparable damage to your career.

"As leaders, we need to create an inclusive culture and environment where everyone can do their best work and where the least empowered person confidently contributes," said Mike. "As a junior officer aboard submarines, I learned early on that authority, responsibility, and accountability are intertwined. They are three corners of the same triangle. To succeed as a team leader, you need to be an excellent example of all three."

TEN *STORGE* LEADERSHIP REVIEW POINTS

1. The Sixth Neuron Secret is: *The Principle of Authority: Tough love leaders are authoritative mentors, not authoritarian dictators.*
2. This principle is based on the Greek word *storge*, often exhibited in the authoritative relationship between parents and children.
3. A *storge* type of love is akin to the "tough love" that is difficult but necessary to help others learn and grow.
4. In practicing this type of love, we should not do for others what they can do for themselves.
5. This principle is logical and aligns mostly with our logical neocortex, which responds best to written words, facts, figures, and data.

6. We should strive to be a confident authoritative leader rather than a "dictator" authoritarian.
7. Authoritative leaders gain the trust and support of teams by earning it rather than demanding it.
8. Leaders who practice this principle and the associated Greek form of love have the courage to delegate, empower, let go, and advise rather than micromanage.
9. The Wizard in *The Wonderful Wizard of Oz* provides a good metaphoric representation and embodiment of this principle.
10. This principle can be summed by these two words: *be authoritative*.

THREE STEPS TO *STORGE* LEADERSHIP

1. *Policy:* Leaders should be required to collaborate with team members to create only three primary goals per quarter that are realistic and attainable and drive toward the firm's overall passion and purpose. Members should then be given authority and autonomy to execute toward the goals.
2. *Procedure:* Leaders should meet weekly with team members to review progress toward each goal to ensure the challenges are not too easy or hard, to review expectations for that week, and deliver praise for progress. (The Neuron Decision Making chapter offers examples.) Leaders need to ensure they do not micromanage, but instead review metrics and the progress their members are making toward the goals.
3. *Practice:* Leaders should be trained, by internal or outsourced coaching experts, to be confidently authoritative, to delegate appropriately and effectively, and to listen and communicate clearly. Visit www.neuronleaders.com to use the *Neuron Personality Profiler* app to assist with customizing communication styles using neuroscience-based messaging.

ONE *STORGE* LEADERSHIP EXERCISE

For this exercise, please answer the following questions. It is best to write your answers on a sheet of paper.

- Do I have the courage to empower and let go, or do I constantly micromanage?

- Am I afraid to lead because I doubt my knowledge, skills, abilities, or authority?
- Am I overconfident and a perhaps a bit cocky, or am I humble enough to listen to my team?
- Am I an example of an authoritative leader like John F. Kennedy or an authoritarian dictator like Adolf Hitler?
- When given authority by others, do I step up and lead, or do I defer to their authority?
- When I am authoritative, will I remember to also be calm, confident, and logical?
- Do I seek to gain the enthusiastic support of my team and a buy-in to the vision, or do I force my will upon others?
- Am I courageous enough to accept honest feedback and criticism, or does my ego force me refuse to or ignore the input?
- What will I do differently after today to practice *storge* love in my life and profession?

I played God today
    And it was fun!
I made animals that men had never seen
So they would stop and scratch their heads
    Instead of scowling.
I made words that men had never heard
So they would stop and stare at me
    Instead of running.
And I made love that laughed
So men would giggle like children
    Instead of sighing.
Tomorrow, perhaps, I won't be God
And you will know it
    Because you won't see any three-headed cats
    Or bushes with bells on ...
I wish I could always play God
    So lonely men could laugh!

—*Dr. James Kavanaugh, from* There Are Men Too Gentle to
Live Among Wolves

CHAPTER **12**

Wise Scarecrow—Neuron Secret Seven

FIGURE 12.1   The Scarecrow

Source: Anna Velichkovsky, Dreamstime.com.

Experience is the only thing that brings knowledge, and the longer you are on earth the more experience you are sure to get.

—*THE WONDERFUL WIZARD OF OZ* (FIGURE 12.1)

NEURON SECRET SEVEN

The Principle of Wisdom: Patience and dependability are the cornerstones of great leadership.

When Sean O'Keefe was born in Monterey, California, in 1956, his parents, like most, had visions of grandeur for their son. As Sean matured, he never gave much heed to those visions, but they found him all the same. Sean's mother and father hailed from New Orleans and persuaded him to attend Loyola University after he graduated from high school. Sean earned a Bachelor of Arts degree and then pursued a Masters of Public Administration at Syracuse University one year later. Unsure of what his next steps should be, he decided to let the gentle waters of fate guide him toward his destiny.

"I recall a great book written by James Stavridis called *The Accidental Admiral*," said Sean. "I may write a book one day called *The Accidental Public Servant*."

In post graduate school, Sean was "accidentally" selected to the inaugural class of the Presidential Management Intern Program and later served as a budget analyst for the Department of the Navy. That accidentally led to a stint with the U.S. Senate Committee on Appropriations staff for eight years, which later earned him a promotion to staff director of the Defense Appropriations Subcommittee.

In 1989, John Tower was President George H. W. Bush's selection for Secretary of Defense, but for the first time in three decades, the Senate rejected the president's nomination. Instead, Dick Cheney got the nod and immediately initiated a search for a Senate staff veteran. Sean was "accidentally" on the radar screen and so accepted the opportunity to serve as the Comptroller and CFO for the Department of Defense. Following a *New York Times* profile about his sharp cost-cutting, Sean earned the title of the "Grim Reaper."

Said Sean, "Secretary Cheney's Deputy Secretary, Don Atwood, was selected from the ranks of the business community after serving as vice chairman for General Motors. Atwood brought a management efficiency agenda to our organization to streamline overhead costs. Some people didn't like the fact that I had been selected as the 'point man' for Secretary Atwood's agenda, but it offered me a pragmatic education on what it takes to implement change management in a large organization."

Sean was later praised for his heavy hand in managing finances for the 1991 Gulf War and, along with Atwood, for encouraging U.S. allies to hand over large sums to cover the war expenses. Over $54 billion of the $61 billion expended for U.S. forces was covered by allied contributions. Sean's demeanor as "one tough hombre" again placed his name in the hat when a serious incident caused a big shakeup at the highest levels of the U.S. Navy.

In September 1991, during the 35th Tailhook Association symposium in Las Vegas, Nevada, over 4,000 men and women attended a two-day debriefing on U.S. Navy and Marine Corps aviation operations. Active military, reservists, and retired personnel gathered in Sin City to eat, drink, and review the success of the air campaigns completed during Operation Desert Storm in Iraq.

Flying for the Navy or Marine Corps is a risky business. If you don't get shot down, your engine could fail, you could get sucked into your wingman's draft, miss the deck during a carrier landing, or just make one tiny mistake. Any of these misfortunes could be your last. Adrenaline and egos run high, as might be expected. Letting off some steam is considered commonplace. Unfortunately, during those two days under a bright Nevada sun, the vented steam fogged far too many windows.

Reports later surfaced, along with incriminating photos, documenting inappropriate behavior. When Tailhook Association President Captain Rick Ludwig returned to the aircraft carrier USS *Midway* in Seattle, he met with his air wing commanders and flag officers to discuss what had happened at the event. Later, 83 women and seven men came forward and filed claims of sexual harassment. Making matters worse, they claimed that several flag officers had been aware of the activities but did nothing.

"The report took over ten months to complete and failed to produce any substantial conclusions," said Sean. "That obviously was not acceptable."

The resulting report, completed by the Naval Investigative Service, blamed only low-ranking enlisted men for the bad conduct and absolved the flag officers. Barbara S. Pope, assistant secretary of the Navy, refused to accept the findings. She stormed into the office of Secretary of the Navy H. Lawrence Garrett III and threatened to resign and go public if he did not "do another report and look at what we needed to do about accountability and responsibility and the larger issues at hand."

"Garrett elected to do another investigation to be conducted by the Defense Inspector General," said Sean. "The next Tailhook report was far more damaging and was released months after Garrett's resignation in June 1992. On a Friday I was comptroller and CFO of the Defense Department. By Monday, when I was selected to relieve Garrett, I was Acting Secretary of the Navy."

Quite by accident, Sean O'Keefe stepped into Garrett's shoes and subsequently went public with the new Tailhook report in September 1992, when it was issued by the Defense Inspector General.

"Picking up the pieces from Tailhook became a tough leadership challenge," said Sean. "Ultimately, I had to make some difficult and serious change management decisions that scuttled or damaged the careers of many naval aviators and several flag officers. Some people didn't like me very much after that, but it was important to demonstrate the naval service commitment and dedication to doing the right thing."

In the wake of the Tailhook incident, the Naval Investigative Service also took a hit. The organization was refocused to the primary task of investigating criminal behavior and received a name change to the Naval Criminal Investigative Service, or NCIS, which spurred one of the most popular shows on television.

President George H. W. Bush appointed Sean O'Keefe as permanent secretary of the Navy, whereupon his Grim Reaper reputation once again came to the forefront. With the Cold War now over, Sean oversaw the requirement to "draw down" Navy and Marine Corps forces and reframe the strategy of naval services to complement the Department of Defense's pragmatic long-term plan. Sean faced difficult choices and strong political winds that pressed him to compromise his integrity. He never did.

"A leader's most important principle must be integrity," said Sean. "You must demonstrate that you intend to live by the same rules you impose on others. If your integrity is compromised even once, it might never be regained."

Sean's reputation for unwavering integrity and dependability later led to his "accidental" selection as NASA administrator (CEO) just three months after 9/11. Many questioned his appointment as he did not have a technology, engineering, or scientific background.

"I was typecast as a bean counter," said Sean, "not a rocket scientist. But what prompted my reassignment from the White House staff as OMB Deputy Director was a financial management challenge at NASA. The commander's intent that President Bush communicated to me was to control costs and run the agency more efficiently."

Sean accomplished that goal by eliminating a $5 billion overrun the administration had inherited for the International Space Station. Construction of the station had been undertaken by a consortium of

16 nations to build the largest laboratory in space, one module at a time. A little over a year later, when the space station obstacles were finally under control, Sean faced one of the most difficult and disheartening challenges of his career—the loss of the space shuttle *Columbia*.

"We'd prepared for the STS-107 mission for months," Sean said. "Commander Rick Husband was an Air Force colonel and a brilliant mechanical engineer. His pilot, Bill McCool, was an experienced Navy commander who had finished at the top of his class at the Naval Academy and flight school. The onboard crew consisted of two Navy captain medical specialists, an Air Force lieutenant colonel as payload commander, an Israeli Air Force colonel who was a legendary pilot in his country, and an Indian-American veteran astronaut aerospace engineer. This was one of the finest crews NASA had ever assembled. They worked hard and trained hard and should never have died on that mission."

STS-107 was NASA's 113th Space Shuttle mission. Originally, it had been scheduled for launch almost 12 months before Sean O'Keefe assumed command of NASA, but technical issues and scheduling challenges had caused several delays.

On January 16, 2003, on the launch pad at Cape Canaveral, three clustered rocket engines thundered and roared and hurled the Space Shuttle *Columbia* toward the stars. Eighty-two seconds after liftoff, a suitcase-size chunk of foam broke free from an external tank and smacked into the *Columbia's* left wing. The hit damaged the craft's thermal protection coating. The *Columbia* Accident Investigation Board determined that more than two weeks after liftoff, when the space shuttle re-entered the intense heat of the earth's atmosphere, the damaged leading-edge section of the left wing channeled the hot gases to enter and ripple through the shuttle orbiter. This caused the *Columbia* to break apart just minutes before the scheduled landing. All seven crew members perished in the disaster.

"I've dealt with several hardships during my career," Sean said. "None were more difficult than delivering the news to the families of the crew after the accident. However, their reaction was awe inspiring. In the midst of the deepest remorse and pain that anyone can endure, they requested that we find out what happened, fix the problems, and rededicate ourselves to the dream of space exploration that their loved ones had died for. Their request became the mantra my team and I lived by every day thereafter."

Sean and his team were forced to make forward-thinking decisions, especially regarding the dependability of the current platforms. One of these was to place the Space Shuttle program on a two-year hiatus while they poured through data, ran simulations, and designed new safety measures, procedures, and materials to prevent future mishaps. During that time, he learned a lot about team leadership.

"First and foremost," said Sean, "I learned how important it is to embrace my responsibility to lead my team by example. I needed to be consistent and dependable, as well as accountable. I couldn't ask my team to be responsible and make tough decisions if I wasn't willing to do the same. After the *Columbia* accident, everyone was painfully reminded that our decisions and actions could cost lives. We had to hold each other accountable to a much higher standard and think about the long-term big picture."

Achieving that higher standard was met with a great deal of criticism in January 2004, when Sean was forced to make another difficult decision. He canceled the Space Shuttle mission to repair the Hubble Space Telescope, which was to be its last before the service life of the telescope expired. Sean reasoned that with the dust still settling on the *Columbia* failure and the investigation board admonishing him to defer shuttle operations until NASA could "prove that it's safe," the risk was too great as only a few of Accident Investigation Board recommendations had been completed. If the shuttle was damaged in any way, there was no means to rescue the crew without risking a mid-space orbit intercept with another shuttle, which had never been done.

The Hubble telescope operates at an altitude nearly 100 miles higher than the International Space Station, so a safe haven rendezvous was not an option. However, time was running out for Hubble. Engineering team experts had determined that the telescope had no more than a few more years of life left if the servicing mission wasn't conducted immediately. A decision needed to be rendered by early 2004 to avoid Hubble's demise. Some agreed with Sean, but many others led by a group of astronomers did not. They felt that the Hubble's contribution to science trumped the risks.

Sean announced his resignation from NASA on December 13, 2004. Seven months later, the Space Shuttle *Discovery* launched from Pad 39B to commence mission STS-114 to the International Space Station while demonstrating the new safety protocols devised after the *Columbia* tragedy. The *Discovery's* crew returned safely to earth less than two weeks later. In May 2009, six years after the loss of *Columbia,* the Hubble engineering estimates proved to be wrong. More than five years after the telescope was predicted to cease operations, a final mission approved by Sean's successor was launched to repair Hubble and extend its service life. Other than short flights to support completion of the International Space Station, this was the last mission ever conducted by a space shuttle.

"After I left NASA," Sean said, "I thought my life would be easier. Little did I know that I was jumping from the frying pad into another fire."

Sean became chancellor of Louisiana State University on February 21, 2005. Six months later, he was "accidently" and literally tossed into the middle of a hurricane. The infamous gale named Katrina swept through the Gulf of Mexico and caused what became known as the world's costliest natural disaster and one of the five deadliest hurricanes in U.S. history. In all, more than 1,200 people died during the storm and subsequent floods. Total costs were estimated at north of $100 billion.

Katrina began her reign of terror by rearing her ugly head over the Bahamas on August 23. She roared eastward toward Florida and earned the official title of "hurricane" when she hit landfall at Hallandale Beach. Warm Gulf of Mexico waters propelled Katrina to a category five. By the time she assaulted Louisiana on August 29, she'd lost a little steam and had been downgraded to a category three. Still, the damage was severe. Katrina wreaked havoc across the Gulf from Florida to Texas, causing levee failures and 90 percent flooding in Mississippi beachfront cities. Casino barges and small boats rammed into buildings while the storm overturned cars and uprooted houses and damaged buildings.

In New Orleans, Katrina caused more than 50 breaches in the city's hurricane surge protection structures, resulting in massive loss of life. More than 80 percent of the area remained flooded for weeks. Those who survived ran from the calamity, but most had nowhere to go.

"We were in shock," said Sean. "The area near LSU had been hit hard, but not nearly as hard as New Orleans. They were only 80 miles away, but they were right on the water and breaches in the inner city canal walls caused flooding in most of the metropolitan-area neighborhoods. Thousands died, and many more were now homeless. I knew we had to do something to help the survivors."

With most hospitals closed after power went out in the 150-mile radius around New Orleans, Sean decided that LSU should open its doors, and its heart, to anyone in the area that needed shelter. He organized teams and instructed them to turn LSU into what was later referred to as the largest acute-care field hospital established in a contingency in the nation's history.

"We turned the basketball arena into a thousand-bed MASH unit," Sean said. "We housed doctors and medical professionals from around the region and the country who came to the campus to assist the diaspora from New Orleans. There was no power anywhere else, but we had a cogeneration facility and emergency generators. People were stifling in the 90-degree heat and suffering severe dehydration."

Sean also had to deal with lots of misinformation. Rumors spread that the area wasn't safe due to reported incidents of rioting, looting, and shootings in the city of Baton Rouge. The claims proved to be false, but they frightened people away. Many of those people needed help and might perish if not properly treated or cared for. Sean immediately organized a town hall–style meeting in the community and did what all great leaders who exhibit unwavering integrity should do. He took full responsibility for his part.

"I told everyone that we were going to start our meeting by denouncing the false rumors. I then apologized to the community for compounding the confusion. I hadn't verified the rumors before permitting the LSU communications team to advise the campus about the situation. It was my responsibility and the buck stopped with me. From now on, we would double our efforts to keep everyone properly informed and work closely with local law enforcement. I then asked everyone to join in the effort to support those who had come to our campus for shelter and treatment."

Sean and his staff worked around the clock for weeks to ensure uprooted and hurt residents were sheltered and cared for. In all, thousands of refugees were taken in and taken care of by hundreds of volunteers, all working under Sean's leadership.

In October 2009, Sean O'Keefe accidentally accepted an offer to become the CEO of EADS North America—the U.S. subsidiary of the aerospace giant now known as Airbus Group. He leveraged his bean-counter expertise and Washington connections to help EADS compete with Boeing to secure a $35 billion U.S. Air Force contract for aerial refueling tanker aircraft. In the midst of that campaign, a different type of aircraft almost took his life and that of his teenage son.

In August 2010, Sean and his son were on a fishing trip near the central coast of Alaska. They were flying in a seaplane near Aleknagik when the plane went down. Alaska's Senator Ted Stevens and four others aboard died in the crash. Nearly eighteen hours after the accident, a team of Air National Guard, Coast Guard, and local medical emergency personnel found the aircraft and arrived at the crash site. It was a miracle that Sean, his son, and two others survived the ordeal.

Apparently, higher powers were not yet finished with Sean. His successes at EADS gained him a seat as chairman of the board in January 2011, but he stepped down just three years later due to lingering issues with the injuries he'd sustained in the 2010 airplane crash. He now speaks publicly on the topic of leadership and teaches at his graduate school alma mater, Syracuse University's Maxwell School of Citizenship and Public Affairs.

"The advice I often express to current and aspiring leaders is that making wise decisions requires diverse input," said Sean. "It's important to listen to other points of view that may be fundamentally different from your own. When you open your mind to other perspectives, solutions, and courses of action, even if you don't initially agree with them, you can begin to expand your thinking and your long-term sagacity. You can begin to see opportunities that you might have overlooked. By inviting different views, you also encourage your team to think outside of what's commonly accepted, and in doing so, they might just astound you. Gaining leadership wisdom does not happen overnight. It is a lifelong pursuit."

PRAGMA LOVE

Sean O'Keefe's experience and wisdom set the stage for the Seventh Neuron Secret: *The Principle of Wisdom: Patience and dependability are the cornerstones of great leadership.*

We talked earlier about Dr. James Kavanaugh's view that becoming who and what we desire requires "long-game" thinking. We can't stroll onto the golf course after taking our first lesson and expect to hit below 60. The ancient Greeks called this *pragma*, a long-term, mature form of love. To explain this type of love, they used examples of couples who have been in committed relationships for many years, who share a deep understanding of and affection for each other. Such an abiding love is only possible when both partners demonstrate a high degree of integrity, trust, and dependability.

This rational form of love appeals to our logical brain, as verified by the word pragmatic, which is a derivative of *pragma*. Team members, guided by consistent examples exhibited by their leaders, can realize this form of love and respect for each other only if they are willing to make compromises, set aside egos, and demonstrate a high degree of tolerance, understanding, and long-term patience.

Erich Fromm, a renowned psychoanalyst, once commented that people often emphasize falling in love when they should be learning how to "stand in love." Although making the right selection up front is critical, in relationships and with members of our team, we often see couples and leaders adopt a "happily ever after" mentality. Despite what we've been programmed to believe from reading kids' books, happily ever after is more fairy tale than reality. There is no such thing on a consistent basis unless we make the effort to give more love than we receive. More than a third of first-time marriages end up in divorce court after less than a decade.

Remember the adage about "Greater love hath no one than this, that he lay down his life for his friends"? We learned that to lay down our lives means to generously give our time to others. If we expect to hire someone, or get into any kind of long-term relationship with anyone, we must be willing to lay down our time and our unrealistic expectations. We must be willing to play the long game. Only in this way can we develop a pragmatic form of love.

Pragma is a form of practical love based on logical reason, sense of duty, and commitment, and an alignment with mutual long-term interests. In personal relationships, physical attraction becomes less important than individual qualities and shared compatibilities, common goals, and staying the course. It's about playing all 18 holes.

Pragma love was far more prevalent than *eros* love when arranged marriages were more common. Modern non-arranged relationships usually begin with an abundance of *ludus* or *eros* love and mature over time into a combination of *philia* and *pragma* love. In some relationships, *eros* and *ludus* are lost and may be replaced by *pragma*. Some believe this is a bad thing, but for many couples who have marriages that last for decades, the initial raging fires slowly subside, but the embers remain warm and comfortable for decades. They have grown to know and love each other deeply. They are now more companions and best friends than passionate lovers. Their initial physical passion has matured into an undying mental and spiritual one.

For leaders, this form of love is about trusting, praising, and depending upon your people. Also, letting them know you are committed to them and you expect the same level of commitment in return. If you want them to hang with you long term, and exhibit undying loyalty, you must show them *pragma*. Since it's logical, the best way to express this is via emails, written and signed letters, award certificates or plaques, on a team presentation slide, etc. Also, it's best to use facts, numbers, details, graphs, and charts. For example, in a presentation or email, you might say, "Fred, thank you for helping our sales team achieve an average 79 percent social selling index on LinkedIn last quarter."

This approach does many things. It speaks to Fred's logical brain, it clearly defines the expectation in quantified terms, and it lets Fred know that his leader is paying attention and using metrics to track and reward desired behaviors.

TRUST EQUALS DOLLARS

In a recent *Harvard Business Review* article titled "The Neuroscience of Trust," Dr. Zak discussed how business leaders struggle with building a culture of trust. He cited a 2016 global CEO survey by Pricewaterhouse Coopers wherein 55 percent of CEOs stated that a lack of trust is a threat to their firm's growth.

We discussed earlier how Dr. Zak conducted a series of experiments and determined that an increase in oxytocin in individuals also reduced their instinctual fear about trusting someone. This is a significant finding because people who work for companies where trust is high as compared to low have 74 percent less stress, 106 percent more work energy, 50 percent higher productivity, 76 percent more engagement, and 40 percent less burnout.

Leaders who are not raising two eyebrows after reading the last paragraph are probably burnt out because they work at a low-trust company. If employees are 50 percent more productive because you, as a leader, created a culture of trust, how might that impact your revenue? Your profits? Your market share? Your stock performance?

How can you raise the oxytocin levels in your employees and foster an atmosphere of trust? Read the chapter in this book entitled The Eighth Secret.

PRAGMA TEAM RECRUITING

For leaders who are involved in the hiring process (and most are), as well as human resources and recruiting professionals, focusing on *pragma* more than *eros* can be invaluable. We may really like that guy we just interviewed. He has a friendly and warm personality. Others on the team also like him. He's smooth and charming and dresses sharp. We're attracted to him, so we hire him.

Then we start to see his warts, the ones we ignored earlier. We liked him, so we turned a blind eye. We didn't take the appropriate time to dig deep enough to determine if he was the best pragmatic choice. We let our emotional brain make the decision and told our logical brain to take a vacation. We allowed someone's effervescent personality to override our principles.

Conversely, we may sometimes get *too* logical. I've frequently seen CEOs in small start-ups hire executives with MBAs from Harvard or Stanford who have impressive titles at large, name-brand firms. Venture capitalists, who sit on the board, often push these CEOs to find such candidates. They look good on paper, and everyone's egos get stroked when the guy says yes. Once onboard, these individuals are like fish out of water.

Most are not used to rolling up their sleeves and hunting for customers or clawing for industry recognition. They've come from an environment where they had dozens of subordinates who were doing most of the "street" work. They had admins and budgets and ongoing business. Starting from scratch is a foreign and difficult concept. When both they and their hiring leader finally realize that it's just not working, months have gone by and opportunities have been lost.

Leaders and recruiters can find greater hiring success by adopting a more pragmatic approach, in similar fashion to an arranged marriage. By focusing on how someone may be the best long-term fit, rather than an ego-stroking, "we look good for hiring them" short-term win, we lower our odds of failure. How does this person's long-term goals, their passion and purpose in life, and their ability to be a great team player fit with our current team? Once the pink cloud has evaporated and we're no longer as attracted to their glittering white teeth, will they be someone that everyone on the team can have a long-term *pragma* relationship with?

Once employees are hired, companies should invest in continuous training to improve skills, confidence, and retention. With engagement and retention dropping like the stock market during a crash, it's surprising that the average company only invests in about 30 hours per year of training for each employee. The result is that over a third believe their lack of training is hurting their productivity.

A few years ago, the management team at Symantec recognized the need to improve sales training and enablement. My team and I were brought in to solve this problem, and we spent the next year designing and creating an entirely new approach to training and enablement across all of their product lines. Their senior director of sales enablement, Matt Weaver, understood that the "old school" approach of focusing on technical product training was inadequate. Sales pros, even the "salty dogs" who'd been selling for years, needed more solution training coupled with good old fashioned sales training. Matt also knew that while the traditional sales training models used by popular sales performance companies were excellent, they were not very customized or modernized. They did not use cutting-edge neuroscience, advanced storytelling techniques, or social-selling tactics for LinkedIn.

While the initial investment was high, the payoff was far higher. The new programs and tools, including a *Dynamic Interactive Sales Playbook*™ that customized content to a prospect's profile, was rolled out to over 4,000 salespersons and 50,000 channel partners across a dozen countries. The feedback, compliments, usage, and results were higher than for any program they'd ever done. Within two quarters, virtually every salesperson had been trained. Lead conversion and closing rates shot upward and so did morale.

Said Matt Weaver, "[Their] team has been a critical partner in my team's success in driving Symantec sales transformation. We set very aggressive targets and timelines to improve the global salesforce's effectiveness and productivity. [Their] team provided us with insights, guidance, and high-quality solutions that enabled us to realize significant gains in our sales team's ability to execute."

Top leaders are not afraid to make appropriate investments in their most precious asset: people. As Captain Jo Dee Jacob told us, "I try to treat people like wonderful Waterford goblets that should be treasured."

Jo Dee and leaders like her understand that they are playing the long game. To retain their best talent long term, they need to think long term, invest in their people and effective training, and practice *pragma* love.

THE PRAGMATIC LEADER

Pete Daly's father served in the U.S. Navy during World War II. After the war, he returned home to Chicago, Illinois, and continued to serve his country in the Naval Reserve. Pete's dad became a member of the U.S. Naval Institute (USNI)—a nonprofit professional military association established in 1873. The USNI is based in Annapolis, Maryland, and offers independent, nonpartisan forums for education and debate on national defense and security issues. The USNI publishes books and articles on naval topics via its Naval Institute Press (NIP)—the publishing company that launched Tom Clancy's breakout novel *The Hunt for Red October*.

Having all those Naval Institute books and magazines in his house while growing up made an impression on Pete. "I fell in love with the Navy, and with my father's encouragement, I decided to apply for a NROTC scholarship and attend the College of the Holy Cross in Massachusetts."

Although he never thought that his scholarship would lead him toward a long-term military career, Pete ended up serving as Surface Warfare Officer for over 30 years, rising to the rank of vice admiral.

One of the most valuable leadership lessons Pete learned occurred when he was a captain serving as the executive assistant to Admiral Tom Fargo, the Commander of the Pacific Fleet. During that time, the *Los Angeles*–class attack submarine USS *Greeneville* (SSN-772) collided with the *Ehime Maru*—a Japanese fishery high school training ship operating near the southern coast of Oahu, Hawaii, on February 9, 2001.

The *Ehime Maru* carried a total of 35 passengers, including 20 crew members, 13 students, and two teachers. The ship's 74-day voyage included a training curriculum for tuna fishing, maritime navigation, marine engineering, and oceanography.

The *Greeneville* departed Oahu on February 9, to conduct a demonstration of submarine capabilities for 14 VIP civilians, congresspersons, media journalists, and other important visitors onboard. As part of the demonstration, the commanding officer ordered an emergency dive followed by an emergency main ballast blow to swiftly propel the sub to the surface. When the *Greenville* surfaced, the submarine struck the underside of the *Ehime Maru*. Nine of the students and crew on the Japanese vessel lost their lives in the tragic incident. The *Ehime Maru* sank to the ocean floor, over 2,000 feet beneath the waves.

Pete recalled that the loss was extremely emotional for all involved, most especially for the families of those lost.

"This kind of situation could have ruined relationships between the U.S. and Japan," said Pete. "Dealing with a tragedy of this magnitude might have been too much for even the most seasoned leader, but Admiral Fargo rose to the occasion. He understood the difference between making short-term decisions to simply deal with the problem quickly versus taking the more difficult pragmatic path to ensure the best long-term outcome. Having served in Japan years earlier, Admiral Fargo appreciated the Japanese culture and pursued a position of transparency to regain their trust."

Fargo knew he needed to include the Japanese in every decision and step along the way to salvage the vessel. He invited Japanese salvage experts to work side by side with U.S. Navy experts. When senior officials in Washington, D.C., expressed skepticism at conducting a Court of Inquiry that could "turn into a circus," Admiral Fargo insisted on one as he knew that maintaining transparency was essential. He even invited a Japanese admiral to sit with American flag officers as a member of the Court of Inquiry.

"That move was an act of genius," said Pete. "Admiral Fargo had to 'manage up' almost as much as he had to 'manage down.'"

Fargo insisted that the Navy needed to recover the bodies *and* conduct a Court of Inquiry. The Court finished in mid-summer 2001; however, the very challenging salvage effort dragged out for many more months. Shortly after the 9/11 attacks on the World Trade Center, the government of Japan acknowledged that the United States had made a full effort on the salvage and could conclude the operation. Admiral Fargo could have accepted that communique as permission to end the salvage efforts, but he instead directed that the Navy continue. In October 2001, the *Ehime Maru* was brought to a shallow depth to allow divers to recover any remains. U.S. Navy and Japanese divers eventually recovered eight of the nine bodies.

"That was one of the best examples of leadership I've ever witnessed," said Pete. "By turning a tragedy that could have caused a serious divide between two countries into an opportunity to build an even stronger bond, Admiral Fargo taught me a valuable lesson about being a pragmatic leader."

The prime minister of Japan later telephoned Admiral Fargo to thank him personally. During the call, the prime minister said that, given the 9/11 tragedy, only the strongest friend and ally would have continued to follow through on the long-term promise to complete the salvage.

Pete believes that transparency and trust can't be summoned in the short term. As Admiral Fargo demonstrated, a good leader must always consider the "long view."

"Your team and your partners will sense your continued dedication and commitment," said Pete, "so they must be genuine. If you are not genuine, you will lose your team's trust."

Pete also believes that the best leaders clearly communicate their organization's commitment to the mission to ensure buy-in and dedication for the long haul. Doing so reflects wisdom and a desire to build and maintain a relationship with your team built upon a patient and consistent *pragma* form of love.

Pete Daly continues to serve his country and fellow Navy veterans as the president of the USNI, which today has over 50,000 members worldwide.

TEN *PRAGMA* LEADERSHIP REVIEW POINTS

1. The Seventh Neuron Secret is *The Principle of Wisdom: Patience and dependability are the cornerstones of great leadership.*
2. This principle is based on the Greek work *pragma*, which is a mature and pragmatic "long-game" form of love.
3. The *pragma* type of love is logical and connects with the logical neocortex.
4. Gaining wisdom requires patience, experience, and the willingness to listen to input from others.
5. This principle is best expressed using written words, numbers, charts, etc. and not by visual and auditory means.

6. Unlike *eros* love, which is about falling in love, *pragma* is about staying in love long term.
7. For leaders, this principle and form of love emphasizes the need to depend upon and praise the people on your team.
8. Recruiters and hiring managers should use *pragma* love to evaluate the long-term team and cultural fit of candidates interviewed.
9. The Scarecrow in *The Wonderful Wizard of Oz* provides a good metaphorical representation and embodiment of this principle.
10. This principle can be summed up with these two words: *be dependable*.

THREE STEPS TO *PRAGMA* LEADERSHIP

1. *Policy:* Leaders should work with teams to create long-term team and individual goals and metrics that not only align with the firm's performance goals, but also with Conscious Capitalism or similar tenets, and the organization's mission, passion, and purpose.
2. *Procedure:* Leaders should meet weekly with team members to review progress toward team and individual goals, and focus on only three primary goals and three projects or tasks for each goal. See the Neuron Decision Making chapter for an example of this.
3. *Practice:* Leaders should be trained, by internal or outsourced coaching experts, on best-practice time and goal management procedures using the Pareto Principle (80/20 rule), as well as strategic processes that focus on long-term pragmatic performance and metrics.

ONE *PRAGMA* LEADERSHIP EXERCISE

For this exercise, please answer the following questions:

- Am I afraid of taking a hard look at myself, and if so, why?
- Have I been open to other people's point of view?
- Do I frequently look for and admire positive traits in others?
- Have I been focused on the negative and been blind to the good around me or in me?
- How have I played the victim, and why do I continue to do so?
- Have I ever opened up and exposed my weaknesses to others I trust?

- Have I been honest with myself about my part in bad situations?
- Am I willing to play the long game and be patient?
- Am I dependable and pragmatic?

You are your own answer,
   Beyond books and seers,
      psychics or doctors
   Beyond the strength that comes
      from what you have accomplished.
Your weakness is as valuable as your strength,
Your helplessness as lovable as your charm.

—*Dr. James Kavanaugh, from* Quiet Waters

CHAPTER 13

Our Helpers

FIGURE 13.1   Our Helpers

Source: Nelosa, Dreamstime.com.

> The purpose of human life is to serve, and to show compassion and the will to help others.
>
> —ALBERT SCHWEITZER

Before we dive into the next chapter, it's important that we first understand how to ask for help and from where we should seek advice and support (Figure 13.1). We learned in the Needs chapter that we must accept that our needs are real, important, and justified. We must also take responsibility for meeting our own needs, and not expect others to do for us what we can do for ourselves. Our subordinates, customers, employer, boss, parents, spouse, government, or anyone else is not responsible for ensuring that our every need is met.

Fortunately, we are not required to face every hardship alone. We have help, and we can and should turn to that help when it's justified.

Constructing a safe and useful support system is vitally important, and not without risk. Not all the input received will be true or optimal, and not all our sources will have our best interests at heart. We need to discern the difference between beneficial and detrimental feedback, and between trustworthy, honest, and caring sources as opposed to those with agendas or unhealthy outlooks on life.

Also, just because a quote, a passage, a chapter, a psychologist, a suggestion, or a course of action worked well for someone else does not mean it will work well for you. Conversely, just because something didn't work for someone else doesn't mean you shouldn't try it, if you are convinced it's the right thing to do.

How can you discern? How can you trust? How can you ensure your support system elements are right for you? Now that you understand better what your true beliefs and values are, and have a clearer picture of your needs, you can begin to discern by holding up the input you receive from your support sources to the light of your truths. If the reflection shines bright, and your heart glows with assurance and conviction, then most likely the input is right for you.

Think about all the sources in your life that give you inspiration and hope. For some, this might be a close friend or relative, a spouse, a sibling, a parent, a pastor or rabbi, a colleague or classmate, the Bible, the Quran, or a wonderful book of poems. Maybe it's a colleague, business partner, mentor, self-help book, a 12-step program sponsor, a support group you belong to, or a former boss. Now reflect on your new list of beliefs and needs and match these against all the sources of help and support you can envision in your life.

If, for example, you previously deleted a religious belief that no longer serves you, then a pastor or priest connected to that religion may no longer be an appropriate part of your support system. However, if that pastor can offer input free of any objectionable opinions, the trust you have built with him or her over the years may offset any concerns. Be sure to evaluate each source of support honestly and completely. These sources will become your lifeline going forward and may be a deciding factor between a fruitful professional life and an unemployment check.

Epictetus once said, "Make the best use of what is in your power and take the rest as it happens." Leaders who try to bend everything and everyone to their will or envision themselves as "lone wolf" superheroes need a reality check. Trying to go it alone all the time will leave you burned out, depressed, and disgruntled. The best leaders understand their own limitations and seek to know the limitations of their team members. There's nothing wrong with striving for perfection until it becomes such an obsession that the return on investment is negative. Spending $1 million of time and effort on a $1,000 problem or project does not ensure that your team or boss will think you walk on water. Instead, your team will become frustrated with the continued nitpicking, and your boss will become concerned about missed deadlines and budget overruns. Do your best with the time and resources you are given and accept the outcome. There are only 24 hours in each day, and we don't need to face each day alone.

We do not need to overcome the struggles in our Hero's Journey on our own. Resources are readily available from our team, friends, colleagues, loved ones, books, tapes, Higher Powers, a God if we believe in one, a neighbor, counselors, our boss, and maybe even our customers.

No matter what our needs may be, we have support systems all around us that we can take advantage of. All of us also have an abundance of resources and help at our disposal. What are they? Who are they? Where do we turn when life's struggles overwhelm us? When the people we engage with, whether personally or professionally, run through our boundaries like a bull through a red cape, where do we go for help?

If we have a spouse, do we turn to him or her for support and understanding, or merely to complain? Venting can be a healthy release, but not if that's all we do. How does your spouse respond? Does he or she react with fear because they are concerned you might lose your job? Do they advise you to ignore your feelings as any action or reaction on your part could trigger the dreaded pink slip? Do you reject someone else's beliefs outright, or listen patiently and try to glean pearls of wisdom from their input that might help you?

Women often have an advantage over men. Most women are wired to attain and nurture relationships and rely on friendships as a part of their support system. Ice cream manufacturers count on distressed women for their very survival. Men are not so lucky. Most have been taught, via someone else's beliefs, that it's not manly to admit to a weakness or cry on someone's shoulder. It's not manly to cry at all. It's not appropriate to discuss personal issues or confess them in any way. When someone does finally open up, the subject is often quickly changed to sports, politics, or work. For men, finding people to trust is not easy, but it is necessary. For women, discerning which friends will be nonjudgmental and maintain confidentiality may be difficult, but also vital.

We need to rely upon others to support us, understand us, encourage us, and even chastise us when appropriate, but it's important to choose our support groups and systems wisely. Bad advice, even though well-meant, can make matters far worse.

Here are a few questions to ask yourself before moving on to the exercise below:

- What or who do I have faith in, completely, and why?
- Who would I trust with my life, and the lives of my family?
- Who always has my back, and never stabs it with a knife?
- Who can I trust with my deepest and darkest secrets?
- Who is my best friend and why?
- Who have I known the longest in my life, and how close are we today?
- What book has inspired me the most, made me cry, or made my heart sing with truth?
- What writings do I treasure the most, and which ones give me comfort in times of trouble?
- What measures have I tried on my own, without help, that have ended in disaster?
- Do I truly believe that I need help at times, and I can trust in that help and support?

EXERCISE

Once you have pondered and answered the questions above and are willing to let go of trying to bend outcomes and people to your will, or go the distance alone, you are ready to create your support list. Spend an adequate and appropriate amount of time doing this exercise, as it can make or break the future of your professional life. Examine your heart, your beliefs, your values, your needs, and your sources of support and help, and complete your list.

To complete this exercise, bring up a notes app on your mobile device, or use a sheet of paper, a notebook, or a document on your computer to create your list now.

Have you completed your list? If not, please do so before continuing.

Now go back and spend at least one minute on each source of support. This ten-minute examination could save you hours, days, months, or even years of frustration in the future, so do not hurry this along. Think long and hard about each person or item on your list, and know in your heart that you believe and trust in this resource implicitly and without reservation. If you have doubts, delete that resource and replace it with another. If you can't get to ten right now, that's okay. You're better off being a few short than having a few suspect sources. Don't be afraid to delete or replace people or items as time goes on.

Your list should be a "living and breathing" one that grows along with you and does not hold you back from completing your journey. You should use this list to help you deal with difficult professional issues and people, including frustrating situations and insubordinate subordinates.

This part of your journey requires faith. I'm not talking about a religious faith, unless that is one of your core beliefs. I'm referring to having the courage to take a few risks. We all fear letting go of our illusions of control. It's like taking our hands off the wheel of the car and allowing the forces of nature to guide us down the road. Whenever we see a tree looming ahead, we desperately want to yank the wheel right or left. We want to be the masters of our own fate. Dr. James Kavanaugh tells us we are destined to lead a life of denial and misery unless we let go and permit our own inner wisdom to guide us. What is holding us back? Fear of failure? Fear of losing control? Fear of the unknown?

Notice that the operative word is fear.

Some say that fear is an acronym that stands for False Evidence Appearing Real, or perhaps "F" Everything And Run. When I heard these sayings, I admit I scoffed a bit. I thought they were just more of those dumb things people say. I now see that perhaps those people were right. Whenever I have honestly evaluated my fears, they have usually turned out to be false whispers that evaporate when held up against the light of truth.

One of our biggest fears involves making needed changes or speaking and living our truth, especially when dealing with professional relationships, including subordinates, bosses, and peers. This exercise will help us let go of our fears, live our truth, and trust in our sources of support to help guide us along the path of our leadership journey.

CHAPTER 14

Dorothy's Revelation—Neuron Secret One Redux

FIGURE 14.1   Dorothy

Source: Anna Velichkovsky, Dreamstime.com.

No matter how dreary and gray our homes are … there's no place like home.

—DOROTHY (FIGURE 14.1) IN *THE WONDERFUL WIZARD OF OZ*

NEURON SECRET ONE (REDUX)

The Principle of Prosperity: To prosper, you must love yourself by being humble and teachable.

Jeff Jones is an executive vice president at SkylineDx BV, a leading biotechnology firm located in Rotterdam, The Netherlands. Today he is responsible for executing complex global strategic plans for market development and commercialization for the firm's medical diagnostic solutions. A few decades ago, his missions were far more dangerous.

"I volunteered for U.S. Navy SEAL teams when I was 20," said Jeff. "I knew the training would be challenging, but I didn't know that I'd be only one of fifteen guys to graduate from a class of fifty-six."

The training Jeff completed was at the Navy SEAL Basic Training Command, or BUD/S, which stands for Basic Underwater Demolition/ SEAL.

Said Jeff, "Most people know that Navy SEAL training is the most demanding, dangerous, and difficult in the world. A large majority who start BUD/S never make it all the way through. They ring the bell and wash out."

The bell Jeff referred to is an old Navy ship bell that's attached to a stanchion in the courtyard. A trainee who has had enough and wants to quit grabs the dangling rope, rings the bell, and then sets down his helmet and walks away. Those who are left standing in the yard, shivering from cold and aching with fatigue, are either more motivated to quit or to do whatever it takes to graduate.

Navy SEAL trainees are divided into small teams that bench press and shoulder heavy telephone poles together for hours. They face dangerous waves and rocky shores while riding in small rubber Zodiac boats. They march, run, and exercise together. At midnight, under dark skies and an uncaring moon, they shiver together along the shore, arm in arm, as the freezing surf threatens to suck them out to sea. Within a few weeks, they either ring the bell or learn how to become brothers in arms, literally.

"Hell Week either defines you or crucifies you," said Jeff. "You learn what you're made of, but you also learn what teamwork is all about."

Hell Week in BUD/S pushes trainees to their limits and beyond. They must endure an entire week of sleep deprivation and extreme mental and physical fatigue. They must depend upon each other to graduate or even survive. Most of the bell ringing happens during this week.

During the infamous Hell Week at BUD/S, and the other long weeks of living hell, Jeff refused to ring the ship's bell. When he finally completed his training and added the coveted ombudsman pin to his uniform, he thought the hard part was over. He soon discovered that it was only beginning.

"SEALs don't make mistakes—at least we're not supposed to," said Jeff. "When we do, someone might die. We are taught to keep anything of value with us at all times. Compasses, maps, whatever. My team was transiting to a mission aboard a C-130 transport and I made the mistake of leaving an important map pouch on the plane. When my officer in charge found out, I learned more about being humble in five minutes than I had throughout my previous twenty-two years of life."

Jeff's officer in charge (OIC) did not become an authoritarian pirate and make Jeff "walk the plank." Instead, he authoritatively told Jeff a Vietnam War story to emphasize how one small mistake can domino into several critical consequences for the entire team.

"Using a combat story to teach me a valuable lesson was brilliant," said Jeff. "When I heard the real-world consequences of unintended mistakes like mine, it hit me hard. Instead of just telling me how I'd let down the other guys on my team, he showed me through a powerful and memorable story. I remember almost every detail of that story even today, and it helped teach me to never make a mistake like that again."

Jeff's SEAL team boarded the USS *Grayback* (SS-208), an old diesel submarine used frequently for clandestine insertion operations. During the six-day underwater transit to their station, haunted by his OIC's story, Jeff was motivated to regain the trust of his leader and teammates.

"I didn't make excuses, and I didn't let it defeat me. I decided that I needed to become humble and teachable and take full responsibility for my mistakes. I also decided that I needed to make amends to the guys on my team. I spent the entire six-day ride recreating every detail of those maps and volunteering for extra duty."

Jeff managed to redeem himself and added another stripe to his sleeve by the end of that deployment. Today, he is grateful for the mistakes of his past and the pain they caused him. In his opinion, pain can either defeat you or help you find the courage and strength to "get back on the horse" and ride again with renewed vigor and commitment. He feels it's important for team leaders not to berate or belittle others for making mistakes, but instead become a mentor by doing three important things.

One, clearly articulate why the action taken was a mistake and why this person let down the rest of the team. Two, use a powerful story to teach this person how such mistakes can cause serious consequences. Three, quantify the potential consequences and outline what needs to be done to correct the mistake and make amends to the rest of the team.

"Leaders need to walk a fine line," said Jeff. "In the teams, we understood that even small mistakes could cause huge problems or even the failure of a mission. In my civilian position, it's not usually that catastrophic. When something goes wrong, I need to temper my emotional and instinctual responses and apply some logic. I need to quantify the consequences and then decide how to respond. I need to ask whether this is 'a hill worth dying over' and ensure the disciplinary actions I take are on a par with the potential consequences."

Jeff has learned that for leaders, being humble equates to being fair. When someone on his team makes a mistake, he recalls the map mistake he made. This helps him to remember that we are all human. While he does not excuse missteps made by those on his team, he also does not "blame or inflame."

"I never attack someone personally for a mistake," said Jeff. "I also don't lose my temper and start yelling at them. That's the worst thing a leader can do. Instead, I first ensure that this person was not set up for failure. I ask whether I or someone on the team did something to contribute to the mistake. Is this person overworked? Do they have all the resources they need? Did we stretch them too far? I then ask the person why they believe a mistake was made. If I hear excuses or blaming, I help them to be brave enough to take responsibility for their part."

Jeff's advice to aspiring leaders, or any leader who wants to continue to grow, is to find another leader that you admire. Observe them, emulate them, and perhaps even ask them to be your mentor. When you do, it's vital to be humble and teachable, for without these two qualities it's almost impossible to learn and to grow.

"Character isn't just a word in the dictionary," said Jeff. "It's an important principle that I believe every leader should reflect. We build character by having the courage to take risks. When we take risks, we will always make mistakes because we're human. When we make mistakes, we need to learn from them. To learn, we need to be humble and teachable. By doing so, we will build character and become better leaders."

THE SECRET OF *EUDAIMONIA*

We reviewed the first part of Neuron Secret One when we embarked on our Hero's Journey. We are now ready to complete our journey by understanding the second part of the first secret. We have reached the end of our Hero's Journey, we have found our way back home, and we have hopefully returned with our discovery—the magical elixir, the MacGuffin, or the prize we sought. Finding our way home, to the heart of our heart where *eudaimonia* resides in its purest form, was not an easy or fast journey. The path was not void of thorns or trials, but the voyage was worth the reward. We are now ready to share our newfound knowledge with our ordinary world.

The elixir I have endeavored to share with you is this: *Leadership is Love*.

As leaders, we must learn how to love ourselves enough to be able to love others. Then and *only* then can we lead. By accepting the role of a leader, we have a profound responsibility to help others, most especially our teams, to become one of the 33 percent that's engaged in their work. Even more so, to be one of top five percent that's inspired, motivated, and highly productive. To accomplish this goal, we need to take our own elixir and help our teams do the same so we can all become better leaders. We can do this by being brave enough to take three giant steps forward:

1. *People before profit*. We explored this truth when we discussed the tenets of Conscious Capitalism, wherein we can be more profitable by placing our passion and purpose above only profitability. Attaining *eudaimonia* requires that we also do this for our people. We must become committed to the wellness, well-being, and happiness of our teams. This goal must supersede making a profit, as crazy as that sounds. Think of it this way: plenty of baseball teams have tried to "buy" their way to a World Series title. They bought the best coaches and players and equipment and whatever and were convinced that dollars were king. Investment is important, of course. Teams who spend nothing gain little, but plenty of teams with less than half the payroll of others have taken it all. In most cases, they won because they achieved a measure of *eudaimonia*. They focused on the players and their well-being. As Randy Jones taught us earlier, they played for each other, not for an owner's balance sheet.

2. *Wellness programs.* We need to fashion a framework and process to foster an environment of *eudaimonia*. It's not enough to simply say to your department heads, "Hey, make everybody happy, okay?" The best leaders invest in coaches with years of experience in creating and implementing wellness programs and mindsets. For example, Dr. Bill Hettler co-founded the National Wellness Institute and created a model for wellness in 1977. He called it the *Six Dimensions of Wellness*. Many CEOs use this model, but also bring in consultants and coaches, such as those from CUSTOMatrix, to create customized and effective change through leadership *eudaimonia* programs to ensure that teams operate at peak efficiency.

3. *Mindfulness metrics.* Once a program is implemented, it should be measured continuously. We live by Key Performance Indicators (KPIs) for just about everything we do in business, and we should do no less for the well-being and mindfulness of our teams. Perhaps with the help of experts in this field, we should create a series of measurements to ensure progress toward something like the *Six Dimensions of Wellness*, which include factors related to social, physical, emotional, occupational, intellectual, and even spiritual satisfaction. The best way to do this is by first understanding each person's neuron profile (you can use the app at www.neuronleaders .com). You'll then have a better understanding of the optimal neurotransmitter balance needed for each person to feel and be at their best. You can even begin to help people adjust their diets and lifestyles to be happier. For example, if someone's dopamine level should optimally be high, drinking too much coffee could lower this and make them feel miserable. Why should you care? Because a happy camper is a productive one. When your teams are not just checked in but also dialed in, when they're firing on all cylinders because they're full of joy and a desire to show up every day and contribute, then profitability soars.

Leadership coach and consultant Jordan Goldrich said, "Many results-driven leaders in our society, especially if their style is abrasive, controlling, or commanding, may react negatively to the concept that 'leadership is love.' They may see this mantra as touchy-feely or New Age psychobabble. Perhaps they need to consider the fact that using the seven ancient forms of love outlined in this book aligns with the practice of holding people accountable. It's also consistent with letting people go when they do not perform. The difference is that the conversation is focused on behavior and consequences. The tone and the words used should not be demeaning, humiliating, or disrespectful."

THE REVELATION

In *The Wonderful Wizard of Oz*, L. Frank Baum concludes with a short but sweet 24th chapter:

> Aunt Em had just come out of the house to water the cabbages when she looked up and saw Dorothy running toward her.
>
> "My darling child!" she cried, folding the little girl in her arms and covering her face with kisses. "Where in the world did you come from?"
>
> "From the Land of Oz," said Dorothy gravely. "And here is Toto, too. And oh, Aunt Em! I'm so glad to be at home again!"

What had changed when Dorothy returned home? Certainly not Kansas. It was as gray and plain as ever. Not her Uncle Henry, who was "milking the cows in the barnyard." Not Aunt Em, who was working in the garden. Nothing had really changed except Dorothy.

The revelation that Dorothy discovered along the path of her Hero's Journey is that she had been focused outwardly. She had previously assumed that in order for her to attain happiness, everything and everyone in her ordinary world needed to change. What she discovered in the Land of Oz—the magic elixir she brought back home—was that nothing needed to change except Dorothy.

Once she set aside her ego, shed the debilitating beliefs of her past, and faced herself in the mirror, she realized that there's no place like home.

Those of us who desire to lead cannot do so by forcing everything and everyone in our world to change. We must instead close our eyes, look inward, and make the appropriate and wise changes to *our* life, to *our* reactions, to *our* expectations, to *our* attitudes, to *our* communication style, to *our* mind and heart, and to *our* leadership style. We can then see a *magical change in us—and perhaps in everyone we lead.*

THE SELFISH LEADER

Recall that Sigmund Freud gave us interesting insights about our ego. He described the Id as our instinctual drive for survival, our Superego as the emotionally derived learned behavior, and the Ego as the logical mediator between the two. We often hear ego referred to as something bad that we should strive to avoid. Ego is neither good nor bad, it just is. It is an attribute that we all have. Asking someone to rid themselves of their ego is like asking them to chop off their head or rip out their heart.

Our ego is neutral. When we allow ourselves to become unhealthy psychologically, we can become egotistical. This is self-serving and can be viewed as a negative trait. When we are healthy, we can have a strong ego drive that motivates us to perform at our best as leaders. This is a positive trait.

We need to set aside our unhealthy egotistical tendencies and form healthy daily habits to allow our positive ego drive to engage our ears and our heart so we can learn, grow, and fulfill our destiny, and help others to do the same.

To effectively make leadership decisions and inspire others, we need to balance our personal, selfish needs and wants against what is right and best for the members of our team and what is in the best interests of our organization. The ability to do this effectively begins with properly taking care of ourselves. If we are unhealthy physically, mentally, or spiritually, our judgment may be cloudy, our patience thin, and our decision-making ability far from optimal. Therefore, to be a better team leader, we need to first focus on our own personal well-being.

To many, this may seem selfish and contrary to what we were taught as children. Shouldn't we be selfless and care more about others than ourselves? Shouldn't we strive to be "servant leaders"? Those in medical professions know that it's virtually impossible to care for patients effectively if you're suffering from malaria. We've all heard the adage that you should first place the oxygen mask on yourself in the airplane before placing it on the small child next to you. On the battlefield, the soldier with the broken leg can't carry his wounded buddy to safety.

Therefore, to be a great leader, we need to be a selfish leader. This means taking better care of ourselves by improving our diet, exercise routines, sleeping patterns, and work habits. Working too hard does not always produce more results and often leads to mistakes, bad tempers, and illness.

When we do make mistakes, the worst thing we can do is to hide them, lie about them, or blame others. History records the decisions made by John F. Kennedy during the Bay of Pigs fiasco in 1961 as "disastrous."[1] Many blame Khrushchev's subsequent brash moves that led to the Cuban Missile Crisis on Kennedy's missteps. Rather than deflect, diminish, or deny, Kennedy had the courage to be honest and open with the American people. This led to what psychologists refer to as the "pratfall effect,"[2] wherein a leader's endearment to others can increase if they admit they are flawed and make amends for the downfalls.

Some historians attribute Kennedy's ability to be genuine, charismatic, and more often than not to make good decisions to his commitment to self-care. Most people are not aware that when Kennedy was three years old, he had scarlet fever. Some say this and other factors led to chronic digestive and back pains that plagued the president throughout his life. He endured years of painful medical tests and rarely complained. Close friends commented that Kennedy never spoke about his problems.

During World War II, Kennedy volunteered for PT boat duty but was turned down due to his ailments. His father pulled some strings to over-rule the Navy's decision. Kennedy silently endured his pain during his 17-month tour in the Pacific where he completed numerous near-suicide missions—including the one where PT-109 was cut in half by a Japanese destroyer.

When Kennedy was later elected president, despite his frequent bouts with pain, he set an example for others by adopting good daily habits. He was an avid swimmer and hit the pool twice each day. Dr. Hans Kraus, a New York orthopedic surgeon, encouraged daily exercise sessions to help Kennedy manage his pain, improve his mental acuity, and maintain the stamina needed to function as the President of the United States.

Each day after lunch, Kennedy took a two-hour nap. J.B. West, head of the White House staff, recalled that "during those hours the Kennedy doors were closed. No telephone calls were allowed, no folders sent up, no interruptions from the staff. Nobody went upstairs for any reason."

Kennedy awoke in the late afternoon and returned to the Oval Office at around 3:30 PM for meetings, briefings, and other duties. He frequently worked until after 8:00 PM but did not force others to do so. Instead, he led by example and became one of history's most revered leaders.

Sidebar

Brigadier General Michael J. Aguilar (USMC Ret) is the first person of Mexican descent to reach the rank of brigadier general in the U.S. Marine Corps. He served in the Marine Corps for 31 years and accumulated over 4,000 flight hours, mostly as an attack helicopter pilot, which earned him the Defense Superior Service Medal, the Legion of Merit, the Bronze Star, the Meritorious Service Medal, and a Navy and Marine Corps Commendation Medal. General Aguilar believes that the best leaders exhibit a specific set of traits and strive to live by an unwavering set of principles. In his opinion, the Marine Corps has done an excellent job of describing these 14 traits and 11 principles (listed below), and he encourages all Marines to exhibit these as leaders and servants of their country.

Major General Bobby Butcher, also a retired U.S. Marine pilot, concurs with General Aguilar. "The best leaders know their people and, most of all, they take care of their people," said General Butcher, who earned the Distinguished Flying Cross, 15 Air Medals, and a Combat "V" Bronze Star. Today, General Butcher is the epitome of a great leader. He has selflessly given his time and talent for the last 17 years serving as chairman of the board for the foundation that supports the Marine Corps Flying Leatherneck Aviation Museum in San Diego, California.

Marine Corps Leadership Principles

- Know yourself and seek self-improvement.
- Be technically and tactically proficient.
- Develop a sense of responsibility among your subordinates.
- Make sound and timely decisions.
- Set the example.
- Know your Marines and look out for their welfare.

- Keep your Marines informed.
- Seek responsibility and take responsibility for your actions.
- Ensure assigned tasks are understood, supervised, and accomplished.
- Train your Marines as a team.
- Employ your command in accordance with its capabilities.

Marine Corps Leadership Traits

- Dependability

  The certainty of proper performance of duty.

- Bearing

  Creating a favorable impression in carriage, appearance, and personal conduct at all times.

- Courage

  The mental quality that recognizes fear of danger or criticism, but enables a man to proceed in the face of it with calmness and firmness.

- Decisiveness

  Ability to make decisions promptly and to announce them in a clear, forceful manner.

- Endurance

  The mental and physical stamina measured by the ability to withstand pain, fatigue, stress, and hardship.

- Enthusiasm

  The display of sincere interest and exuberance in the performance of duty.

- Initiative

  Taking action in the absence of orders.

- Integrity

  Uprightness of character and soundness of moral principles; includes the qualities of truthfulness and honesty.

- Judgment

(continued)

(*Continued*)

The ability to weigh facts and possible solutions on which to base sound decisions.

- Justice

  Giving reward and punishment according to merits of the case in question. The ability to administer a system of rewards and punishments impartially and consistently.

- Knowledge

  Understanding of a science or an art. The range of one's information, including professional knowledge and an understanding of your Marines.

- Tact

  The ability to deal with others without creating offense.

- Unselfishness

  Avoidance of providing for one's own comfort and personal advancement at the expense of others.

- Loyalty

  The quality of faithfulness to country, the Corps, the unit, one's seniors, subordinates, and peers.

FIVE LEADERSHIP LESSONS

Drew Martin is the chief information officer for Jack in the Box, a Fortune 1000 company with 2,250 locations worldwide. They are one of the nation's largest hamburger chains, serving over 500 million hungry eaters each year. Prior to working for Jack in the Box, Drew learned a lot about leadership while working for PepsiCo, where the company emphasized three key leadership categories related to vision, agenda, and collaboration.

Said Drew, "PepsiCo encouraged leaders to clearly define a vision, create an agenda with goals while inspiring teams to reach them, and create an atmosphere of cooperation by treating people with respect."

Drew also believes that it's important for leaders to surround themselves with excellent advisors. Leaders should be humble enough to realize that they rarely have all the answers and should welcome and listen to the opinions of others. They should also be teachable enough to seek advisors who may disagree with their viewpoints. You will often learn more from others who are not like-minded as they can force you to "think outside the box."

When Drew joined Jack in the Box, he discovered that the company's executives encouraged their leaders to embody the leadership lessons taught by Norman Brinker, the late founder of Jack in the Box, Chili's, Bennigan's, and Burger King restaurants. Five of these lessons were outlined in an excellent article written by Jeff Campbell, former president of Burger King USA, in a February 2017 article. They are paraphrased below.

1. *Leading by Example:* Teach others by setting the right example rather than only issuing explicit orders.
2. *Leadership by Inclusion:* Rather than prescribe actions to subordinates, a leader should provide the objectives and allow team members to design the best paths to achieve them.
3. *Leadership by Understanding:* Seek to understand your team's strengths, weaknesses, and tendencies.
4. *Leadership by Identification:* Create clarity about the firm's purpose, mission, and values, and encourage innovation.
5. *Leadership by Optimism:* Maintain a positive attitude and a winning mindset.

NEURAL PATHWAYS

Executive coach and consultant Jordan Goldrich said, "Leaders who desire to embody the seven types of ancient love discussed in this book, in both their professional and personal lives, may find this difficult because of how our brains are wired. Partly because of genetics and partly because of learned behaviors and thought patterns, it's not easy to change our responses to events that generate negative and judgmental thinking and feeling."

Jordan notes that experts have learned a great deal about the human brain in the last few decades, which offers us new processes for making desired changes. For example, today we have functional magnetic resonance imaging (fMRI) systems that enable us to monitor the electrical impulses and blood flow within our brains in real time. We now know that our thoughts and actions are mediated by impulses in our brain that travel through systems (highways) of neurons that fire in tandem. Scientists call these "neural pathways."

"The more utilized and therefore larger a neural pathway becomes," said Jordan, "the more resistant it is to change. You can't get rid of your established neural pathways that govern your habitual thoughts, feelings, and behavior. Your brain is wired to produce thoughts and feelings that trigger habitual responses to people and events."

In Jordan's forthcoming leadership book, *The Least You Can Do*, he discusses how the structure of the human brain is "set in its ways" by the time we reach young adulthood. However, we can rewire our brain by focusing on, and mentally rehearsing, new thoughts and feelings that trigger behavior more consistent with our desired values.

This process is called neuroplasticity, which deals with the brain's ability to reorganize itself by creating new neural pathways throughout our life. The good news is, our brain can develop new neural pathways that are programmed to produce different thoughts, feelings, and behaviors. As we seek to drink our own elixir and implement new habits, these neural pathways will enlarge. Eventually, they will become more dominant and offer us greater choice and control over how we think, act, and react.

SECOND LIFE

Urban Miyares met the love of his life in New York City in the early 1960s. She lived five blocks away in the Yorkville area of Manhattan. They were only 13, but Urban's heart was smitten. He graduated from high school, got engaged, and then had his dreams dashed upon the rocks of life.

"I got drafted," said Urban. "That was in 1967, during the height of the Vietnam War. I finished basic training in South Carolina and joined the Army ninth infantry division as a rifleman."

Urban had previously completed training at the Non-Commissioned Officers Academy in Fort Pope, Louisiana, so the Army advanced him to the rank of sergeant. Urban grabbed a pack of malaria pills, his helmet, and his rucksack, and boarded a plane. In the delta of South Vietnam, he trudged through rice paddies, hacked through elephant grass and thick brush in rubber tree plantations, swatted giant mosquitoes, and gained a fearful respect for bamboo viper snakes.

"The whole time I was in country," said Urban, "I felt dizzy and nauseous. I lost a lot of weight, I couldn't sleep, and I was constantly exposed to the horrors of war. The doctors diagnosed me with malaria. Then they said it was heat prostration, stress, or maybe peptic ulcers. They gave me Maalox and sent me back out into the field."

One morning while on patrol, Urban felt sick and weak. His knees buckled and his mind lapsed into a dreamlike state while walking along the dyke of a rice paddy. He heard shouting, M60 machine gun fire, explosions, and then the sensation of flying before he blacked out. Two days later he woke up in a Saigon military hospital. An IV jutted from his arm and a solution bottle hung from a metal pole nearby.

A nurse walked in and said, "You're one lucky grunt."

When Urban asked why, she said, "A medic found you alive in a KIA body bag."

Urban never discovered the name of that medic until 38 years later when he met Brian Leet, who'd been an advancement medic stationed at a basecamp near the 9th Infantry Division. He'd been tasked with toe-tagging dead soldiers. When he opened Urban's bag, he heard a whooshing sound. He leaned in close and realized that the "dead guy" was still breathing. Leet immediately rushed Urban to the 17th Field Hospital in Saigon where he was diagnosed with Type I diabetes.

Urban's diabetes soon caused peripheral neuropathy in his legs. Doctors at the Valley Forge Military Hospital told him that he might not live more than another decade or two. In 1968, the care and treatment for diabetes was archaic at best. Urban was discharged from the Army in December 1968 and returned to his life in New York City.

"I tried to find a job, but I got turned down everywhere. They told me, 'We're not hiring a needle-toting, baby-killing Vietnam veteran at this company.'"

Left with no choice, he scraped together his last nickel and started his own company. It failed, and so did two other businesses he launched. When Urban discovered that no one was willing to offer help or assistance for disabled veterans, he vowed to one day help other veterans with their business endeavors. To help others succeed, however, he knew that he'd first have to prove that *he* could succeed. Despite his physical and psychological debilitations and the complications with his diabetes, he put his head down and went to work. Then he was thrown another curve ball. He went blind.

"Because of my other ailments, I wound up having several mini-strokes," said Urban. "Those eventually caused my blindness. I began to wonder if the Army medics were right; that I'd only have a few more years to live."

Urban could have given up. He could have thrown in the towel, admitted defeat, and reconciled himself to the fate he'd been handed by the evil universe. Unable to look at his own gray eyes in the mirror, he instead looked deep into his soul and prayed for an answer. He was tortured day and night by post-traumatic stress disorder from his Vietnam experiences. His diabetes and blindness restricted his ability to work, think, or get around. He suffered constantly from the neuropathy in his legs. Unsure if he'd ever get past first base, he decided to swing for the fence.

Urban pursued his entrepreneurial endeavors with passion and finally found success. He gained recognition nationwide and received a presidential commendation for his business accomplishments. Finally, having achieved a modicum of success, he decided that it was time to fulfill his promise to help other disabled veterans live their dreams.

As providence would have it, a fellow disabled veteran asked Urban for help to start a new business. Then another disabled friend called with a similar request, and Urban saw a lightbulb go off in his mind's eye.

"I started a nonprofit called the Disabled BusinessPersons Association," said Urban. "I connected with others working in the Veterans Administration to start a pilot program to help disabled veterans start companies or find jobs."

Urban Miyares was pronounced dead when he was 20 years old. When he came back to life, they told him he would not live past the age of 40. He is now 70. He can't see. He's had a stroke, had his thyroid removed, had a kidney transplant, has a spinal cord injury, and has a hearing impairment. He has neuropathy in his legs and needs assistance to get around. Despite these impairments, his mind is sharp and his spirit is strong and he has helped launch dozens of companies.

"I think people sometimes forget that I'm blind," said Urban. "I laugh when they ask me to pass the salt."

Urban found new life in serving others, mostly his fellow veterans. He got involved in sports activities for disabled persons and broke the record in the early 1990s for the fastest downhill skiing record set by a blind person—63 miles per hour. He then convinced the U.S. Department of Veterans Affairs to sponsor a National Summer Sports Clinic where almost 100 disabled veterans cycled, sailed, kayaked, and surfed to earn awards in a series of competitive but friendly races.

"All of the participants had PTS, spinal cord injuries, amputations, brain injuries, visual or auditory problems, or neurological disorders," said Urban. "When you have a disability, life becomes a team sport. Helping each other get through it is the best therapy I know. A lot of my fellow disabled veterans feel abandoned and lost, and I know just how they feel. Compared to what many of them have had to endure, I consider myself pretty lucky that I was given a second chance in life."

Like Dorothy, Urban was swept up by a tornado that landed him in the Land of Oz. He died there, came back to life, and then discovered that there's no place like home. He also discovered the secret of life and brought it back to an ailing world.

"Leadership is all about love," said Urban. "Without it, you can't lead anything or anyone."

Today, despite his disabilities, Urban is a leader with a heart filled with love. His Disabled BusinessPersons Association has helped hundreds of aspiring and current business leaders overcome their disabilities to lead productive, fulfilled, and joyous lives.

Urban will never actually see any of the disabled people he has helped. "That's okay," he said with a tear in his eye, "I can see them in my heart."

TWELVE *EUDAIMONIA* LEADERSHIP REVIEW QUESTIONS

1. Can I love myself enough to have realistic expectations for my own capabilities and performance, and can I be kind to myself when I make mistakes?
2. Am I willing to shed my unhealthy or debilitating beliefs and take the next step in my journey?
3. Have I accepted the fact that I cannot control or manipulate anyone else's behavior or attitudes?
4. Do I understand that those I lead are people, just like me, who may be acting on unhealthy beliefs and learned behaviors and are doing the best they can?
5. When I have tried to change, control, or manipulate people, places, or things, have I always been successful?

6. How do I feel when things don't go my way or others don't act exactly as I believe they should?
7. Am I looking for a quick fix to improve my leadership skills, or am I willing to play the long game?
8. Am I willing to let the coin of life fall as it may, or do I still want to control outcomes to my benefit?
9. Do I constantly seek approval and affirmation from others; am I bitter when it's not given?
10. Am I frequently indulging in an unhealthy personal lifestyle but expecting a healthy professional life?
11. Do I set unrealistic expectations for others and then get angry when they don't measure up?
12. Do I understand that this second part of the first secret can be summed by these two words: *be wise*?

ONE *EUDAIMONIA* LEADERSHIP EXERCISE

If we are currently employed or have an income, let's take a moment to be thankful for what we have. For this exercise, we're going to list ten reasons why we are grateful that we are employed or have an income. If you're not employed or have an income, imagine that you now have that perfect job or business and complete the list anyway. What you list might be as simple as "my profession lets me provide for my family" or "aspects of my business are truly fulfilling" or "I'd be bored if I didn't have a job." Be imaginative here. Dig deep, and come up with ten great reasons why your situation is a benefit to your life. To complete this exercise, bring up a notes app on your mobile device, or use a sheet of paper, a notebook, or a document on your computer to create your list now.

Have you completed your list? If not, please do so now before continuing.

For those brief few moments of time, while filling out your list of ten reasons to be grateful, did you once have a negative thought about your current situation? If you did, that's okay. Remember that this is a journey and not a race or a quick fix. Before you can move forward, you must be willing to admit the following:

• I accept that I'm not perfect, and I'm willing to learn and grow and progress toward becoming the best leader I can be.

- I have *not* been granted the capability or responsibility to change my boss, my subordinates, or my peers.
- I must be willing to let go of the illusions of my past and open my mind to new knowledge, experiences, and actions.

If you're still having difficulty with any of these statements, go back and re-read this chapter. The next time around, spend more time digging deeper into the concepts presented and how they relate to you.

> I asked the river
>> Where he was going
>>> and how he would know
>>> when he got there.
> He only laughed at me
>> Splashing across the rocks.
> I asked the mountain
>> When he was high enough
>>> and how he would know
>>> when he reached the heavens.
> His echo only laughed
>> Like thunder in the valleys.
> I asked the trees
>> How long they would live
>>> and how they would know
>>> when they were a forest
> Their leaves only shook with mirth
>> In the joy of a sudden wind storm.
> Finally I was silent,
>> As if there were no one else to please,
> And I spent my time laughing,
>> With the river, the mountain,
>>> and trees.

—Dr. James Kavanaugh, from Quiet Waters

CHAPTER 15

The Neuron 3-Act Play

FIGURE 15.1 It's as Easy as 1, 2, 3

Source: Norbert Buchholz, Dreamstime.com.

> It is an ancient need to be told stories. But the story needs
> a great storyteller.
>
> —ALAN RICKMAN

Aristotle taught us via his ancient *persuasion model* that to persuade we
must also be an effective communicator so we can impart a clear vision
and our "commander's intent." One of the most effective ways to do this is
by using compelling and engaging stories because "facts tell and stories

sell," and leaders are frequently tasked with "selling" their vision and themselves to their teams.

We learned about the Hero's Journey in the Dorothy's Journey chapter. We'll now examine some elements of this three-part (Figure 15.1) journey structure from a neuroscience-based perspective in relation to how it aligns with another effective and age-old format called the three-act play. This approach, when combined with neuroscience-based messaging, creates the *Neuron 3-Act Play*™, which has been proven successful across thousands of leadership situations for dozens of firms large and small.

We've been telling stories since the dawn of time. When told well, stories usually follow the three-act play format often employed in the plays of Shakespeare, the poetry of Aristotle, the fables of Aesop, and movies directed by Alfred Hitchcock. Dr. Paul Zak conducted a study during which his team monitored the release of the molecule oxytocin. As we recall, this chemical stimulates feelings of love. Dr. Zak discovered that we can evoke a loving response—like that bestowed upon family members or pets—when we frame our message within a properly structured story. This works best when we tell the story using the right kind of framework and approach.

Humans thrive on stories. They engage our minds and help us connect ideas, understand ourselves and others, and learn complex concepts. The lessons learned through stories are far more memorable and often leave a deeper, more impactful, and longer-lasting impression on our minds. They speak more directly to our emotional and instinctual brains and have a higher retention factor than logic-based presentations.

For example, Nordstrom dramatically bolstered their brand and reputation by way of the popular story about the customer who returned a snow tire. The Nordstrom customer service rep cheerfully handled the situation and made the customer happy even though Nordstrom doesn't sell tires. When our brains hear this story, we get a boost of "like me" dopamine and "trust me" oxytocin, which solidifies the Nordstrom branding message of "we value customers."

Neuroscience explains why stories are more engaging and stay with us longer than the black-and-white copy we read in a textbook or see on a PowerPoint slide. Researchers in Spain, while conducting studies in 2006, discovered that certain words such as "rose" or "mint" were understood by the language-processing area of our brain, but also activated networks in the olfactory regions that process odors. Our brains actually smell a rose when we read a description about the sweet fragrant sent. Don't believe me? Imagine a bright yellow juicy sour lemon. You're biting into the citrus pulp of a bitter lemon right now and the sour juice is flowing across your taste buds. Are you salivating yet? If not, perhaps you've been trained by the CIA to trick lie detector tests.

Words unassociated with our senses, such as "button" or "coat," don't stimulate anything. You're fastening the button on your shirt right now. Feel anything? Didn't think so.

Motion words also have an interesting effect on our brain. If we're reading a good thriller, for example, and the author is describing a high-speed chase, certain words will trigger our motor cortex—the part of our brain that controls muscular movement. Researchers used an fMRI system to show that when individuals read the words "kick," "pick," or "lick," brain areas that control their feet, fingers, or tongue started tapping or licking.

Jeffrey Zacks, the director of the Dynamic Cognition Laboratory at Washington University in St. Louis, said that neuroscientists and psychologists are concluding that stories can create a mental simulation of the events described. Zacks and his team conducted a study in 2009 where fMRI scans were used to record various regions of the brain that were stimulated when participants read short stories. This study revealed that when we become engrossed in fictional events happening to a story character, we feel and react as if they are real. Whether it's real or we're reading about it in a good book, the same areas in our brain light up.

A well-told story activates areas in our brain that allow us to translate the story into our own experiences and concepts. This is called neural coupling. Also, our mirror neurons will help us feel what the protagonist feels. Finally, when our brains process the facts being told, the Broca and Wernicke areas of our brains are activated, along with our motor, sensory, and frontal cortex.

STORY STRUCTURE

Dr. Paul Zak validated that when we're experiencing a story with a dramatic arc, our brain pumps out two neurochemicals: oxytocin—the love hormone we read about previously that's involved with emotions, trust, and bonding—as well as cortisol—a stress hormone that sharpens our powers of concentration. When Zak conducted one experiment, he noted that when participants viewed an emotionally charged father and son story, many of them became more open to charitable donations.

Zak said, "We discovered that to motivate a desire to help others, a story must first sustain attention—a scarce resource in the brain—by developing tension during the narrative. If the story can create that tension, then it is likely that attentive viewers or listeners will come to share the emotions of the characters in it, and after it ends, are likely to continue mimicking the feelings and behaviors of those characters."

Zak also found that an effective storytelling structure that will stimulate these neurochemicals is the tried-and-true Freytag's Pyramid (Figure 15.2).

Gustav Freytag was a nineteenth-century German novelist who noticed several common patterns hidden in the plots of well-written stories. He created a diagram depicting a typical structure and used a pyramid to diagram the story plot. Freytag determined that to emotionally engage readers, good stories needed to include rising action, a compelling climax, and a satisfying resolution.

Gustav's diagram is very similar to the three-act play format that we humans have used to tell stories since a Neanderthal speared that first bison and lived to tell about it. Shakespeare used this structure for many of his stories including comedies, histories, and tragedies.

How can leaders use the three-act play to impact and inspire others to follow a vision, embrace a firm's passion and purpose, and willingly

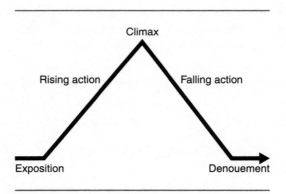

FIGURE 15.2   Freytag's Pyramid

Source: Graphic created by author.

complete difficult tasks? As we learned from former Navy SEAL Jeff Jones in a previous chapter, we can tell impactful and memorable stories.

ACT I

Whenever I tell a story to persuade a subordinate, peer, superior, or large audience, my goal in Act I is to get them to "like me" or the protagonist emotionally by increasing the dopamine level in their brains. This neurotransmitter makes us feel good and lays the foundation for trust—which is essential in persuading anyone.

Dr. Garcia-Fresco said, "Emotions are stored in your memory centers together with the events that triggered those emotions. The more emotional events we experience in life, the more memories we form. Subconsciously our decisions are influenced by stored events and the emotions they elicit. Our brains love patterns. If we have a memory of an event that triggered a happy response, whenever we encounter a similar event, our brain will subconsciously guide us to make a decision so that it can enjoy that happy feeling again."

In Act I, we are displaying a combination of emotional and playful *ludus*, as well as generous *agape* love. In the "story" we are telling, we begin by immersing our audience into the ordinary world as described in the Hero's Journey format.

Great writers understand that it's critical within the first few chapters of a book to grab the reader's attention and connect them emotionally with the protagonist. This could be you, or a customer, employee, stakeholder, or fictional character that illustrates your point. The operative word here is *emotional*. In this act, we need to primarily appeal to the emotional brain. We need to tug on heartstrings and create a "sympathetic character." Writers often use an associative technique to do this. For example, you might show your protagonist imparting kindness or love to someone, or having that bestowed upon them. It could be something as simple as petting a dog or helping an old lady across the street.

Our emotional brain is more visual, so we need to refrain from using lots of copy, facts, figures, graphs, and so on. Dr. Garcia-Fresco said, "We are very visual creatures. We process visual inputs much faster than anything else, hence a visual image can elicit a quicker decision. You can use storytelling to paint a picture of a present memory in their minds which will most likely trigger the resurgence of a similar memory they had or even create a new, pleasant one."

We need to describe the protagonist's ordinary world in colorful and visual detail and show them as either unhappy or neutral, but not yet fulfilling their life's passion and purpose. We then turn up the gas and create a "call to action." This is a situation in which the protagonist becomes motivated to act. The hero usually refuses the call to action until a mentor convinces him or her to take that first step into Act II.

For example, to help a team embrace the passion and purpose that drives a pharmaceutical firm to succeed, I might use a story about a mother who was in a happy ordinary world until her son, Johnny, was diagnosed with a serious disease. The disease has just become the antagonist. Mom got a call to action because of something the antagonist did, but she is so distraught that she can't take that first step to explore treatment options. Finally, a doctor friend convinces her to embark on her Hero's Journey to find a cure for little Johnny.

Act I should cover about 25 percent of our entire story.

ACT II

In Act II my goal is to get my audience to "trust me" or the protagonist by raising the oxytocin level in their brains. This "love" chemical helps build instinctual trust and can lower norepinephrine and cortisol levels, which our bodies produce when we are subjected to fearful, dangerous, stressful, or untrusting situations. Strange as this may sound, our objective is to initially raise norepinephrine and cortisol, temporarily, by raising the stakes in our story along with tension, anxiety, and fear. As Dr. Zak discovered, increasing cortisol also sharpens our powers of concentration. In this act, we are employing a combination of curious and passionate *eros* and courageous and honest *philia* love.

"In actuality, your decisions result from the reptilian brain influence: you need to connect to the basic instinctive part of the brain before you even try to rationalize with people," said Dr. Garcia-Fresco. "We all want to believe that we make rational and thoughtful decisions, but reality shows that all of our decisions begin as emotional or instinctual decisions using our reptilian or emotional brains. We then take a second step to rationalize it in our rational brain. This means that our core decision making relies on our primal instincts and emotions first."

In the case of our fictional story, our mom is at first emotionally influenced by her doctor mentor, but then she must face a horde of instinctual obstacles on her own. To ratchet up the tension and raise the stakes, the best writers use time as a plot element, wherein our heroin is running out of time and must find the MacGuffin before it's too late. The MacGuffin in our example story is the cure for Johnny. The antagonist disease is progressing rapidly and little Johnny is losing the battle. Mom is frantically exploring options but is thwarted at every turn by other bad guys. These might be snake oil companies who promise cures but then steal the money and disappear. Pacing is critical in this act. We should use more active verbs, shorter sentences and paragraphs, and speed up the action.

By the end of Act II, our heroine is finally pointed in the right direction by a nurse who has heard about a miracle cure. The nurse was informed by a sales rep from our pharmaceutical company. Spurred by this nurse, Mom decides to research our firm and its capability to arrest this disease.

By offering a glimpse of hope toward the end of this act, we can lower cortisol and raise oxytocin and therefore trust, which will set us up for Act III.

Act II should be about 50 percent of our story.

ACT III

In Act III, my goal is to get my audience to "believe me" or my protagonist by becoming more logical and authoritative. I will do this by raising their serotonin and GABA levels as this has a calming effect on our minds, which can help make us more receptive to logical information. To accomplish this, I will use a combination of authoritative *storge* and dependable *pragma* love and impart more facts, figures, and choices. Studies have shown that positive visualization can increase serotonin levels in the brain, and one of the best ways to do that is by becoming engrossed in an engaging story.

In our fictional story, mom is learning about the cure, she's ready to trust us, but she became so jaded and confused in Act II that she's not sure which choice to make. In the meantime, the doctors report that Johnny has precious little time left. In fact, they've just discovered that there's now less time than previously thought. If she does not find a cure soon, Johnny will perish.

Mom is forced to dig deep and find an inner strength that she didn't even know she had. She must now give it her all and do whatever it takes to save her son. She takes a leap of faith and decides to trust our firm to provide a treatment. At this late stage, there are no guarantees, but we are her best logical hope. In a thrilling climactic scene, little Johnny almost doesn't make it but is saved in the last second by competent doctors and the medication provided by our company.

In this act, we seek to offer calm assurance by raising serotonin and GABA levels in the brains of our audience. For example, when we read a great mystery novel, we are amazed at how the protagonist logically brings together all the clues and facts and deductively catches the killer.

In our story, mom returns to her ordinary world, with Johnny by her side, and is compelled to bring the "magical elixir," our medication, to all who reside there. She becomes an evangelist and spokesperson for the company, and in time, thousands of lives are saved. How did this happen? Because one sales rep truly believed that our company's products can and will save lives. She became motivated to inform as many doctors and nurses as possible, and one of those nurses told our protagonist. Thus, little Johnny is alive, happy, and healthy.

Act III should take up the remaining 25 percent of our story.

The story above is one example of how to use the Neuron 3-Act Play (Figure 15.3) to impart an organization's vision, passion, and purpose, and emotionally charge employees to willingly embrace the "commander's intent" and become evangelists for their products or services.

In workshops, I dive much deeper into using the Neuron 3-Act Play and the use of neuroscience in leadership, sales, and marketing applications. In these workshops, I also discuss three important additional ingredients.

Principle of Threes

There's a reason why we say "one, two, three," "ready, set, go," and "let's go on the count of three." A three-act play has three acts because our brains like it that way. While some plays do have five acts, closer observation reveals that the two additional acts are really "subacts" and these stories still have three main parts: the beginning, the middle, and the end.

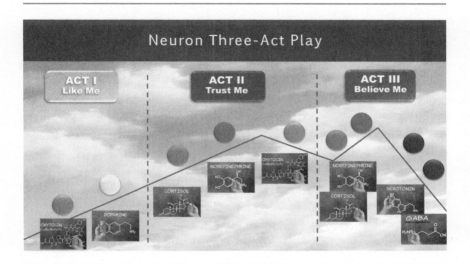

FIGURE 15.3   Neuron 3-Act Play

Source: Graphic created by author. Photos from Zerbor, Dreamstime.com.

The human brain is genetically wired to think in threes. We don't like processing more than three things at a time. Marketers who flood customers with a dozen "value propositions" obviously are not aware of this basic principle of human nature. When leaders present to teams or board members, they are best to focus on only three main points at a time. Each PowerPoint slide should have no more than three bullet points. If you are imparting emotionally and instinctually charged information, using emotionally and instinctually charged pictures and few or no words, is best.

Principle of Contrasts

Within every story and presentation, we should use contrasts. The human brain likes to see a before and after picture, a transition from where one is to where one might be. We want to visualize a character arc that takes us from our ordinary not-so-great world to a shiny future where we find the magical elixir and bring it home to share with others.

When we tell a story, it's all about contrasts as we move the characters through their Hero's Journey. In presentations, we are best to use side-by-side pictures with a mediocre or bad situation on the left and nirvana on the right. No words are needed, as this will appeal to the emotional brain (wouldn't you love to be here instead of where you are?) and the instinctual brain (do you really want to risk losing the opportunity to gain nirvana?).

"Comparing and contrasting gives people a point of reference. It also allows people to compare with their own personal experiences. The more contrast you show, the more obvious your point becomes," said Dr. Garcia-Fresco.

Principle of Escalation

Within the three-act play, every story must escalate. To quantify this, let's assume for our story we are using a tension dial with a 1-to-10 scale (10 is the highest). In Act I, in our ordinary world, our hero is hovering at around 1 or 2. Something happens to nudge her out of her comfort zone and the tension goes to a 3 or 4. In Act II, we escalate quickly up to a 7 or 8 by increasing the stakes in the game. When we reach the story climax in Act III, we should be at a 10 where the protagonist and antagonist battle it out. We can then de-escalate back down to a 1 or 2 as our hero delivers the magical elixir and all is well in the land.

For more information on the The Neuron 3-Act Play, visit www.neuronleaders.com.

CHAPTER 16

The Eighth Secret

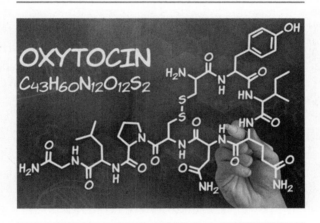

FIGURE 16.1   Oxytocin

Source: Zerbor, Dreamstime.com.

> I think a leader has to really be a balanced, whole, and a
> healthy person … in order to be the best leader on the job.
>
> —MIKE DUKE, FORMER WALMART CEO

You've just learned about the Seven Secrets of Neuron Leadership, but there are really eight. We've all heard about the eight wonders of the world: here is the eighth and most important neuron *secret* of the world:

Everything beautiful, glorious, and ingenious, and everything diabolical, horrific, and devastating that humankind has ever created is heavily influenced by one chemical and one neurotransmitter in our brains.

I realize that a host of brain experts and creative painters will line up at my door to cut off my fingers for making this statement, but the evidence is clear. The neurotransmitter is dopamine and the brain chemical is oxytocin (Figure 16.1).

We learned earlier that many neuroscientists believe that our personalities are related to three primary neurotransmitters that modulate brain activity in predictable patterns and influence how we humans act and react to the world around us. Again, the neurotransmitters are norepinephrine, serotonin, and dopamine.

Our neurotransmitter chemical levels are either high, medium, or low, and if our levels are out of balance, we can become psychologically or physically unhealthy. For example, a serotonin deficiency can cause migraine headaches, nausea, appetite issues, depression, and anxiety. Something as simple as drinking too much coffee can affect our dopamine levels and make us grumpy.

When we do something that gives us pleasure, like complete a project, create something beautiful, or show kindness and mercy, we do so because it increases our dopamine level and makes us feel good. Not being allowed to pursue our dreams deprives of us dopamine. We can become unhealthy and prone to addictions such as drugs, alcohol, control, money, power, sex, or work. We continue to feed these bad habits because doing so gives us a temporary dopamine rush.

To human beings, dopamine and oxytocin are almost as important as food and water, for without them our souls can eventually dry up and wither away. Our mental and physical health might decline, make us susceptible to disease, and rob us of the will to live.

I provided an example earlier of a friend in a sales leadership role who eventually left his job to pursue a happier, healthier lifestyle even though it came with a pay cut. He did so because he was miserable. He was not pursuing his passion and purpose in life. He no longer got a dopamine high or oxytocin rush from his profession.

How many of us have failed to pursue our dreams, our passions, our purpose in life because we felt guilty? Were we doing what we thought was best for others? Perhaps we martyred ourselves for a perceived greater good without realizing we'd made everyone else miserable because we were. Maybe we lacked enough *philautia* self-love to have the courage to follow our hearts, or maybe our dopamine level was out of whack because we remained in an unhealthy environment or relationship, or we were unaware of specific healthy actions we could take to raise our dopamine and oxytocin levels. In this chapter, I outline 10 ways you can raise both.

Sidebar

I mentioned earlier that neuroscientist Dr. Paul Zak had conducted experiments showing the connection between raising oxytocin levels and increasing trust in work environments. Dr. Zak offers eight management behaviors that foster trust that are measurable and can be managed to improve performance:

1. Recognize Excellence—publicly reward top performers
2. Induce "Challenge Stress"—create moderate job stress via attainable goals
3. Ensure Work Autonomy—trust workers to complete projects in their own way
4. Enable Job Freedom—allow people to select the most rewarding projects
5. Share Company Information—a well-informed employee is a happier employee
6. Build Relationships—less task-orientation and more relationship-orientation
7. Encourage Wellness—facilitate personal growth along with professional growth
8. Show Vulnerability—leaders should ask for help to encourage cooperation

---

RAISING DOPAMINE

Here are 10 ways you can raise dopamine levels in yourself and in the brains of your team members, thereby making everyone feel positively giddy:

1. *L-Tyrosine*. This is an amino acid that helps raise dopamine levels in the brain. It can provide a "feel-good" boost while helping to

alleviate stress and minimize stress-induced something ... what was it again? Oh yeah, memory loss. L-Tyrosine can be found at most vitamin stores.

2. *Creativity*. Spark your team's creative energies by holding brainstorming sessions, assigning them creative tasks, and praising their creative accomplishments. Inspire creativity instead of stifling it, but be sure to "pull the chain" if someone spends too much time finger-painting and not enough time working.

3. *Exercise*. Goes without saying. Encourage exercise, long walks around the office, bike rides, whatever. Some companies hold periodic stretch and mini-yoga "at your desk" sessions every day. It looks funny but it works.

4. *Music*. It also works, but it's temporary and may activate your brain's chemical dependencies. For addictive types, music is a two-way street. It can boost your feel-good dopamine level but cause withdrawal when you take off your headphones.

5. *Addictions*. This is a tough one because all of us are addicted to something. We get a dopamine rush when we satisfy our addictions, and hit a valley when the rush is over. If we're addicted to work or being in control, as a leader we may be inclined to push our teams too hard so we can get a rush. When they all quit, so does the rush.

6. *Diet*. Stop eating tons of sugar and processed foods. No more white bread or candy bars or mocha frappuccinos. They're deadly. Try whole grains (not wheat bread), Stevia sweetener, palm sugar, or agave syrup instead. You can also try curcumin, ginkgo biloba, or L-Theanine.

7. *Meditate*. We mentioned this earlier. An interesting way to do this is revealed in a subsequent chapter, so keep turning those pages.

8. *Streaking*. I don't mean taking your clothes off and running naked around the office. Although this might raise eyebrows, it won't raise dopamine. Okay, maybe it will for you, but I mean get a streak going. For example, with a local sports team that's winning, a contest, a fundraising drive, subscriber numbers, or website visits, and so on.

9. *Win*. Winning is a great way to raise dopamine levels. When we accomplish something, like completing an important task or closing a deal, we get a nice dopamine boost. Having task or goal checklists for your team may help with this, provided the goals are attainable on a frequent basis.

10. *Buy something*. Most women are probably smiling and nodding at this one. Shopping raises dopamine? Buying a new pair of shoes gives you a rush? What a revelation. Imelda Marcos bought 3,000 pairs of shoes. I think she's in the *Guinness Book of World Records* for having the highest dopamine level on the planet.

RAISING OXYTOCIN

Could it be that virtually all wars, books, songs, paintings, inventions, medical breakthroughs, and financial epiphanies were created due to this brain chemical? We want more of it, so we do what it takes to increase it. When we lack enough of it, a nasty hormone takes control and turns us into a diabolical maniac.

Aside from having sex or delivering a baby, how can we increase our own—or someone else's—oxytocin levels? There are many ways and we'll explore 10 right now.

Before we do, I need to invoke a reminder that it is morally wrong to manipulate or coerce anyone to do anything. The following suggestions are offered as ways to improve relationships and help people feel happy and fulfilled, not as ways to trick them into doing your bidding. Please use these with respect, caution, and discretion.

1. *Giving*. This is why the principle about generosity is so important. Giving something to someone increases your oxytocin level, but only if it is from your heart and carries no expectation of reciprocity. When we give, we receive happiness and health in return because our oxytocin level increases. From now on, don't pass by that Salvation Army guy out in front of Walmart, but instead dig into your pocket and put a few bucks into the bucket. Volunteer your *time* for a worthy cause. In doing so, you'll feel better and live longer. Giving does not need to be in a monetary or hourly form. Give a compliment, a courteous gesture, a pat on the back for a job well done, or just a smile. You'll pump up your oxytocin level and that of the person you interact with. At work, sponsor charitable drives, visits to homeless centers as a team-building exercise, or outings to charitable events. Encourage your team to be generous. They will feel better and respect you as a leader for helping them help others.

2. *Hugging*. Along with touching, this releases oxytocin. Hugging is a tough thing to do in office environments where men and women interact, but if done in a proper setting with more than two people in the room and in a genuine and respectful way, it can be quite powerful for increasing the oxytocin hormone and helping you and your team feel happier. By showing even a small modicum of platonic affection, others will feel appreciated and their oxytocin levels will soar. This does not mean you need to have hug fests every five minutes, or sponsor campfires where everyone sings kumbaya, but hugging occasionally in appropriate settings can have immediate and long-lasting positive effects.

3. *Petting*. When we pet an animal, like a cat or a dog, our brain releases oxytocin. That's why we feel better when Charlie the cat sits on our lap and rubs his furry head into our hand. Interestingly, oxytocin is also released in the pet. That's why they love us so much. Our magical hands increase their oxytocin level. While we may not be able to bring a pet into the office, we can emulate this effect via mirror neurons by having a few pictures of pets here and there. These may remind people of their own pets and how they feel during a petting session. In my workshop sessions, I teach marketers how to use this secret to get customers to love your brand almost as much as their dog.

4. *Exercising*. Jogging, walking, biking, or other outdoor activities have been scientifically linked to increasing oxytocin levels. Walking while talking with someone else is one of the best ways to accomplish this as it raises the levels in both of you. Try this on for size: instead of a one-on-one meeting in your office, go for a walk with the other person. You'll bond better and feel better while raising oxytocin levels in both of you. Embarking on an adventure with someone also boosts your respective levels. That's why an adventurous vacation can help strengthen a relationship. That's also why some companies invest in adventurous team-building exercises. They work because everyone's oxytocin levels are energized along with their batteries.

5. *Shooting*. Pacifists may reject this one, but it does work. Maybe because it's an adventure, who knows. There's something about slamming a magazine into a Glock 17, chambering a round, aiming the gun at the target, and blasting that paper full of loud holes. It's

exhilarating. It's primal. It's fun. It can also be expensive, but a lot less costly than a heart attack.

6. *Laughing*. When we laugh, oxytocin rushes through us and the evil lord cortisol is vanquished. If your stress levels are soaring, or you're feeling depressed, watch a funny movie or YouTube video, go to a comedy club, listen to a fun-filled recording (there are plenty on the web), or crack open a book of jokes. Likewise, for your team, encourage them to tell a good joke (a clean one, of course) prior to the start of a meeting. This will help crack the ice, set the tone for a more harmonious meeting, and raise everyone's oxytocin levels so they are more receptive to the information being delivered. The best orators know this intuitively, which is why they usually open their presentations with a funny story.

7. *Chatting*. Preferably on the phone rather than in a chat room. Talking while walking is better, but when you can't walk together then at least talk together. Pull your head out of your text app and use your phone in a primal, unconventional way. Dial a number and start talking. Better yet, do it in person by forming or joining a support group that meets frequently and allows everyone to chat for at least an hour.

8. *Meditating*. Try interacting with your mobile phone without using your thumb even once. Challenging, isn't it? Use your forefinger to tap on a music app, fire up something soft and soothing (not Led Zeppelin or Kiss), close your eyes, and meditate. Your nasty cortisol level will melt away, replaced by a warm and fuzzy wave of oxytocin. If we could only bottle this stuff and sell it. There's a ton of scientific research that shows how meditation lowers stress, increases memory and cognitive abilities, and makes us happier. The latter is because it increases our oxytocin levels. Just set aside at least 10 minutes each day to clear your head, with or without the music. Then give something away, hug someone, pet a pet, shoot a gun, jog a few miles, and call up a friend and tell them all about your oxytocin-enriched day.

9. *Eating*. Not just eating, but eating right. Yeah, I know, our doctors always admonish us to do this, and we always ignore them and then we feel bad while we're slowly killing ourselves. It's a thing. Here are a few simple tricks that will help us do a better job of following our doctor's orders. Try this recipe: boil some eggs, or if you're lazy, pick up a few preboiled ones from the store. Smash them up, yolks and all

(I won't go into all the new evidence that yolks got a bum cholesterol wrap, you can research this yourself). Next, smash in a banana and sprinkle in some black or cayenne pepper. This tasty combo is easy to make, easy to eat, and it's a proven oxytocin booster. When you're done with that little snack, open your refrigerator and say cheese, please ...

10. *Cheesing*. Is that even a word? More importantly, are there miracle foods that can instantly make us feel happy and improve our relationships by raising our oxytocin and dopamine levels? Yes, there are, and this powerful final secret can save a relationship, a customer, and your job all in the same week. We talked about eggs, bananas, and pepper, but chocolate and mayonnaise also help boost oxytocin, as do certain cheeses. Here's why ...

SAY CHEESE, PLEASE

Have you savored a genuine Parmigiano-Reggiano or Dutch farmhouse Gouda and marveled at the crunchy bits that taste like salt? Those are actually small crystals of tyrosine inside long casein molecule amino acid chains.

Certain quality cheeses, like a mouth-watering manchego or tongue-tingling cheddar, are filled with tyrosine. Since our bodies are incapable of manufacturing this amino acid, most of us have low levels and need frequent "boosts." A section of our brain called the olfactory bulb contains an enzyme that reacts with tyrosine to form neurotransmitters, including norepinephrine and dopamine.

Our sense of smell is also located in the olfactory bulb, which is related to our limbic system. Cheese presses our emotional "happy button" by stimulating our oxytocin and dopamine levels, which makes us smile.

Cheese makes everyone smile, you might say, but it also makes everyone fat. Sure, if you eat a whole pound of Brie or Havarti with every meal you'll soon look like the cow from whence the cheese came, but moderate amounts can be healthy.

Cheese is made from milk, which is almost 90 percent water, and contains significant amounts of minerals and proteins. Aged cheese has very little lactose and is essentially concentrated milk, but delivered in a healthy "predigested" form. Most importantly, cheese contains tyrosine.

When eaten in moderation, tyrosine-filled cheese is the ultimate feel-good food that can stimulate your oxytocin and dopamine levels and make you feel happy. When you're happier, your relationships improve and your leadership style is easier for the troops to digest. Things might also go a bit smoother with your boss or board. So, cheese is not only healthy, but might also help you get a raise ... or at least keep you from getting fired.

You can determine your *Neuron Personality Profile* type and download a detailed description of your traits along with specific leadership suggestions and exercises by visiting www.neuronleaders.com. There you can also find a detailed chart that will help you determine your personal optimal neurotransmitter levels and review specific diet and health recommendations to improve your balances, and therefore your ability to lead.

NEURON EXERCISE

In our leadership roles, our heads fill up daily with millions of impressions, facts, figures, data points, names, tasks, and more. Our world is a cornucopia of nonstop stuff. Our email inboxes are overflowing, our phones are constantly buzzing, and our calendars are completely full. We're in overload mode, and the tsunami never stops. How do we deal with these constant storms?

We can find an "eye" and hang out for a while.

We must find a quiet time and place to meditate and clear our minds daily. If you're like me and find this difficult, here's a way to simplify the practice of meditation: Do you remember the acronym you learned in high school physics class when studying the colors of the spectrum? If not, it's ROY G. BIV, and it stands for Red, Orange, Yellow, Green, Blue, Indigo, and Violet. These are the colors of the spectrum.

Light vibrates at various wavelengths, which is what creates different colors. Likewise, research validates that colors can have a profound effect on our brains.[1] We can learn to gradually lower our mental wavelength by closing our eyes and first visualizing the color red. Once we clearly see that color in our mind's eye, we can lower our wavelength one step further by visualizing the color orange and so on until we reach the color violet. At that point, we are vibrating at the lowest wavelength and will find it easier to clear our minds of all thought. With the color violet floating across our mind's eye, we will feel the weight of the universe lift from our shoulders. We will feel peace and serenity sweep over us like a warm ray of sun. We will find the practice of meditation to be easier and far more effective.

You should meditate for at least ten minutes each day. If you can't find at least ten minutes, then you are obviously far too busy riding your high horse while swinging a lasso and trying to yodel. Meditating and praying daily will help you become more in tune with yourself. It will help clear your mind of all that built-up clutter and allow you to focus on the leadership tasks of the day. You'll feel better, think better, act better, and lead better.

CHAPTER 17

Neuron Decision Making

FIGURE 17.1 Decisions

Source: Citalliance, Dreamstime.com.

It is only in our decisions that we are important.

—JEAN-PAUL SARTRE

This chapter covers how to utilize the *Neuron Decision Matrix*™ and the *Neuron Priority Planner*™ to make and implement important leadership decisions and tasks (Figure 17.1).

I mentioned earlier that I've spent the past decade as an executive coach and consultant working with C-level and VP-level executives at dozens of leading firms worldwide. In most cases, these executives are excellent decision makers who exhibit calm confidence when deciding courses of action. Most do a great job of also seeking input from their team and inspiring them to follow the courses selected. Some, however, when subjected to environments of high stress, can make emotionally or instinctually charged decisions that lead to disaster.

Aristotle taught us that to be persuasive, we need to engage all three parts of our brain. Making a decision is all about persuasion. We need to persuade ourselves that we're making the right and best decision, and then we need to persuade our teams to execute on those decisions. The best way to do this is to ensure that all three parts of our brain get an equal say in the matter. I've designed a Neuron Decision Matrix that can help us do that more effectively. Here's how it works.

First, be sure that you have already clearly defined your personal or company mission, passion, and purpose. This should become the most important factor in making every important decision. Will the decision you make drive you toward your vision, or away from it?

Once you know where you're headed, draw three vertical lines on a whiteboard, a PowerPoint slide, or wherever to create three columns. Label the first column *Emotional*, the second *Instinctual*, and the third *Logical*. In the *Emotional* column, create purpose and passion statements that are emotional in nature, for example: "Our overarching purpose is to bring joy to millions of people by allowing them to connect and communicate easier with our solutions."

Do the same in the *Instinctual* column. You might write: "Our passion is to help our customers avoid risks and harm via solutions that offer greater security." Finally, write your *Logical* statements, for example: "Our goal is to provide affordable solutions that are 50 percent more efficient than any others."

Now, when making a major decision, place the document you've just created front and center. Brainstorm decisions with your team and list all of them on a whiteboard. Include everything, whether you think they are good, bad, or ugly. Refrain from making comments or expressing opinions about any of them, but do seek to clarify them so they're understood by all.

Once you have a plethora of decision points on the board, examine each one against the backdrop of your firm's passion, purpose, and vision. Does it take you toward or away from your destination? Narrow your decision choices down to three finalists, because again, the human brain works best when given only three options to choose from.

Now, draw two intersecting lines on the board, one vertical and one horizontal, to create four equal quadrants. Label the upper left quadrant *Emotional*, the upper right one *Instinctual*, the lower right one *Logical*, and the lower left *Summary*.

Look at decision possibility number one. In the upper left quadrant, list three emotional reasons why this decision is a good one (fulfills your firm's purpose) and three reasons why it's bad. Do the same for the Instinctual and Logical quadrants. Be sure they are actually *Emotional*, or from whichever category they pertain to. The object of this exercise is to engage all three parts of everyone's brain to make more balanced decisions. Once you have three good and bad reasons in each quadrant, rank them all with a number between one and five, with five as the most important to you and your team. For example, if reason number one resonates strongly (i.e., it aligns well with your passion and purpose), then rate it as a five. Use negative numbers for the three reasons you should not make this decision. It's important here to be as honest as possible. While a leader can help guide a team, he or she should not try to manipulate or coerce others into "doing their bidding" by scoring a reason a certain way.

Once all the reasons have been scored, do the math. Select the most important "should do it" and "should not do it" reasons from each quadrant and place them in the fourth bottom left quadrant. Then, add up the positive numbers for the three "should do it" reasons and compare it to the total of the negative "should not do it" numbers. Which number is higher? There's your answer. If the "should do it" number is higher, go for it. If not, don't do it or re-evaluate.

In the visual example shown in Figure 17.2, I use the decision to buy a convertible automobile or not. Some of the "should do it" reasons are less stress, less repair risk, and high maintenance costs for my current car. I compared those against the "should not" reasons of more stress, more financial risk, and higher payments. The "should" reasons won so it's obvious that I should buy that convertible.

Neuron Decision Matrix

Should I buy a convertible?

1. Less Stress - 5 2. More Motivated - 5 3. More Fun - 3	1. Less Risk (Handling) - 3 2. Great Deal - 3 3. Less Risk (Maint) - 4
1. More Guilt - 4 2. Bigger Ego - 3 3. More Stress - 5	1. More Risk (Speed) - 3 2. More Risk (Financial) - 3 3. More Risk (Even Better Deal) - 2
13 1. Less Stress - 5 2. Less Risk (Maint) - 4 3. High Maint Cost - 4	1. High Maint Cost (Current Car) - 4 2. Affordable in Budget - 3 3. Professional Need - 2
12 1. More Stress - 5 2. More Risk (Fin) - 3 3. High Payments - 4	1. High Payments - 4 2. Sacrifice other Items - 3 3. Higher Cost (New vs. Used) - 4

FIGURE 17.2   Neuron Decision Matrix

Source: Illustration created by the author.

NEURON PRIORITY PLANNER™

The Greek philosopher Seneca once wisely said that we should "Count each day as a separate life." Each new dawn brings with it the promise of a new beginning. There is much we can and should learn from the past—especially our mistakes—but we gain more ground by focusing on only one day at a time. Long-term goals are important and should align with our mission, passion, and purpose, but I recommend having each team and individual create only three primary weekly tasks per goal and updating these daily to ensure progression toward each goal rather than making a long list of "checkoff" tasks. Doing the latter can be overwhelming and lead to busy work instead of important work.

I use the *Neuron Priority Planner* tool and methodology daily and teach client teams how to do this in workshops and webinars. My clients love it and swear by it. You may recall the "Time Management Grids" offered by Stephen R. Covey in his book *The 7 Habits of Highly Effective People*. Covey popularized a matrix grid with four quadrants. This matrix was actually created by President Eisenhower, who once

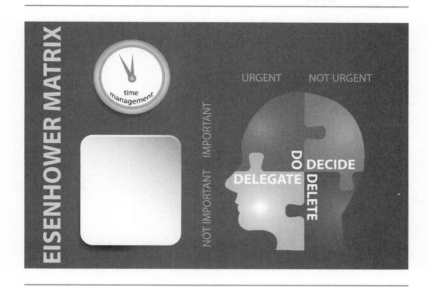

FIGURE 17.3 **The Eisenhower Matrix**

Source: Jaroslav Frank, Dreamstime.com.

said, "What is important is seldom urgent, and what is urgent is seldom important" (Figure 17.3).

Eisenhower placed tasks or projects that were *Urgent and Important* in the upper left quadrant of the matrix for immediate action. *Not Urgent and Important* items went into the upper right quadrant for further decision. *Not Important but Urgent* in the lower left for delegation, and *Not Urgent and Not Important* in the lower right for deletion.

This grid has proven effective for millions and is an excellent and simple way to keep your priorities straight. However, Eisenhower created this grid decades before modern neuroscientists had a more mature understanding of how our brains work. Also, long before we had such an abundance of social media, web content, and communication sources. In today's dynamic and hectic world, we need a better way to simplify our projects and tasks and prioritize our time. It's not enough to make four lists in four quadrants and check them off as you go. That might have worked in the seventies and eighties, perhaps even in the nineties, but not anymore.

The simplified spreadsheet version of the patent-pending *Neuron Priority Planner* is free and available at www.neuronleaders.com.

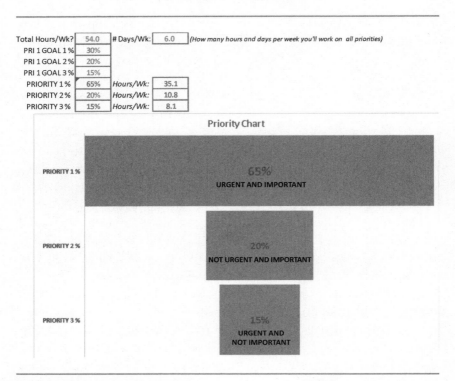

FIGURE 17.4   Priority Chart

Source: Illustration created by the author.

My team and I have also created more sophisticated and customized web and mobile app versions for clients. Here's how it works:

Recall that our brains think in threes, not fours. Therefore, a four-quadrant grid is not ideal. Instead, let's use three boxes to represent Priority 1, 2, and 3 Goals (Figure 17.4). These are *not* projects or tasks, they are goals that are directly related to our overarching passion and purpose. Goal 1 is the most important thing we can do to take a giant stride toward accomplishing the passion and purpose, vision, or mission we've identified for our organization, department, or team. Think of this as *Urgent and Important*. Keep this simple, clear, and use only one sentence.

Goal 2 is the second most important thing we can do to reach our objective, which might be akin to *Not Urgent and Important*. Goal 3 is the third thing, perhaps akin to *Urgent and Not Important*. There is no box for *Not Urgent and Not Important.* Listing things in this box forces our mind to spend time thinking about the things we should not be thinking about. Do we really need to waste time writing down what we should delete?

Next, we need to decide what percentage of our personal or team time will be devoted to each goal. The experts who impart Lean and Six Sigma expertise often talk about the age-old 80/20 Pareto Principle wherein 80 percent of the effects come from 20 percent of the causes. Translated for our purposes, 80 percent of our time should be spent on 20 percent of our projects or tasks—those that will gain us 80 percent of our objective.

I recommend spending 60 to 65 percent of your time on Goal 1 items, around 20 percent on Goal 2, and 15 to 20 percent on Goal 3. Note that Goals 1 and 2 add up to around 80 percent, which is in sync with the Pareto Principle. Now comes the fun part.

Tab two in this spreadsheet allows you to type in a sentence for your Priority 1 Goal 1. Under this, you can list three projects to accomplish this goal. Under each project, you list three immediate tasks to complete the projects. Why only three? You guessed it, our minds prefer threes. Long lists of 20 tasks are far too complex. This approach provides a good way to "train your brain" to simplify your projects, tasks, and your life. If you work at it, you can find a way to structure or combine tasks to create only three immediate ones. The operative word here is *immediate*. There may be other tasks that are long term. If so, on the spreadsheet example (found at www.neuronleaders.com), there are tabs for each month. You can list various future projects and subtasks there.

For my own personal version of this, I only list tasks I will accomplish this week and update them daily. To the right of each task, I list who will do this, me or someone else or several people. I also type in how many hours I will devote to that task. These add up to show me how many total hours I'll spend on all Priority 1 Goal 1 tasks.

I do this for my Priority 2 and 3 Goals, as well as my Priority 2 and 3 tasks. When done, I click on the Dashboard sheet where a large graph shows me how much time I will devote for each area today or this week (Figure 17.5). Also listed is each project under each priority.

For team purposes, I use a version of this in our weekly meetings (Figure 17.6). We first review our overall passion and purpose as a reminder of why we're all in the meeting in the first place. Then we

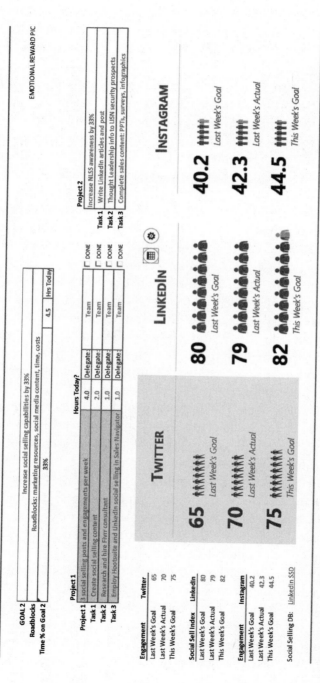

FIGURE 17.5 Dashboard Sheet

Source: Illustration created by the author.

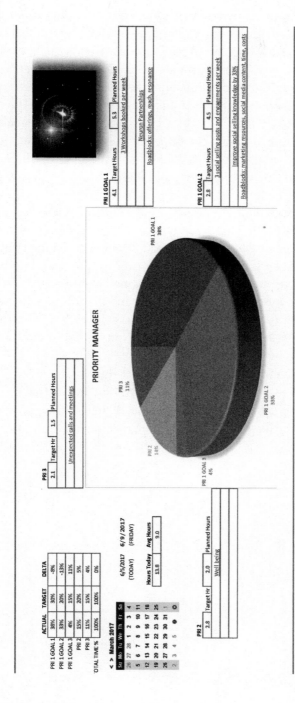

FIGURE 17.6   Neuron Priority Planner

Source: Illustration created by the author.

review each goal and the amount of time we're spending on each. We adjust this as needed. On each goal sheet, we review a graph that depicts our progress toward each goal. We look at last week's goal, last week's actual, this week's goal, month-to-date, and year-to-date metrics. The focus is on our trending. Are we making the progress we desire?

On each sheet are two visuals in the upper right section. One shows a "reward" picture of what we'll receive if we accomplish our goals. This speaks to our emotional brain. The other photo depicts a consequence if we fail to meet our goals. This taps on our instinctual brain. All the numbers and charts on the page appeal to our logical brain, so all the neuron bases are covered.

This is one example of how to simplify and prioritize your goals, projects, tasks, and life. There are others, but I encourage using only three boxes, circles, or whatever, and quantifying a percentage for each. Also, be sure to keep track of how much time you're spending in each area. I was shocked when I did this. I'm ashamed to admit that I was concentrating far too much time on Priority 2 and 3 stuff, usually because some of these were more interesting or fun. While it's a good thing to take an occasional fun break (*ludus* love), it's not good to flip the 80/20 rule on its head.

The above illustrates that time and task management are mostly logical but should also include some emotional and instinctual elements. This is primarily related to *pragma* love as it needs to align with and drive us toward our long-term goals, vision, passion, and purpose.

CHAPTER **18**

Conclusion

FIGURE 18.1 Lightbulb

Source: Tanewpix, Dreamstime.com.

> President Eisenhower once said that "The supreme quality of a leader is unquestionable integrity." Being highly ethical in everything you do is critical because your team will reflect the examples you set.
>
> —GORDON ENGLAND, FORMER DEPUTY SECRETARY OF DEFENSE, DEPUTY SECRETARY OF HOMELAND SECURITY, AND SECRETARY OF THE NAVY

The author of this story is unknown. He or she tells of a group of alumni from a leading university that held a reunion at the house of their former professor. By now they were all well into their lofty careers, so the conversation soon lapsed into complaints about work, stress, and bad leaders.

The professor listened patiently and then finally shook his head and went to the kitchen to make coffee. He returned several minutes later with a pot and a large tray filled with an assortment of cups. The mix on the tray included paper, plastic, porcelain, metal, glass, crystal, and bone china. Some cups were plain and ordinary, and others were decorative and exquisite.

The former students hovered around the tray to select a cup from the assortment. The first one picked exquisite bone china. The second person picked expensive crystal, the third one picked decorative porcelain, and so on. Those who picked last appeared disappointed at being left with only plastic or paper.

The professor poured each person some coffee from the pot. He then smiled and asked the alumnus who had picked first why he had chosen that particular cup. The former student, a young man in a pressed shirt, trimmed hair, and polished shoes, shrugged and said he liked the way it looked. The professor turned to the guest who had picked second and asked the same question. The young woman, adorned in expensive clothing, gave a similar answer as the young man. The last of the alumni simply said they were left with no choice but plastic or paper; otherwise, they would have chosen something different.

The professor gazed at his guests for a long moment and then said, "Those of you who picked cups first, all chose the more ornate, exquisite, and expensive-looking ones. Those who chose last seemed disappointed and commented that they would have selected something 'better' if given a choice."

The former students glanced at each other and then back at their professor. Their eyes were filled with confusion and curiosity. One of them asked, "What's wrong with our choice of cups?"

The professor smiled and said, "We all want the best for ourselves, but focusing on external glitter is often the source of our problems and stress."

"I don't understand," a young woman said.

The professor asked the students to set their cups on the counter. They complied. He picked up a paper cup from the tray and filled it with coffee. He then handed it to the young man who had chosen first. "Drink this."

The young man took the cup and drank.

"How does that coffee taste?"

"Fine," the alumnus said.

"Is there any difference between that coffee and the brew in your ornate cup?"

"No," the man said, "why should there be?"

"Precisely," said the professor. "There is no difference at all."

The room fell silent as the alumni stared at the cups they had chosen.

The professor continued. "The container adds no quality to the taste of the coffee. An expensive cup simply costs more and may even detract from the richness of the brew. What you all really wanted was coffee, not cups. Yet those of you who were left with plastic or paper were jealous of the others. Why is that?"

No one responded. Most lowered their gaze and studied their shoes.

The professor picked up the pot. "Life is like this coffee. Your jobs, money, cars, houses, and toys are like the cups. They are symbols of your success. They do not define, determine, or dictate your quality of life. When we focus outwardly on the cups, we often fail to look inwardly at the joy of our coffee."

The professor went back into the kitchen and returned with a stack of paper cups. He handed one to each of his former students and then filled them with coffee from the pot.

"As your professor, the most important lesson I can teach you is to view your life like this coffee. The happiest and wealthiest people don't focus on the fanciest cups. They are grateful for the cups they have, and even more grateful for the richness of the coffee they have been served."

The professor raised his paper cup and offered a toast. "Live simply, love generously, care deeply, and speak gently. And remember, your life is like this coffee."

FINAL EXERCISE

If we are grateful for what we have and where we are today, but are also willing to make progress each day toward a better understanding of ourselves and those we interact with, our personal and professional lives will be miraculously changed. We will experience life through a new lens, and we will transform our personal and working relationships. Finally, we will experience an abundance of true joy, happiness, success (Figure 18.1), and fulfillment every day, including our work days.

If there is only one thing you remember as you close the cover on this book, I hope it is this: ***Leadership is Love.***

Again, for those who are uncomfortable with this, I encourage you to explore the business value of becoming a Conscious Capitalist. For those who are ready and willing to embrace this concept, I hope you will consider making three important changes in your life:

1. Find your passion and lay down your *time* for a worthy purpose
2. Recite the following every morning and again every night before retiring:

    Be Humble, Be Playful, Be Generous, Be Passionate, Be Courageous, Be Authoritative, Be Dependable, Be Wise

3. Be a mentor and lay down your *time* for others in need

FINAL REQUEST

It is my sincere hope that you have enjoyed this book and found within these pages some knowledge, insights, and wisdom that will help guide you on your leadership journey. If for whatever reason the concepts, principles, stories, or writing were not to your liking, I ask that you be kind with your public remarks. Remember, dozens of military veterans graciously offered us their wisdom and experience, and any negative comments, even if you believe they are deserved, may also reflect badly on these veterans.

My gracious and wise late mother once told me, "Son, if you can't say something nice, don't say anything at all."

Today: Be Humble, Be Playful, Be Generous, Be Passionate, Be Courageous, Be Authoritative, Be Dependable, Be Wise.

Notes

WHAT'S YOUR TYPE?

Please visit www.neuronleaders.com and use the **Neuron Personality Profiler™** for free. You will be asked a few simple questions to determine your **Neuron Personality Profile**. This is a giant step beyond the typical Myers-Briggs or Enneagram assessment as it's based on the ancient Greek Enneagram observational science combined with more modern neuropsychology science and uses visual elements that will appear more to your emotional and instinctual brain.

A second set of questions in the **Profiler** will help determine the **Neuron Personality Profile** of someone you interact with, such as a subordinate, peer, or supervisor. You can answer the questions for them, or have them answer the questions on their own.

Once done, you and they will see a detailed outline of your individual profiles. This is far more detailed than other profiles you might have received from other sources and includes primary fears, motivators, leadership tendencies, healthy and unhealthy traits, optimal neurotransmitter levels, recommended diets and lifestyle changes to remain optimal, and helpful hints to improve your leadership approach.

You will also be able to download a document that offers helpful insights about others you engage with, such as subordinates, as well as suggestions and tips to better understand the other person's fears and motivators, along with optimal words and phrases to use, do's and don'ts when engaging with them, and much more. Included is information about their primary attributes and professional tendencies, along with a personality trait exercise and a detailed neurochemical analysis. Also, recommendations for diet, supplements, exercise, and lifestyle changes to maintain a healthy neurotransmitter balance and recognize unhealthy behaviors.

INTRODUCTION

1. Bouree Lam, "Why Do Workers Feel So Unhappy? Just One-Fifth of Employees Report Believing That Their Workplaces Strongly Value Them," *The Atlantic*, November 4, 2014.

CHAPTER 2: WHAT LEADERS NEED TO KNOW ABOUT THE BRAIN

1. Paul D. MacLean, *The Triune Brain in Evolution: Role in Paleocerebral Functions* (New York: Plenum Press, 1990).

CHAPTER 3: WHAT LEADERS NEED TO KNOW ABOUT PERSONALITIES

1. Randall Beck and Jim Harter, "Managers Account for 70% of Variance in Employee Engagement," *Gallup Business Journal*, April 21, 2015, http://www.gallup.com/businessjournal/182792/managers-account-variance-employee-engagement.aspx.
2. Nate Boaz and Erica Ariel Fox, "Change Leader, Change Thyself," *McKinsey Quarterly*, March 2014.
3. Rob Markey, "Set Perfection as the Goal: Leadership Lessons from Former Vanguard CEO Jack Brennan," Net Promoter System, April 25, 2016, http://www.netpromotersystemblog.com/2016/04/25/set-perfection-as-the-goal-leadership-lessons-from-former-vanguard-ceo-jack-brennan/.

CHAPTER 5: PLAYFUL TOTO—NEURON SECRET TWO

1. Erin Griffith, "Amazon CEO Jeff Bezos: 'I've made billions of dollars of failures,'" *Fortune*, December 2, 2014, http://fortune.com/2014/12/02/amazon-ceo-jeff-bezos-failure/.

CHAPTER 6: GENEROUS TIN WOODSMAN—NEURON SECRET THREE

1. Rainer Strack, Jean-Michel Caye, Thomas Gaissmaier, Christian Orglmeister, Eddy Tamboto, Carsten von der Linden, Sebastian Ullrich, Pieter Haen, Horacio Quirós, and Jorge Jauregui, "Creating People Advantage 2014-2015: How to Set Up Great HR Functions: Connect, Prioritize, Impact," *BCG Perspectives*, December 1, 2014, https://www.bcgperspectives.com/content/articles/human_resources_creating_people_advantage_2014_how_to_set_up_great_hr_functions/.

2. David A. Garvin, "How Google Sold Its Engineers on Management," *Harvard Business Review*, December 2013, https://hbr.org/2013/12/how-google-sold-its-engineers-on-management.

3. Daina Beth Solomon, "Amazon Report Sparks Debate," *Los Angeles Times*, August 15, 2015, C3.

4. Jeff Vrabel, "Why Are There So Many Bad Bosses? Some People Are Natural-Born Leaders. Others Are Cruel, Inhuman Monsters," Success, Towers Watson Global Workforce Study, 2012.

CHAPTER 8: PASSIONATE WIZARD—NEURON SECRET FOUR

1. "Employee Job Satisfaction and Engagement: Optimizing Organizational Culture for Success," Society for Human Resource Management, April 28, 2015, https://www.shrm.org/hr-today/trends-and-forecasting/research-and-surveys/pages/job-satisfaction-and-engagement-report-optimizing-organizational-culture-for-success.aspx.

2. Charles Duhigg, "What Google Learned from Its Quest to Build the Perfect Team," *New York Times*, February 28, 2016, https://www.nytimes.com/2016/02/28/magazine/what-google-learned-from-its-quest-to-build-the-perfect-team.html?_r=1.

CHAPTER 11: AUTHORITATIVE WIZARD—NEURON SECRET SIX

1. Dov Eden, "Leadership Expectations' Pygmalion Effect," *Leadership Quarterly* 3, no. 4 (1992): 271–305; A. S. King, "Self-Fulfilling Prophecy in Training the Hard-Core: Supervisor Expectations and the Underprivileged Workers' Performance," *Social Science Quarterly* 52 (1971): 369–378; A. S. King, "Expectation Effects in Organization Change," *Administrative Science Quarterly* 19 (1974): 221–230; D. Eden and A. B. Shani, "Pygmalion Goes to Boot Camp: Expectancy, Leadership, and Trainee Performance," *Journal of Applied Psychology* 67 (1982): 195–199.

2. "23 Employee Motivation Statistics to Silence Naysayers," Blackhawk Network, August 2015, https://www.hawkincentives.com/insights/23-employee-motivation-statistics-silence-naysayers.

3. Alan G. Ingham, George Levinger, James Graves, and Vaughn Peckman, "The Ringelman Effect: Studies of Group Size and Group Performance," *Journal of Experimental Social Psychology* 10, no. 4 (July 1974): 371–384.

CHAPTER 14: DOROTHY'S REVELATION—NEURON SECRET ONE REDUX

1. Bay of Pigs, W. Craig Reed, *Red November: Inside the Secret U.S. – Soviet Submarine War* (HarperCollins, May 10, 2010).

2. Steven Bergals, "The Entrepreneurial Ego: Pratfalls. A Clinical Psychologist Explains Why It's Good for Every Leader to Stumble Through Pratfalls," *Inc.*, September 1, 1996, https://www.inc.com/magazine/19960901/1796.html.

CHAPTER 16: THE EIGHTH SECRET

1. Ravi Mehta and Rui (Juliet) Zhu, "Blue or Red? Exploring the Effect of Color on Cognitive Performances," *Science*, February 27, 2009, 323 (5918):1226-9.doi: 10:1126/science.1169144.

Further Reading

Amthor, Frank. *Neuroscience for Dummies*. Hoboken, NJ: John Wiley & Sons, 2012.

Baron, Renee, and Elizabeth Wagele. *The Enneagram Made Easy: Discover the Nine Types of People*. New York: HarperCollins, 1994.

Benson, Nigel, Joannah Ginsburg, Voula Grand, Merrin Lazyan, Marcus Weeks, and Catherine Collin. *The Psychology Book: Big Ideas Simply Explained*. New York: DK Publishing, 2012.

Braverman, Eric R. *The Edge Effect: Achieve Total Health and Longevity with the Balanced Brain Advantage*. New York: Sterling, 2005.

Cannon, Jeff, and LTCMDR Jon Cannon. *Leadership Lessons of the Navy SEALS*. New York: McGraw-Hill, 2003.

Clifton, Jim. *The Coming Jobs War*. New York: Gallup Press, 2011.

Covey, Stephen R. *How to Develop Your Personal Mission Statement*. Grand Haven, MI: Grand Harbor Press, 2013.

Covey, Stephen R. *The Seven Habits of Highly Effective People: Powerful Lessons in Personal Change*. New York: RosettaBooks, 2013.

David, Oscar. *The Enneagram for Managers: Nine Different Perspectives on Managing People*. Writers Club Press, 2001.

Hazeldine, Simon. *Neuro Sell: How Neuroscience Can Power Your Sales Success*. London: Kogan Page Limited, 2014.

http://adaptiveneuroscience.com/2015/10/12/neuroscience-of-selling/

http://archive.fortune.com/magazines/fortune/bestcompanies/snapshots/1615.html

http://fortune.com/2015/04/02/quit-reasons/

http://fortune.com/2015/10/29/happy-productivity-work/

http://hbswk.hbs.edu/item/the-subconscious-mind-of-the-consumer-and-how-to-reach-it

http://journals.plos.org/plosone/article?id=10.1371/journal.pone.0056934

http://mastershtm.sdsu.edu/2017/02/09/5-lifelong-leadership-lessons-learned-norman-brinker/

http://neuroeconomicstudies.org/images/stories/documents/barraza2015_heart_of_story.pdf

http://news.bbc.co.uk/2/hi/business/8352389.stm

http://psychology.jrank.org/human-behavior/pages/cmxyrs57zk/neocortical-functions-neural-bases.html

http://selfdeterminationtheory.org

http://usatoday30.usatoday.com/money/companies/management/2006-06-06-shy-ceo-usat_x.htm

http://webcenters.netscape.compuserve.com/whatsnew/package.jsp?name=fte/quitjobs/quitjobs

http://webspace.ship.edu/cgboer/genpsyneurotransmitters.html

https://www.americanprogress.org/wp-content/uploads/2012/11/CostofTurnover.pdf

https://books.google.com/books?id=j_5-9zWaBI0C&pg=PA696&lpg=PA696&dq=
jimmy+carter%27s+involvement+with+the+submarine+cruise+missile+program&
source=bl&ots=mjZToS9kXz&sig=1YBAtErpioRGcy-JdsRaXbwDkb0&hl=en&sa=
X&ved=0ahUKEwjW5Y2PjoLUAhVD74MKHccWDFEQ6AEISzAH#v=onepage
&q=jimmy%20carter's%20involvement%20with%20the%20submarine%20cruise
%20missile%20program&f=false

https://breakingmuscle.com/learn/understanding-our-adrenal-system-norepinephrine

https://ctsmithiii.wordpress.com/2012/02/16/4-tenets-of-conscious-capitalism/

https://en.wikipedia.org/wiki/Amygdala

https://en.wikipedia.org/wiki/Norepinephrine

https://en.wikipedia.org/wiki/SSM-N-8_Regulus

https://en.wikipedia.org/wiki/Thirteenth_Amendment_to_the_United_States_
Constitution

https://forbes.com/pictures/fjlj45fkfh/9-hp/#499a4b9c119a

https://introvertdear.com/news/introverts-and-extroverts-brains-really-are-different-
according-to-science/

https://leilajameel.wordpress.com/2013/04/03/neuromarketing-the-future-2/

https://medlicker.com/789-low-dopamine-causes-symptoms-diagnosis-and-treatment-
options

https://musingsonmormonism.wordpress.com/2012/09/17/easily-the-most-fascintaing-
and-illuminating-comparison-of-introversion-and-extroversion-ive-ever-seen/

https://www.americanprogress.org/wp-content/uploads/2012/11/CostofTurnover.pdf

https://www.barna.com/research/the-different-impact-of-good-and-bad-leadership/

https://www.boundless.com/biology/textbooks/boundless-biology-textbook/osmotic-
regulation-and-the-excretory-system-41/hormonal-control-of-osmoregulatory-
functions-232/epinephrine-and-norepinephrine-867-12114/

https://www.brainyquote.com/quotes/quotes/t/thomasaed132683.html

https://www.britannica.com/topic/Parallel-Lives

https://www.classy.org/blog/science-of-storytelling-marketers/

https://www.enneagraminstitute.com/

https://www.forbes.com/pictures/fjlj45fkfh/9-hp/#709ddb88119a

https://www.forbes.com/sites/christopherhelman/2013/10/29/the-worlds-happiest-and-
saddest-countries-2013/#1cdca1982a8f

https://www.integrativepsychiatry.net/neurotransmitter.html

https://www.integrativepsychiatry.net/serotonin.html

https://www.ncbi.nlm.nih.gov/pmc/articles/PMC2819196/

https://www.nytimes.com/2015/10/22/science/quantum-theory-experiment-said-to-
prove-spooky-interactions.html

https://www.psychologytoday.com/blog/the-athletes-way/201505/how-do-your-genes-
influence-levels-emotional-sensitivity

https://www.sciencedaily.com/releases/2015/05/150507135919.htm

https://www.sciencedaily.com/terms/neocortex.htm

https://www.youtube.com/watch?v=Og64L31FWlk

https://www.zanebenefits.com/blog/bid/312123/employee-retention-the-real-cost-of-losing-an-employee

Kleinman, Paul. *Psych 101*. Avon, MA: Adams Media, 2012.

Krznaric, Roman. *How Should We Live?: Great Ideas from the Past for Everyday Life*. Katonah, NY: BlueBridge, 2013.

Lapid-Bogda, Ginger. *Bringing Out the Best in Everyone You Coach: Use the Enneagram for Exceptional Results*. New York: McGraw-Hill, 2010.

Lewis, James P. *Project Leadership*. New York: McGraw-Hill, 2003.

Olsen, Marti. *The Introvert Advantage: How to Thrive in an Extrovert World*. New York: Workman Publishing Company, 2002.

Palmer, Helen. *The Enneagram in Love & Work: Understanding Your Intimate & Business Relationships*. New York: HarperCollins, 2010.

Riso, Don Richard, with Russ Hudson. *Personality Types*. New York: Houghton Mifflin, 1996.

Schein, Edgar H. *Organizational Culture and Leadership*. Fourth edition. San Francisco, CA: Jossey-Bass, 2010.

Thomas, Tina. *Who Do You Think You Are?: Understanding Your Personality from the Inside Out*. New York: Morgan James Publishing, 2016.

www.apa.org/monitor/oct05/mirror.aspx

www.apa.org/topics/personality/sciencedaily.com/releases/2015/05/150507135919.htm

www.benbest.com/science/anatmind/anatmd10.html

www.businessinsider.com/how-stress-at-work-is-costing-employers-300-billion-a-year-2016-6

www.collective-evolution.com/2016/01/20/10-ways-to-increase-dopamine-levels-in-the-brain/

www.customatrix.com

www.drjoecarver.com/clients/49355/File/Chemical%20Imbalance.html

www.dutchdailynews.com/dutch-kids-ranked-happiest-in-the-world/

www.ei-resource.org/articles/mental-and-emotional-problem-articles/easy-and-natural-ways-to-raise-low-serotonin-levels/

www.encyclopedia.com/science-and-technology/biochemistry/biochemistry/serotonin

www.goodtherapy.org/blog/psychpedia/dopamine

www.healthline.com/human-body-maps/vagus-nerve

www.hp.com/hpinfo/abouthp/values-objectives.html

www.inc.com/maeghan-ouimet/real-cost-bad-bosses.html

www.jneurosci.org/content/30/14/4999?sid=4fc5d5f7-b722-40f5-8bf2-7e6254efd6bc

www.jneurosci.org/content/35/16/6506

www.medicalnewstoday.com/articles/275795.php

www.netpromotersystemblog.com/2016/04/25/set-perfection-as-the-goal-leadership-lessons-from-former-vanguard-ceo-jack-brennan/

www.news-medical.net/health/Dopamine-Functions.aspx

www.news.com.au/business/worklife/survey-finds-two-thirds-of-responders-have-a-horrible-or-average-boss/story-e6frfm9r-1226116143100

www.nvtsi.org/

www.nydailynews.com/news/national/70-u-s-workers-hate-job-poll-article-1.1381297

www.ohio.edu/people/hartleyg/ref/fiction/freytag.html

www.onrec.com/news/statistics-and-trends/new-study-reveals-fun-at-work-can-boost-productivity-and-reduce-sick-days

www.telegraph.co.uk/women/family/raise-worlds-happiest-children-time-went-dutch/

Zak, Paul J. *Trust Factor: The Science of Creating High-Performance Companies*. New York: AMACOM, 2017.

Other Books by W. Craig Reed

www.wcraigreed.com
www.neuronleaders.com

Index

Page references followed by *fig* indicate an illustrated figure or photograph.